S0-BCA-137

Ancient Civilizations, Geography, Art, and English

Lessons 19 - 36

Oak Meadow, Inc.
Post Office Box 1346
Brattleboro, VT 05302-1346
www.oakmeadow.com

Copyright © 2000 Oak Meadow, Inc.
All Rights Reserved

Without limiting the rights under copyright reserved above, no part of this publication may be reproduced, stored in or introduced into a retrieval system, or transmitted, in any form, or by any means (electronic, mechanical, photocopying, recording, or otherwise), without the prior written permission of Oak Meadow, Inc.

Social Studies/Art/English~~~~~~Lesson 19

BARBARIANS AND CELTS

Vocabulary Words

Your vocabulary words relate to the material you are studying in Social Studies. Define each of them without using the root word, and use them in a sentence in a way that shows you understand the meaning. Try to think about them in the context of your Social Studies work. If you are unable to find a word in your best dictionary, look in an encyclopedia.

province	**salvation**	**ungodly**
aisle	**thatch**	**brooch**
divination		

Spelling

Select ten words from your written material this week for spelling words. Learn each of these words and use each one in a complete sentence. Practice your spelling words in preparation for a quiz.

Grammar

1. Write sentences in which you use the seven contractions listed in the section called "Contractions" in your *English Manual*. Think of three more contractions and use each one in a sentence.

2. Make an outline before writing your summary on Day 5. Refer to the section called "Outlining" in your *English Manual*.

Days 1 & 2

During the period between 3000 and 1000 B.C., while some great civilizations were building tombs, temples and palaces, inventing writing and creating laws, the people in Europe were leading simple lives in small villages and farms. They built their homes of wood and uncut stones, using thatch and turf for the roofs. Villages of three or four homes would share communal pens for cattle and pigs, and food storage huts built on stilts to prevent animals from getting in. A wall of tall strong stakes was built to protect villages from invaders. Crops were grown in the outlying fields, which were made by cutting down the forest and clearing the land. Isolated farms, some with stone homes big enough to house fifty people, raised cattle and sheep, and grew wheat and barley.

Stonehenge

We do not know much about these people, except that they left behind great stone monuments that can still be seen today. No one knows exactly why they were built, but some believe they had religious purposes. Others claim that they were a method for measuring and keeping track of the movement of the sun, moon and planets. In about 2800 B.C., work was begun on one such monument, now called Stonehenge, located in southern England. At first Stonehenge was merely a circle of pits dug in the ground with a round ditch and a bank built around them. Later, bluestone from Wales was added in two circles. In around 1600 B.C., workers using logs as rollers pulled the massive stones we see there now into place. Straight-sided upright stones called *sarsens* formed the outer ring of the circle, with crosspieces making a complete circle around the top. Inside the ring there are even larger upright stones standing in pairs with a single stone joining them into an arch called a *trilithon*. Although Stonehenge is the most famous of these monuments, similar upright stones formed in groupings can be seen in France and Ireland. Some of them are in the form of avenues, with two rows of stones lined up side by side.

Other structures left by the earliest European civilization are circular burial mounds where personal possessions were left in the graves with the deceased. Circles of stones were laid on the ground along the slopes and beyond. Burial sites like these have been found in Spain, Germany, and near the Black Sea.

Eventually, these early people discovered tin mines, and mixed the tin with copper to make bronze. In this way they were able to make stronger tools and weapons. This was the beginning of the Bronze Age in Europe.

The Celts were an ancient people from the area of modern Austria who spread during this time into what is now France, Portugal, Spain, Italy, and the British Isles. They were among the earliest people of Europe to make iron. The metalwork of the Celts survived into the Middle Ages. They also developed an elaborate style of art featuring patterns of interwoven curves and spirals. A special feature of these designs was to start with a single thread of metal and wind and twist it into a pattern. Even today, many people like to have wedding rings made out of "Celtic knots" as this kind of pattern symbolizes longevity and continuity. These elaborate spirals and curves are known as Celtic La Tène art, and it is seen on manuscripts and stone sculpture, as well as on ironwork.

Because of their skill as metalworkers, Celts often wore a lot of elaborate jewelry, including large brooches, solid gold wristlets, and necklaces. They liked to wear bright clothing, especially woolen cloaks that were sometimes striped or checked. Men often shaved their cheeks, but kept a long mustache.

Celts were organized into tribes, with a chieftain as leader. They were fearsome warriors, using their knowledge of ironmongering to make weapons, armor, and war chariots. They made huge curved trumpets that made a terrific noise in battle. The Celts liked to display all their jewelry in battle. Battles were often a matter of tribes meeting and boasting of their deeds and bravery, ending with a fight. Sometimes battles were settled with the two opposing leaders fighting each other one-on-one.

Celtic Designs

Women had rights and were generally treated with respect. They cooked in large iron kettles that hung over the fire into the center of the home by a chain. Houses were made with interwoven branches covered with clay, and a thatched roof of hay. Most Celts were farmers, others were metalworkers or miners.

The learned, priestly class of the ancient Celts were called Druids. Druids worshipped many different gods, and performed animal and human sacrifice. It is believed that the stone monuments such as Stonehenge were an important part of Druidic celebrations. Celts also threw offerings to the gods, such as jewelry and weapons, into streams and lakes.

Early Celts had no writing, but in the 1st century A.D. they often used a primitive form of writing called *ogam*. When the Romans conquered much of Europe between 300 B.C. and 100 A.D., the Celtic culture was generally absorbed into the melting pot of the Roman Empire. The Celts in what we now call England, Ireland and Scotland, however, preserved much of their own culture. After about 500 B.C., the Celts switched to the Latin alphabet, and many ancient Celtic myths and legends were recorded. Later manuscripts in this style contained intricate drawings of animals along with the writing, such as are seen in the Book of Durrow, written about 680 A.D.

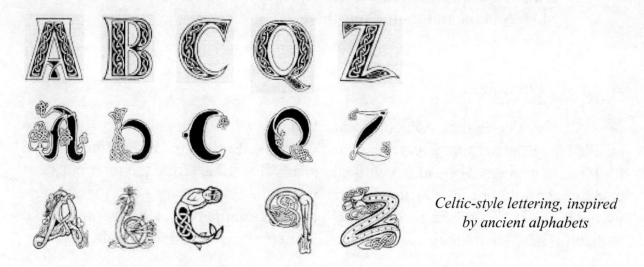

Celtic-style lettering, inspired by ancient alphabets

1. Look at the countries of Europe on your map, so you understand the locations discussed in this lesson.

2. **This and the next assignment may involve a trip to the library. Borrow a book of Celtic mythology, or use the internet sources below. See if you can find the *Mabinogion*, a translation of famous Welsh folk tales. Otherwise, any Celtic story collection is fine. Start reading your book of Celtic myths or stories, and continue reading it through the week. You will be summarizing one at the end of the week.**

3. **Choose one of the following art projects:**

   a. **Look at pictures of Celtic metalwork, and then draw your own design containing elaborate spiral and curved designs interwoven. Remember to keep the thread single, weaving through itself over and over to make the pattern.**

   b. **Find and look at pictures of Stonehenge. Then either draw or paint your own picture, or make a diorama. Try to draw or build the stones to scale and locate them as accurately as possible. Pay attention to the surroundings of Stonehenge, as well as to the stones themselves. Fill the whole page if you making a painting or drawing. If you are making a diorama, one method for making stones is to carve them from pieces of styrofoam and then paint them.**

Days 3 & 4

The Goths, Franks, Visigoths, and Vandals were Germanic barbarians who invaded the Roman Empire and helped to destroy it. "Barbarian" is the Roman name for foreign invaders. They, along with other barbarian tribes, were the forerunners of many modern Europeans. During the first half of the first century A.D., the area that was highly settled by them included what is now Scandinavia, north Germany, and Holland. These communities are commonly referred to as "early German."

Many early Germans lived in a type of longhouse, a house which was divided lengthwise to include several aisles. The middle aisle was a central hall, used for gatherings. One end of the outside aisles was divided up into small stalls for cows and other domestic animals. The other end of the house was used for the family, and was usually one large, open room without any aisles.

Another common building style was a sunken hut. It was a hollow area dug into the ground, with a roof. The floor was usually packed earth, but occasionally wooden planks were used. A wooden structure with a slanted roof was built over it by tying poles to a ridgepole on top, and slanting them downward to the edges of the hollow. The roof was filled in with various thin planks, and then covered with a sort of mud plaster. The top was covered with thatch. These huts were much smaller than the longhouses, and were more often used as workshops than homes.

Early Germans ate a lot of grains, such as barley and wheat. They made porridge and mixed it with leafy plants. Meat was not a major part of their diet, although they did use milk and cheese. The meat they ate was usually wild game, aquatic birds, and fish. Beer was brewed from barley, and flavored with herbs. It was a common drink for all ages.

These people were excellent warriors, but they also loved music and gambling. They especially enjoyed feasting and dancing, and were known for several sword and spear dances that were performed by young men. Ancient dice that have been discovered are very much the same as what we use today, with numbers on opposite sides adding up to seven. The early Germans also made a sort of bowling game on ice, using long knuckle-bones from a horse or cow which were knocked down by a round piece of bone that was flung across the ice.

The Germans of those days were physically much larger than the Romans. They usually had blue eyes and blonde or reddish hair. Red hair was considered to be a sign of strength in war, and some warriors even dyed their hair red. Men's hair was often very long, braided in a single braid or tied into a knot worn behind the right ear.

Clothing nearly always included a woolen cloak. It was fastened at the right shoulder with a brooch, and could be used as a blanket or for extra warmth during the day. Besides the cloak, men wore pants and a tunic.

The life of women was not an easy one in this culture. They could be bought like slaves, and were often not even allowed to sit at the same table as their husbands. Sometimes, when the husband died, the woman was also expected to sacrifice herself.

Religion was an important part of life among the early Germans. War-gods were especially revered, and the gods of the Vikings in Scandinavia also became intertwined with Germanic religion. Tiwaz, Wotan, Odin, and Thor are the names of some of the important gods of the time. When the people needed guidance, they often turned to divination. One method involved having a priest interpret the neighs and snorts of sacred white horses who were kept just for that purpose. Of course, this wasn't easy!

Little by little the Germans and other barbarian tribes became Christians. Usually this happened because as they conquered groups of Christians and traded with Christian merchants, they became interested in the new faith.

On the next page is a sample of the Lord's Prayer in the language of the Goths. Bishop Ulfias, a barbarian Goth, translated parts of the Bible in order to bring his religion to other barbarians. He developed this special alphabet, which combines the ancient runes which were used for divination with Roman and Greek letters.

4. **Put the rest of northern Europe on your map, including Denmark, Norway, Sweden, Finland, Poland, Lithiuania, Estonia, Bylerus, and the Ukraine, if you have not already done so.**

5. **Choose one of the following:**

   a. **Draw your own rendition of one of the two types of houses built by the early Germans.**

   b. **Build a model of an early German house.**

   c. **Play a game similar to the kinds just discussed. You can make up a dice game, or play a commercial dice game. You might enjoy making up your own bowling game, even if you can't play it on ice.**

   d. **Using letters you see in the Gothic Lord's Prayer shown on the next page, it might be fun for you to create your own message that somehow relates to the material you have studied in this lesson. Use the Gothic script, and provide a translation for your teacher. If you would prefer to just copy the prayer in Gothic script, that would be fine.**

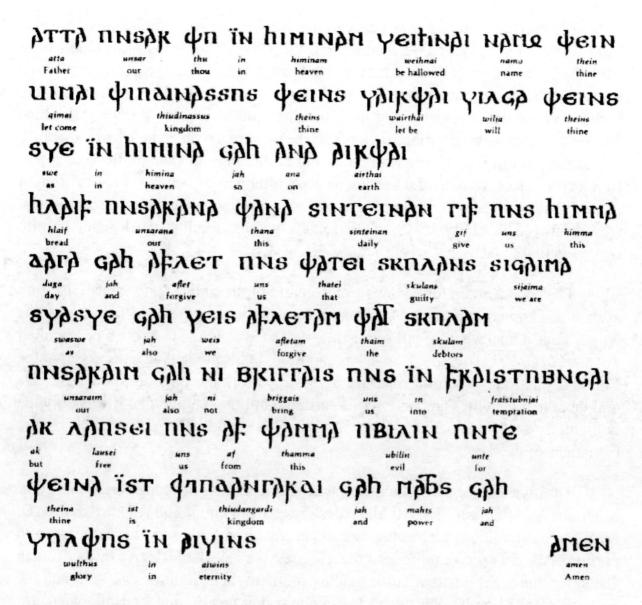

Gothic	atta	unsar	thu	in	himinam	weihnai	namo	thein
English	Father	our	thou	in	heaven	be hallowed	name	thine

Gothic	qimai	thiudinassus	theins	wairthai	wilja	theins
English	let come	kingdom	thine	let be	will	thine

Gothic	swe	in	himina	jah	ana	airthai
English	as	in	heaven	so	on	earth

Gothic	hlaif	unsarana	thana	sinteinan	gif	uns	himma
English	bread	our	this	daily	give	us	this

Gothic	daga	jah	aflet	uns	thatei	skulans	sijaima
English	day	and	forgive	us	that	guilty	we are

Gothic	swaswe	jah	weis	afletam	thaim	skulam
English	as	also	we	forgive	the	debtors

Gothic	unsaraim	jah	ni	briggais	uns	in	fraistubnjai
English	our	also	not	bring	us	into	temptation

Gothic	ak	lausei	uns	af	thamma	ubilin	unte
English	but	free	us	from	this	evil	for

Gothic	theina	ist	thiudangardi	jah	mahts	jah
English	thine	is	kingdom	and	power	and

Gothic	wulthus	in	aiwins					amen
English	glory	in	eternity					Amen

6. Continue reading from your collection of Celtic myths or stories.

Day 5

The Roman Empire grew so large before it collapsed that it stretched from the Middle East to Great Britain. As you may remember from the end of Lesson 16, in 290 A.D. it was divided into two sections: the Western Empire and the Eastern Empire. This made it easier for the emperor to control, especially after he shifted more of the power from Rome, in the Western Empire, to the city of Constantinople in the Eastern Empire.

For two hundred years the peace of the Western Roman Empire was disturbed by uprisings of the subdued Germanic and Celtic tribes. The Goths and Vandals were attracted by the warmer climate, rich farmland, and plentiful resources. Eventually, the Celts and Germanic tribes were in turn being chased by the Huns, another fierce barbarian tribe which was coming from the direction of Eastern Europe. The Huns pushed the other barbarian tribes right across the two great rivers which had previously restrained most invasions: the Rhine flowing north, and the Danube flowing south. Roman provinces fell one after another as wave after wave of barbarian wars brought more and more of them in. Europe was invaded over and over again by the barbarians, who destroyed whole towns and killed many people. Finally, the Roman Empire collapsed in 476 AD.

The people of the former Western Roman Empire didn't feel safe. Civilization as men had known it for a thousand years seemed on the verge of collapse. Aurelius Augustinus, a man we now call Augustine, was a Christian who wrote a book called *The City of God* shortly after Rome was captured. In his book, Augustine assured the Christians that they could never truly be destroyed by the ungodly barbarians. He told them that the cities and empires of earth did not matter, and that it was only the individual's salvation which was important. This book was well received by the Christians of the day.

The invasions of the barbarians started the beginning of a long period in history called the Middle Ages. The Middle Ages lasted from about 500 A.D. to 1500 A.D. Many Roman traditions such as law, art, and language partially survived in the western portion of the collapsed empire after the fall, preserved to a large degree by the Roman Catholic Church. The barbarians brought with them their traditions as well, and the cultures blended with each other. The modern day celebration of Halloween, for example, can be traced to a mixture between an ancient Celtic new year festival which honored Samhain, the Celtic lord of death, and the Christians' All Saint's Day or Allhallowmass, which honored the souls of the dead.

7. **Write a summary of one of the Celtic stories you have read. Illustrate your story if you would enjoy doing so.**

8. **Have your Home Teacher give you a spelling quiz. Review any words you miss and add them to your ongoing list for further study.**

Extra Book Ideas:

Wise Child and *Juniper*, by Monica Furlong
The Sacred Jewel, by N. Faulkner
Fingals' Request, by M.A. Polland
Dragon Slayer: The Story of Beowulf, The Eagle of the Ninth, The Shining Company, The High Deeds of Finn MacCool, Knight's Fee, The Silver Branch, and *Tristan and Iseult*, by Rosemary Sutcliff
The Wizard Children of Finn, by M. Tanner
Beowulf - A New Telling, by Robert Nye
Beowulf the Warrior, by Ian Serraillier
Stonehenge from "The Mystery of?" series, by Harriette Abels, Crestwood House, Mankato, Minn., 1987

Extra Project Ideas:

• Build a model of an early Barbarian or Celtic village.

• Research the Tollund bog in Jutland. What has been found in it?

• Look at some runes (used for divination), and make up your own. Carve some in small pieces of soap, or paint them on smooth, flat stones.

• Find out more about the Huns and their leader, Attila.

• Research and make a map showing where different tribes of Barbarians started and ended up in different parts of Europe.

• Learn more about the early Celts.

• Find out more about the ancient burial sites of Europe, such as Los Millares in Spain, Helmsdorf in Germany, Brenig in Wales, and Kernonen in France.

• Find out about the ancient German city of Wasserburg, which was built from the shores of a lake.

Social Studies/Art/English~~~~~~~Lesson 20

MIDDLE AGES

Vocabulary Words

Your vocabulary words relate to the material you are studying in Social Studies. Define each of them without using the root word or any other form of the word, and use them in a sentence in a way that shows you understand the meaning. Try to think about them in the context of your Social Studies work. If you are unable to find a word in your best dictionary, look in an encyclopedia.

excommunication	**illuminate**	**sacrament**
unison	**monastery**	**abbey**
gospel	**impact**	**diocese**
liturgical/liturgy		

Spelling

Select ten words from your written material this week for spelling words. Learn these words and use each one in a complete sentence. Practice your spelling words in preparation for a quiz.

Grammar

1. **A pronoun is a word used in place of a noun. Write a sentence for each of the following pronouns: I, my, mine, me, our, ours, we, us, you, your, yours. Other pronouns can be found in the section called "Pronouns" in your *English Manual*.**

2. **Beginning this week, you will begin working on a research report that is due at the end of Lesson 24. Start by gathering at least three different resources. Begin taking notes on 3" x 5" cards, putting only a small amount of information on each card. This will make it easier to organize your notes later. See Social Studies Day 1 for a list of topics.**

Day 1

During the early part of the Middle Ages, people in Europe were struggling to recover from the destruction and turmoil caused by the fall of the Roman Empire. But at the same time, the Germanic, Celtic, Christian, and Roman cultures were being woven together. This new civilization was called the "medieval civilization." Medieval means "Middle Ages." The Middle Ages lasted one thousand years, from the fall of the Roman Empire in 476 A.D. to about 1500 A.D.

Many of the invading Germanic and Celtic tribes had already heard of the gospel of Christ from travelers of the East. Many of the invaders converted to a form of Christianity called Catholicism. During the Middle Ages, the Catholic Church grew in size and strength, replacing the Roman Empire as the unifying force in Western Europe. Had this not been the case, the course of Christianity and the history of Western Europe might have been very different.

The Catholic Church had a huge amount of power, and was responsible for guiding people in all matters of faith and religion. If a person wasn't baptized in the Roman Catholic Church, they weren't considered a real member of society. If someone was excommunicated, they lost all their property and other rights as well. The Church had something to say about every aspect of everyone's lives.

There are several scholars who made a big impact during the early years of the Middle Ages. They are St. Ambrose, St. Jerome, and St. Augustine.

St. Ambrose was a bishop who believed that the only way women could truly be happy and live good lives was if they devoted their lives to God, giving up all worldly interests. He said that married women with children have nothing but pain and trouble in life. Also, he felt strongly that wives must obey their husbands in everything, and never wear any kind of cosmetics, jewelry, or other "ornaments."

St. Jerome was an early Biblical scholar who translated the *Bible* into Latin. Latin, which was the language of the Romans, became the official language of the Church. This *Bible*, called the *Vulgate*, was the official Roman Catholic *Bible* for centuries. A commonly told story about St. Jerome says that he lovingly removed a thorn from a lion's foot, and the lion was forever grateful. Pictures of him often show a lion at his side.

St. Augustine was the author of *The City of God,* which was mentioned previously. He taught that the only things in life which really matter are two mystical cities - the city of God and the city of the devil. He said only God knows who belongs to which city, based on the pureness of their hearts and lives. Augustine believed that the church's job was to preach the gospel and that the government's job was to keep peace so the church could do its job. He said the church is more important than the government, but that the two need to cooperate.

St. Augustine

Many people took the writings of St. Augustine to heart, and society began to organize itself accordingly. The churchmen were called the "First Estate" of God, the nobles who ruled and fought were called the "Second Estate", and the commoners, who did the work, were called the "Third Estate."

The Catholic Church, as the first estate, was the head of it all. The head of the Catholic Church was the Pope, and everyone believed he was the voice of God. There was no other higher power, at least not on earth. The first Pope of the Catholic Church was St. Peter, and it is believed he is the one to whom Christ gave the keys of heaven and hell. According to Catholicism, every Pope after St. Peter inherited his powers. The center of the Catholic Church was (and still is) the Vatican, located in Rome. Even though at first most Catholics were in what is now Germany and nearby lands, people would travel from all over to appeal to the Pope at the Vatican. As such, the Vatican became the busiest administrative center in Europe.

Bishops were the churchmen who oversaw the business of the Catholic Church in the various areas of Europe. Every Bishop did his work at a cathedral, where special thrones were built for them. The Bishop ruled over all the priests, monks and nuns in the

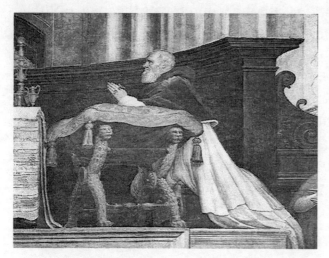

Pope Julius II praying at the Vatican

bishopric or diocese. The Bishop held a court at which all religious matters were decided, and only such a court could try another churchman for a crime. People were regularly fined for such misbehavior as refusing to go to church or gambling in the churchyard. Even disputes over marriage contracts and wills were decided by the Bishop, because, after all, only the Church was allowed to perform marriages and funeral

From left to right, a pope, a cardinal, an archbishop, and a bishop from the 15th century

rites. Excommunication was a real fear, because it carried the threat of being turned away by God and society, not only in this life, but in the next as well. It meant that one could not marry or have a funeral, and that one was going to Hell.

The Archbishop was an official of the church who oversaw the Bishops in his geographical area. They were very powerful and got their orders directly from Rome. If someone did not like the decision of a Bishop, they could appeal to the Archbishop. If they did not like what the Archbishop decided, they could then appeal to the Pope. Often the Archbishop became the right-hand man of the local king or ruler, for without the permission of the Catholic Church, rulers were fearful of ending up in Hell for making the wrong move. As you can see, the Catholic Church was the main political power as well as being responsible for everyone's spiritual life.

Bishops oversaw the parish priests, and it was the priests who actually spread the Word of God to the people. The local priest ran the local church. The priests administered the sacraments and taught parishioners the Lord's Prayer, the Ten Commandments, and all the important aspects of their faith. Some people thought it was bad luck to run into a priest first thing in the morning. Every town or village had a parish priest, and a town's church was always the largest, best-built and most ornate building.

Other church leaders of the time also left their mark. St. Benedict was an important force in the creation of monasteries. When he was twenty, Benedict went to live in a cave high on a cliff in the Italian countryside. He stayed there for three years, praying and living simply. A friend lowered down bread in a basket for him every day so he could eat. He eventually decided that he could serve God better by living with a group of others devoted to prayer and hard work, so he started a monastery. The original Benedictine Abbey was in Monte Cassino, near Naples, Italy. His "rule" (guidelines for the lives of monks and nuns) was so successful that it became the basis for much of Christian monastic life. It involved a combination of prayer, reading of the *Bible* and other sacred writings, and hard physical work. He believed that "idleness is the enemy of the soul."

Monks taking the Rule

Many monasteries sprang up across Europe, each wanting to follow the rule. Monks and nuns served the Church by living apart from society and devoting their lives to God and good works. They wove their own cloth, grew their own food, and made their own wine. They cared for the sick in monastery hospitals and taught children in monastery schools. Many monasteries were economically successful, becoming well known for producing the best wool or the best wine, or the best of something. If a monastery became too wealthy, some monks or nuns would find its life too soft and contrary to the rule, and would break away to form new monasteries.

1. **Choose a research topic from the list below, and go to the library to choose at least three resource materials. You may also make use of the internet sites given below. Each of these topics is touched on during the weeks you are studying the Middle Ages. Your job is to go into depth on your chosen topic. This paper is due at the end of Lesson 24, and should be a minimum of five pages long, plus a cover page, at least one illustration, and a bibliography. (Review the section called "Bibliographies" in your *English Manual*.)**

   Topic Choices:

   Knights and the Crusades

   The Muslim Empire

   Women in the Middle Ages

   Monasteries (founders, orders, and lifestyles)

   Castles and castle life

   Architecture and the building of Cathedrals

   Manors and village life

Days 2 & 3

Pope Gregory the Great, in the Sixth Century, believed firmly in the positive aspects of literature, painting, and music. Some Christians felt that it was not appropriate to paint religious pictures, as it somehow took away from the reverence one should have for God. Gregory, however, said that "Painting can do for the illiterate what writing does for those who can read." His support for the arts opened the door for many marvelous works of art to be created.

The people of a medieval town took great pride in the beauty of their church. Much later author Victor Hugo said of them, "In the Middle Ages, men had no great thought which they did not write down in stone." It is true that their churches and

Romanesque

cathedrals were great works of art in themselves. Recorded in carvings and paintings on the walls and ceilings were poems, stories of saints, historical facts, and philosophical beliefs. Most people couldn't read the Bible for themselves, but the stories were told through intricate carvings and beautiful windows of colored glass.

Two important styles of architecture developed during the Middle Ages: Romanesque and Gothic. The Romanesque was inspired partly by the arches the ancient Romans used widely in their architecture. The building itself was often square and solid-looking. It was not very tall, and arches would grace all its openings. Rows of patterns in a zigzag or chevron shape would decorate the arches. Much of the Romanesque architecture was built in the more northern areas of Europe, and is sometimes called Norman.

The Gothic style tended to be very graceful and elaborate. It was named after the barbarian Goths, even though the Goths had nothing to do with it. It got the name Gothic because there were those who believed that anything that was not Roman or Greek was barbaric, and so considered this new form of architecture barbaric. In the Gothic style, the arches over windows and doors would come to a delicate point at the top. Churches had tall towers built on the front which were ornately decorated with pointed spires. As time went on, the Gothic style became more and more ornate, delicate, and lofty. This later kind of architecture is sometimes called "Perpendicular."

Stained glass church window

Churches were often a mix of architectures, with Gothic features being added onto Romanesque. Sometimes a Gothic tower would simply be added onto the front of a Romanesque church. Many medieval churches and cathedrals are still standing, and you can see the mix between the two styles.

Christian worship services had long included music. This music was simple, and was a blend of music from the Roman, Greek, and Hebrew traditions. It was sung in unison, unaccompanied by any instruments, with a sort of free, flowing rhythm. It was commonly called "plain song." Pope Gregory organized and codified it to insure that it would be sung in the way he considered proper, and actually sent trained teachers throughout the churches to teach the chants. This music is now known as Gregorian Chant, and it is the official liturgical music of the Roman Catholic Church. Over the centuries, new melodies have been composed, and sometimes harmonies have been added.

Manuscript

This illuminated manuscript shows a monk making a manuscript

The only people who wrote books during the Middle Ages were the monks in certain monasteries. The monks produced hand written books of the Gospels and other spiritual writings. If more than one copy was needed, they were copied by hand. Such religious books were called *illuminated manuscripts,* and they were remarkable works of art. Some monks added beautiful pictures and designs to these manuscripts, using gold and silver. Some monasteries were devoted entirely to writing manuscripts, and the monks became specialists in the different styles. The work was so exhausting and laborious that it was considered an incredible feat for a group of monks to produce even a couple of hundred books in many years' time. A monk might devote over a year to copying one *Bible.* They believed that "for every letter, line, and point, a sin is forgiven..."

The *Book of Kells* is a famous example of a Celtic manuscript. Made at the end of the 8th century A.D., it contains the four gospels from the New Testament and a variety of other writings. It was beautifully drawn in vivid colors by Irish monks.

2. Choose one of the following projects:

a. Listen to some samples of plainsong, or chant. Good examples that are easily available include "Chant" (or other recordings by the Benedictine Monks of Santa Domingo de Silos) and "An English Ladymass" (or other recordings by the Anonymous Four). Tell your teacher how you enjoyed this music. It's probably very different from what you usually listen to!

b. **Look in your library or encyclopedia for pictures of *illuminated manuscripts*. An example of the artwork from the *Book of Kells* is shown here. Make a beautiful manuscript with colored pencils and a piece of parchment. The content of your manuscript can be a short poem or verse. A proverb or other quote from the *Bible* would also be appropriate. Make the first letter large, elaborate, and heavily decorated, as in the manuscripts you see. Decorate around the edges of a piece of parchment, using a border pattern entwined with images appropriate for your poem or quote. Use colored pencils, gold paint, or pen to further decorate your manuscript.**

c. **Look at pictures of Romanesque and Gothic churches and cathedrals. In two paragraphs, describe both kinds of architecture and give examples of each. Draw an example of each kind of arch used.**

d. **Look at pictures of stained glass windows in medieval churches and cathedrals. Then make your own "stained glass" window with torn or cut pieces of colored tissue paper. Use the image of a saint or a scene from a Bible story if you wish. Arrange your picture on wax paper, tracing paper, or other see-through paper. Paint over it with liquid starch. Let it dry, and then apply a light layer of white glue if you want the picture to be a little glossy. Hang it in the window for the light to shine through it. Take a picture to share with your teacher.**

3. **Continue reading from your resources for your research paper, taking notes as you go. Use 3" x 5" cards, putting one piece of information on each one.**

Days 4 & 5

The Norsemen (or Northmen) were ancestors of the Norwegians, Swedes, and Danes of today. They were later given the name *Viking*, because in their language to go *a-viking* meant to go and fight as a pirate or warrior. The Vikings became a dominant force in the Middle Ages after the fall of the Western Roman Empire. They regularly invaded parts of England, France, Germany, Ireland, Italy, Russia, and Spain to steal treasure and capture slaves. At first they liked to raid monasteries for their wealth, and later they started to settle in the areas they took over. Vikings loved to fight; the expression "to go berserk" comes from a particularly fierce kind of Viking warrior called a "berserker" who would foam at the mouth, gnaw at his shield, and not even bother to wear armor in battle because he was in such a frenzy to fight. Vikings often murdered men, women, and children alike, and then burned whatever wasn't worth stealing. When they began raiding Europe in about 800 A.D., a monk wrote, "For nearly 350 years we and our fathers have lived in this lovely land, and never before has such a terror appeared in Britain as we have now suffered from a pagan people, nor was it thought that such an attack from the sea was possible."

They fought with axes and several types of swords, as well as bows and arrows. Sometimes they wore armor made from layers of animal hides. They wore helmets, but not with the horns on them as is popularly believed, for such horns would have presented a real danger to their comrades in battle. The horned helmets were reserved for ceremonial purposes. Their shields were wooden and round, with a round, metal piece called a "boss" in the middle to protect their hands should the shield splinter or break. The Vikings loved their weapons and often gave them beautiful names. They also liked to carve them elaborately.

Because the sea almost entirely surrounded the lands of the Vikings, the sea was very important to them. They were excellent shipbuilders who developed new techniques, allowing their ships to go further and faster than other ships. This helped them with their raiding parties throughout the Baltic, North, and Mediterranean Seas. They even built ships at the head of the Volga and Dneiper Rivers and sailed into Eastern Europe and Russia as far as the Black and Caspian Seas. The city of Kiev in the Ukraine was founded by Vikings. They also boldly sailed west from Scandinavia, settling in Iceland. Later a Viking explorer named Eric the Red sailed further west and discovered Greenland. Even though he saw nothing but snow and ice, he named it "Green" in the hopes that others would settle there. Eric the Red's son, Leif Ericson, sailed all the way to North America in the 900's, and was the first European to land there. Vikings tried to settle in what is now Newfoundland, calling it Vinland, but they probably left after running into trouble with the Native Americans living there.

Viking ships were called longboats. They were not very deep, and were made to go in shallow water as well as rough seas. They were about 75 feet long and up to forty men could live in one. They were made out of oak planks with animal fur and tar to fill the cracks and make them watertight. They had a single square sail that was used when the ship was out at sea. When it was stormy, the Vikings used the sail to protect themselves, as there was only one deck at the bottom and no other decks to get underneath. Vikings preferred to stay fairly close to shore, however, and row with long oars that came out of the hull of the ship. When coming into harbor, they liked to hang their shields over the edge of the ship all in a row. They used a heavier oar mounted at the back at one side to steer the boat. The shape of the boat was long, graceful, and curved, and most had ornate carvings. At the prow in the front Vikings often would carve a fearsome figurehead, such as a dragon, snake, or raven's head.

The Vikings became skilled navigators, using the positions of the sun and stars to plot their course. The raven became a symbol of the Vikings because of this bird's ability to find land even when far out to sea. Ravens would be carried on the ships to be released if the sailors weren't sure where land was. They would sail in the direction the ravens flew, knowing that land was not far away.

At home, many Vikings were farmers who grew grains, fruits, and vegetables, and raised cattle, sheep, pigs, and goats. From their raids, many Vikings had obtained slaves, who did the hardest and worst labor, particularly the farm work. Vikings also made their living by metal working, shipbuilding, and woodcarving. Vikings were tremendous hunters, killing deer, bears, seals, and even whales for food. They used the hides and antlers to make tents, bedding and tools. They used animal bones to make everything from combs and spoons to ice-skates.

Although Vikings were fierce to others, they tended to treat their families well. Viking women had more rights than many other women in history. They could own land, and shared in their husband's wealth. When the husbands were away on his raids, wives took charge of the farm and slaves. A Viking woman carried the keys of the house and farm on her belt, and if her husband refused to let her, she had the right to a divorce.

Children were not educated, and Vikings did not read or write. Children helped with the practical work and girls were taught how to spin, weave, cook, brew beer and preserve food so they could be prepared for marriage. Vikings were usually free to marry who they wished. Sometimes early in the marriage, the wife would go with her husband on raids.

Vikings lived together in a longhouse. It was one big room and was usually dark and smoky, as there were no windows. A hole in the roof over the open fire let out smoke. At one end of the longhouse there would be tables and benches for eating and working. The loom would be set up there as well. Everything from clothing to ships' sails were woven by the women and girls on the loom, and every spare minute was spent there. In the middle of the longhouse there was a long open firepit that was used for cooking and baking. At the other end of the longhouse were the sleeping quarters. Only the husband and wife had an actual bed, everyone else slept on platforms built along the side of the longhouse. Benches were also built along the sides of the remaining walls. Belongings were kept in chests.

A farm usually had other buildings as well. Slaves slept in a separate small house, huddled together on the floor, with no fire. In addition there was a barn for animals, a shed for farm tools, and a food storage hut. Sometimes there was also a separate workshop for metalworking and woodworking. The buildings were all made of stone, with thatched roofs.

Law and order was kept amongst Vikings through an event called a "thing." These were open air meetings where the local men would gather and settle lawsuits and crimes. Everyone had their say and when an agreement was reached, they would clash their weapons together. Often punishment was a fine of some sort, but the most serious penalty was banishment. It was reserved for crimes such as murder. Because Vikings cared so much about their families, banishment was considered horrible. Usually the banished man had to leave and run away immediately, so as not to be killed by others wanting to take revenge for his crime.

Funerals were elaborate affairs in Viking society. Wealthy Vikings were often buried in a ship, because they believed that this made the journey to the land of the dead much safer and more comfortable. The ship contained supplies for the journey, sometimes including the deceased person's dogs and slaves. Many interesting artifacts and beautiful works of art have been discovered in burial ships.

The Vikings worshipped a number of gods. The most important ones were Odin, Thor and Frey. Odin was the god of war and wisdom. Vikings believed that Odin always carried two ravens with him, named Huggin (meaning "thought") and Munnin (meaning "memory"), to fly around the world and report back to him. Odin also had warrior maidens called "Valkyries" who would choose the warriors who died heroically in battle and take them to the Hall of the Slain in the land of the gods, where they could fight all day and feast all night forever. This was the Viking idea of heaven.

Thor was the god of thunder, lightening, wind and rain. He swung a mighty hammer and raced across the stormy skies in a chariot pulled by goats. He was a favorite of the slaves, for they believed he could keep evil spirits away.

Frey was the god of nature. Vikings would hold sacrifices to Frey to make sure the crops grew. His sister, Freya, was the goddess of love and dead women. A warrior slain in battle who did not make it to the Hall of the Slain would go to Freya's fortress of dead women.

Eventually contact between the Vikings and European Christians led to the end of the Norse religion, which was not very well organized. Becoming Christian meant that Vikings started to change their ways. They started trading rather than raiding, and there is evidence that they traded as far away as Arabia and Egypt. Vikings created settlements in the lands they invaded, married other people, and learned new customs and languages. Eventually the Vikings were absorbed into the rest of Europe.

4. **Review your map and find the Scandinavian and Eastern European countries and the Caspian and Black Seas. Add Iceland and Greenland to your map.**

5. **Choose one of the following projects.**

   a. **Choose one of these topics to write a short story about. Be sure to include the feelings of your main character and lots of detail. Topics are: one day in a longboat on the way to a raid, one day in the life of a Viking girl about to be married, one day in the life of a slave, or a Viking funeral. Write at least page.**

   b. **Go to the library and find pictures of a Viking longboat. Then make a model of one using thin cardboard and cloth. Be sure to include oar holes, oars (with toothpicks or straws), bottom deck, a mast and sail, and a detailed figurehead and tail. A nice touch would be to have the Viking raiders' shields mounted on the edge. Paint your ship to give it detail. Take a picture for your teacher.**

   c. **Find a book of Norse myths. *D'Aulaires Norse Gods and Giants* is one very good option. Read some of the stories, and then describe three or four of the characters you meet, with one written paragraph for each.**

6. **Continue reading from your sources for your research paper, writing notes on 3" x 5" cards as you go.**

7. **Have your Home Teacher give you a spelling quiz. Review any words you miss and add them to your ongoing list for further study.**

   Extra book ideas for Lessons 20 - 24 on the Middle Ages:

   King Arthur & His Knights, by P.S. Allen
   Page Boy of Camelot (or Page Boy for King Arthur), by E. Stone
   The Door in the Wall: Story of Medieval London, by M. de Angeli
   Where Valor Lies, by A. & C. de Leeuw
   The Magna Carta, by J. Daugherty
   The Long Pilgrimage and Watch Fires Over the North, by G. Finkel
   Robin Hood and His Merry Men, by J. Finnemore
   Adam of the Road, by E.J. Gray
   Guardians of the Forest, by J.E. Hood
   A Proud Taste for Scarlet and Miniver, by E.L. Konigsburg
   The Maude Reed Tale, by N. Lofts
   Robin Hood of Sherwood Forest, by A. McGovern
   The Road to Damietta, by Scott O'Dell
   The Merry Adventures of Robin Hood, by Howard Pyle
   The Minstrel Knight, by P. Rush
   White Rose and Ragged Staff, by E. Seibert
   Trumpets at the Crossroads, by N. Reinherz
   Joan of Arc, by Ross
   Joan of Arc, by Williams
   The Crystal Cave, by Mary Stewart
   The Sword In the Stone, by T.H. White
   Knights and Castles and *Feudal Life*, by Walter Buehr
   The Medieval Knight, by Martin Windrow
   Cross Sections: Castles, by Stephen Biesty
   The First Book of Medieval Man, by Donald Sobol
   The Writer's Guide to Everyday Life in the Middle Ages, by Sherrilyn
      Kenyon
   Life in a Medieval Village, by Frances and Joseph Gies
   The Middle Ages, by Giovanni Caselli

The Age of Chivalry, by Charles T. Wood

Vikings! by Magnus Magnusson

The Viking World, by Jacquelin Simpson

A Viking Sailor "How They Lived" series, by Christopher Gibb, Rourke
    Enterprises, Vero Beach, 1986

Venetian Adventurer: Being an Account of the Life and Times of Marco Polo,
    and *The Book of Messer*, by Henry H. Hart

The Middle Ages from the "History of Everyday Things" series, by Giovanni
    Caselli, Peter Bedrick Books, New York, 1988

Cathedral; The Story of Its Construction, and *Castle*, by David Macaulay,
    Houghton Mifflin, Boston, 1973

Food and Feasts in the Middle Ages, by Imogen Dawson, New Discovery
    Books, NY, 1994

The Luttrell Village; Country Life in the Middle Ages, and *Walter Draguns
    Town*, by Shelia Sancha, Thomas Y. Crowell, NY, 1982.

Knight, by Christopher Gravett, and Medieval Life, by Andrew Langley,
    "Eyewitness Books" series, Alfred A. Knopf, NY

"Look Into the Past" series, *The Vikings*, by Jason Hook, *The Anglo-Saxons*,
    by Roger Coote, and *The Normans*, by Peter Chrisp, Thompson Learning,
    NY

A Medieval Castle, and A Medieval Cathedral, by Fiona MacDonald, "Inside
    Story" series, Peter Bedrick Books, NY

A Strong Land and Sturdy; *England in the Middle Ages*, by Richard Barber,
    A Clarion Book, The Seabury Press, NY, 1976

Castles, by Beth Smith, Franklin Watts, NY 1988

Castles, by Jenny Vaughan, Franklin Watts, NY, 1984

Living in a Castle, and *Living in a Crusader Land*, by R.J. Unstead,
    Addison-Wesley

The Cathedral Builders, "Peoples of the Past" series, by Marie-Pierre
    Perdrizet and Eddy Krahenbuhl, Millbrook Press, 1992

The Great Book of Castles, by John Monks, Rourke Enterprises, Vero Beach,
    FL, 1989

See Inside a Castle, by R.J. Unstead, Warwick Press, 1986

Life In a Medieval Village, by Gwyneth Morgan, and *Building the Medieval
    Cathedrals*, by Percy Watson, "A Cambridge Topic Book" series, Lerner
    Publications, Minneapolis

The Bayeaux Tapestry; The Story of the Norman Conquest, 1066, by Norman Denny and Josephine Filmer-Sankey, Atheneum, NY 1966

Merry Ever After; The Story of Two Medieval Weddings, by Joe Lasker, Viking Press, NY, 1976

A Tournament of Knights, by Joe Lasker, Thomas Y. Crowell, NY 1986

A Crusading Knight, "How They Lived" series, by Stewart Ross, Rourke Enterprises, Vero Beach, FL, 1987

A Medieval Feast, by Aliki, Thomas Y. Crowell, NY 1983

The Crusades "World History Series" by Timothy Levi Biel, Lucent Books, San Diego, 1995

A Crusading Knight: How They Lived, by Stewart Ross, Rourke Enterprises, Vera Beach, 1987

The Middle Ages, by Catherine Oakley, Gulliver Books, Harcourt Brace Jovanovich, New York, 1989

The Middle Ages, by Trevor Cairns, Lerner Publications, Minneapolis, 1975

Queen Eleanour; Independent Spirit of the Medieval World, by Polly Schoyer Brooks, J.P. Lippincott, New York, 1983

Extra Project Ideas:

- Learn to sing some plainsong or chants.

- Watch the movie "Brother Sun, Sister Moon."

- Read about the life of St. Francis. What is he known for today? Memorize the well known prayer that is attributed to him.

- What do you think of Benedect's "rule"? Do you believe monastery life is a good way to serve God? These internet sites have examples of the "rule" for various orders:

- How do you feel about excommunication from the Church? Do you think this is a good way to keep people from misbehaving?

- Read a book of Norse mythology. *D'Aulaires Norse Gods and Giants* is one recommendation. Write your own Norse myth using these characters behaving in the way you learn they do.

- Build a model of a church or a cathedral from the Middle Ages. Look at pictures for ideas.

- Find out about the various vestments (official clothing) of the Pope, the Archbishop and the Bishops. Draw pictures showing them and their names.

- Look for examples of Gothic and Romanesque architecture in your local buildings and churches. Although America had not yet been populated by Europeans in the Middle Ages, many early American buildings follow these styles.

- Read more about the Vikings. Make a map showing their travels, draw pictures of their jewelry.

- Make yourself some Viking armor and weapons and decorate them elaborately, or find out about Viking names.

- Find out more about Eric the Red, Leif Ericson, their explorations, and Vinland. Write a short biography about them.

Social Studies/Art/English~~~~~~Lesson 21

MIDDLE AGES

Vocabulary Words

Your vocabulary words relate to the material you are studying in Social Studies. Define each of them without using the root word, and use them in a sentence in a way that shows you understand the meaning. Try to think about them in the context of your Social Studies work. If you are unable to find a word in your best dictionary, look in an encyclopedia.

tenant	**heraldry**	**legendary**
proxy	**characterize**	**vassal**
conscience	**feudal system (or feudalism)**	
armor		

Spelling

Select ten words from your written material this week for spelling words. Write each of these words correctly five times and use each word in a complete sentence. Practice your spelling words in preparation for a quiz.

Grammar

1. **Write ten complete sentences. Shade the subject of each sentence in blue and the predicate in red. Refer to part 3 of the section called "Sentences" in your *English Manual* for information on subjects and predicates.**

2. **Throughout the week, you should continue to read your resource books for your paper and take notes. You should be finished with your research by the middle of next week.**

Day 1

King Arthur was a legendary king of England during the Middle Ages. Stories about him were rampant during the 5th and 6th centuries, although they weren't actually written down until later. There probably was a real King Arthur, but there have been so many stories about him that nobody knows the truth. The stories say that King Arthur and the knights of his Round Table did many brave and good deeds.

In addition to the brave and good deeds they did, King Arthur and his knights were also on a very special quest to find the Holy Grail. The Holy Grail was the cup used by Jesus at the Last Supper, shortly before he was crucified. The Celts, who had become Christians by now, believed that the Holy Grail was magic, and would provide food and drink for the person who held it. Some say the Grail is a simple dish of stone, but others say it is a beautiful golden cup studded with jewels. Some stories say the Grail vanished into heaven, while others say it remains to be found.

The Knights of the Round Table with the Holy Grail

Some people believe that King Arthur did exist, but that he was actually a man named Charlemagne, who was an early king in the Middle Ages. After the decline of Rome, some of the Germanic barbarians called "Franks" migrated westward and settled in the Roman territory which we now call France. In 768 A.D., Charlemagne became King of the Franks. Charlemagne was very tall - over 6' 4" - and blond. His voice was very high pitched. He had a long nose, a short neck, and a big belly.

Charlemagne was a devoted Christian who tried to make life better for everyone. He loved learning, and started many schools. He encouraged new methods of farming which helped the soil to remain more fertile. It involved planting a series of different crops in the fields, so the soil could be replenished by a variety of nutrients, instead of being depleted by planting the same thing over and over.

On Christmas Day in the year 800 B.C., Pope Leo III of the Catholic Church crowned Charlemagne "Emperor of the Romans," which in fact meant he ruled much of Europe. Charlemagne's empire represented a blend of Germanic customs, Christianity, and Greco-Roman culture. This combination came to characterize Europe in the Middle Ages.

Holy Roman Emperor
Charlemagne

Charlemagne's empire split after his death in 814 A.D. He had given different parts of his empire to his sons, but they were weak rulers who fought with each other to try to win more land for themselves. Around this time was when the Vikings began their raids against the rest of Europe. Part of the reason why the Vikings were so successful with their invasions was because there was so much fighting going on between Charlemagne's successors that they could not even agree to work together to keep the Vikings at bay.

In 911 A.D., in an attempt to keep peace with the Vikings, King Charles III of the French lands decided to give part of his land to a Viking named Rollo. The deal they made was that in exchange, Rollo would become a Christian, support the king, and keep other Vikings from coming into France. Eventually Rollo's descendents became the Normans, and the part of France they lived in was called Normandy. Normandy was the northern area of France, across the English Channel from England.

1. **Look on your map and locate England and France. Look for the English Channel and the area in France that is Normandy.**

2. **Start reading *Tales of King Arthur,* which is included with this curriculum. By the end of this lesson, you should have it finished and be ready to write about it.**

3. **Continue reading your resources for your research paper, and taking notes.**

Day 2

Medieval people saw the world as being very organized, with everyone in the places God had ordained for them. The feudal system was the method used to organize land, wealth, duties, and freedoms. We already saw in the previous lesson that the Catholic Church was considered the First Estate of God. The Second Estate consisted of the nobles who ruled and fought one another. They were also the landowners. The rest of society was called the Third Estate, which was divided into several groups: peasants who worked the land, craftspeople who brought their skill wherever they went; and the merchant guildsmen, which included shopkeepers and bankers.

The way the feudal system worked is that every man had a lord to whom he owed loyalty, service, and obedience. In return, the lord gave back protection. This was the basis of the feudal way of life. At the top of the feudal system was the king who cared for the land entrusted to him by God, and in return his job was to rule wisely. In the same way, the nobles had the use and responsibility for pieces of the king's land, and owed him certain duties in exchange. They then allowed lower nobles to use parts of their land, and so on down the chain to the tenants at the bottom. Tenants had the use of just a few acres, but still had to swear loyalty and obedience, and pay rent or services to the noble just above them.

One of the most important services given by nobles in exchange for land was to provide military assistance and protection to the lord above them. Nobles also had to help settle disputes and carry out punishments. A vassal was expected to be loyal to his lord even unto death; he might have to give his horse to his lord during a battle, or to be taken prisoner as proxy for his lord. On the other hand, each lord was responsible for the safety and well being of his vassals. The system was like a ladder, with duties and responsibilities toward the person above and the person below. Any level of noble could be a vassal to someone higher up on the ladder. The phrase, "No man without a master; no land without a lord," expressed it well.

The feudal system of medieval Europe placed power in the hands of the strongest local lords with large estates. The lords sought allies among their fellow nobles, and in exchange for military assistance, a lord would grant land to a lower level noble who became his vassal. Knights were vassals to their lord, and young nobles were trained to be knights.

There was a lack of strong rulers during the time of the Viking invasions. Because of this, the lords and their armies often fought one another, trying to gain power for themselves. Because they lived in violent times, feudal lords built castles. The castles of medieval Europe were not palaces, which are designed for luxurious living. Castles were designed mainly as fortresses that were used to defend against enemy armies. The local people looked to their local lords for protection. Castles were big enough so that the people from the outlying farms could take refuge in them during times of trouble.

Because castles were built for defense, it often took a long time to capture one. Such battles where a lord and his army would attack another's castle was called a siege. At first they would make a formal request for surrender. If this was refused, then there were several ways to carry out a siege. One was to encircle the castle, allowing no one to come and go, and wait for the people inside to starve until they gave up. This could take a long time because castles usually kept themselves very well supplied. Another way was to take the castle by force. Sometimes attackers would try to dig tunnels underneath and enter from below, or cause the wall to fall down. A third approach was to try to break the castle walls using huge battering rams or catapults, which were machines somewhat like a giant slingshot, that would hurl large stones at the walls. A fourth method was to try to climb the castle walls with ladders or a moving tower on wheels with a drawbridge at the top that could be lowered onto the top of the castle walls.

Storming a castle

Castles had tremendous defenses against attack, however, and did not fall easily to the enemy. High towers gave plenty of view to see the enemy approaching, and the towers would jut out of the castle walls to give the defending archers a clear way to shoot down the enemy at the walls. There was usually a ditch of some sort around the castle that had to be crossed by the enemy. The ditch might have spears jutting up out of it to make crossing difficult. Sometimes a ditch was filled with water to prevent the enemy from digging under the walls. A water-filled ditch was called a moat. Sometimes a heavily fortified structure called a barbican was built out into the moat, and it would have to be taken over before the attackers could even get to the gatehouse. The gatehouse was thought to be a weak spot, so it was strongly reinforced. A drawbridge prevented access to it in times of siege. Also, an iron gate-like door was lowered in front of the gatehouse door to protect it. If the enemy should somehow get into the gatehouse, small openings called murder holes were used to shoot arrows down into the passageway at the enemy below. Windows were made small and narrow to prevent missiles from coming in, while allowing archers to shoot out without being seen or exposed.

4. **Borrow a book from your library that tells you more about castles. Three good resources are *The Castle Book* by Michael Barenstain, Stephen Biesty's *Cross Sections: Castle*, and the book and videotape *Castles* by David Macaulay. There are other books listed at the end of Lesson 20. Then choose one of these projects:**

   a. **Draw a castle on a large piece of paper. Try to make your picture as accurate as possible. Include the various parts of the castle, such as the gatehouses, the corner towers and walls, the chapel, the barbican and causeway, the moat, the great hall, the stables, the garrison, and the keep.**

   b. **Write a description of several parts of a castle and what they were used for. Include as much detail as you like.**

   c. **Write a short story about being involved in a siege against a castle. Are you inside the castle, trying to defend it, or are you part of the enemy attacking it?**

5. **Continue reading *Tales of King Arthur*.**

6. **Continue reading your resource books and taking notes for your paper.**

Days 3 & 4

Although castles were built for defense, lords and nobles lived in them as well. Therefore, they needed to be a place where they could live, sometimes for months, in case of siege, without needing outside help. It is worth looking at what life inside the castle was like.

The center of castle life was the Great Hall. Here all meals were eaten, meetings were held amongst the nobles plotting their political moves, and court was held to mete out punishments for wrongdoing against the nobles or lords. At one end was the dais, a raised platform where the lord and his lady would sit with their guests. This was also where celebrations and dancing took place.

Somewhere off the Great Hall was a room called a solar. The solar was usually the most comfortable room in the castle, and it was where the lord would spend most of his time. Often it was his bedroom as well. Special smaller meetings took place in the solar.

An important person in the castle was the steward. He acted as the nobleman's assistant, and often stood in his place for such things as hearing petitions for justice or relief from those seeking help from the lord. The steward also managed the smooth running of the castle.

Supplies for the castle, such as cattle, poultry, produce, and grain were brought to the castle and stored in huge storerooms. The butler and the pantler were men who were in charge of making sure there was plenty of food and drink. Food was prepared by many workers : cooks and bakers, dairymaids to make cheese, butter and cream; brewers to make beer; and a scullery to keep track of the dishes and pots. The taster made sure the food was not poisoned before the lord and his family were served. Huge kitchens with several fires and ovens were kept busy with the hustle and bustle.

Castles were in constant need of repairs, so carpenters and masons were kept to repair walls and roofs. There were grooms to care for the horses, a farrier to build and repair wagons, a falconer to train and care for the hunting hawks, and a blacksmith to shoe horses and make tools. The marshal made sure all the rooms were ready for visitors, and kept the serving pages and the maids busy at their tasks. Spinning and weaving rooms were kept going all day to make cloth. An accountant kept track of the finances. The armorer had the very important job of making sure all the weapons in the castle were kept in perfect condition and ready for fighting at all times.

Living inside the castle was not very comfortable. Floors were cold stone with layers of straw or rushes would be put down to provide some comfort. Debris and garbage was often simply tossed onto the floor, and cleaned up every few weeks when the straw or rushes were swept up and replaced. There was little natural light, because the windows were few and far between, often only slits, to help protect against the enemy. As everything was made of stone and there was little sunlight, it was often cold, and activity was usually located around the fire. People slept under animal furs to keep themselves warm.

Tapestry is an art form that developed in the Middle Ages as a method for bringing warmth and comfort to the castle. Noblewomen spent hours carefully needlepointing huge canvas-like cloths which were hung on the walls to keep out drafts. Beautiful pictures were created, usually telling a story, perhaps about a famous battle, or a fanciful tale of unicorns and other creatures. They were very elaborate, and it often took a noblewoman and her women attendants years to make just one tapestry.

Life for the noblewoman mainly involved assisting her husband in the running of the castle. If he was away on business or at war, it was up to her to manage the household and servants, oversee the finances, and even organize the castle's defense if it was attacked. Many noblewomen were well educated, able to read, write, and speak foreign languages. However, some men thought it was dangerous to teach women to read, and even well educated women were expected to follow such occupations as spinning wool and weaving.

Marriages were almost always arranged by the parents for their children. Often such arrangements were more like a property contract, where land and goods would be exchanged as part of the marriage. Marriages were often politically motivated, as an attempt to get one lord to stop fighting another. Furthermore, the feudal system proscribed that if a child's father died, the noble on the next rung up the ladder had the right to make the marriage arrangements for that child. This meant that the child was very much at the mercy of the nobleman's political maneuvering. Despite this, there is much evidence that wives and husbands often grew to love each other, writing to each other fondly when they were apart.

The knights were noblemen who were the warriors for their lord or king. "War is a jolly thing," wrote one 14th century poet, and the people loved to hear tales about the chivalrous deeds of knights in battle. The word "chivalry" comes from the French word for "knight" and refers to the qualities of the ideal knight of the Middle Ages: noble, courteous, devoted to helping the weak and oppressed, and valorous to one's foes in combat. Despite these ideals, many knights did not really live up to them. The ideal of chivalry also put a special emphasis on behaving courteously to women.

Sometimes a knight would kneel and show homage to a noblewoman (as well as to his noble), vowing to be her protector. This code of behavior led to the idea of courtly love, where a knight would swear his devotion and love to his lady, even if it was never acted upon in an intimate way.

Tapestry from the Middle Ages

A young son of a nobleman would spend his growing up years working to become a knight. When he was about eight, he would be sent away to the castle to serve as a page. There he would learn to read and write with other boys. He would learn manners and good social graces, singing, dancing and religious studies. He would also learn how to ride while wearing armor.

As they grew older, pages practiced using weapons by using wooden ones on each other, to limit the damage they could cause. They also practiced riding a horse while carrying a lance and trying to hit a revolving wooden target with it. When he grew older, a page would become a squire, and each knight had a squire to attend him. Squires would take care of the knight's horses, weapons,

A married lady

and armor, thereby continuing his learning. He would also continue with his religious studies. When he was ready, the lord would "knight" the squire in a special ceremony, which included an overnight vigil of prayer and meditation, a ritual bath, and an oath of loyalty to the lord or king. Sometimes one was knighted for having shown bravery in battle, and occasionally the king or lord would knight someone to inspire them just before battle.

Coats-of-arms

Knights in battle armor needed some sort of badge to show their fellow soldiers who they were and whose side they were on. These emblems were called "Coats of Arms." Each noble family adopted a Coat of Arms, which was painted on their shields. When two noble families intermarried, their descendants liked to show the emblems of all their ancestors on their shields. Heralds had the job of helping the leaders of armies to organize battles and keep lists of Coats of Arms.

Knights participated in tournaments in order to practice and hone their skills for battle. Two teams of knights would fight each other in a mock battle, over a large expanse of fields and open hills. Sometimes foot soldiers participated as well. At first, when tournaments began in the 1000's, real weapons were used, and the losing knights would have to give up their horses and armor, so a very good knight could make a fine living in tournaments. Later, blunt weapons and special armor was introduced, and knights began to joust as a part of the tournament. In jousting, two knights would face each other on horseback, and each would charge at the other at full speed, trying to knock the other off his horse with a single blow of a long lance. If the joust was a "joust of war" to settle a dispute, a sharp lance was used, and the loser often died. Otherwise knights preferred to use blunt lances.

Tournaments were also a spectator sport, with judges and ladies in the stands to watch. Coats of Arms were in full display, featured in banners waving in the breeze. Each knight also had an attendant bearing a banner for him, as well as his squire to assist with the weapons, armor and horse. Knights wore large decorative crests on the top of their helmets. In the stands, ladies often carried or wore the colors of their knight. Although popular with people, the Catholic Church frowned on tournaments because of the bloodshed.

The games of chess, checkers, and backgammon were developed during the Middle Ages, and they were especially popular amongst the knights. Because power and war were so much on the minds of the nobles of the Middle Ages, the ability to strategize for battle was prized. These games were considered a way to keep the mind sharp

A tournament

for battle. Darts were also a popular game, developed to help a knight's aim.

Europe in the late medieval times (1050 - 1485) was culturally rich. The favorite subjects for songs, poems, and pictures were love and war. Art and music were very popular with nobles and their courtiers. Some lords kept private musicians to play for them while they feasted or strolled in their gardens. Court jesters or clowns were kept for entertainment.

Everyone enjoyed listening to poets and wandering minstrels. Poet-musicians called troubadours wrote short verses and songs about the pleasures of life and love. Troubadours were usually lower-level nobles pledging to honor and serve their lady as loyally as they did their lord.

7. **Choose one of these projects:**

   a. Play one of these games: checkers, chess, backgammon, or darts.

   b. Go to the library and borrow a book on heraldry, such as *Heraldry: The Story of the Armorial Bearings* by Walter Buehr. If this is not possible, then look up heraldry in the encyclopedia and find out the terms for the different parts and colors of the Coat of Arms. Then make up a Coat of Arms for your own family, choosing an image and colors that seem to describe the qualities of your family. Transfer this to a cardboard shield and paint it, or paint it on good quality art paper and frame it. Send the drawing (or a photo) of your Coat of Arms to your teacher.

   c. Design and make a small tapestry. Choose an image that seems appropriate for your Middle Ages studies, such as knights in battle, or a unicorn in a flowered clearing, or a scene of courtly love. Make your design with colored pencil on paper before you begin. There is more than one way to make the tapestry. You can choose needlepoint, patchwork quilting, or embroidery. You may also simply draw it - carefully, in a detailed picture. You may have to make a trip to a craft supply store. There are many books available that will show you the basics of these kinds of needlework. Continue to work on your tapestry throughout your studies on the Middle Ages if you need to. Send a copy of your design to your teacher in the meantime.

   d. Write a song or a poem. Describe the deeds of a chivalrous knight, the battles he heroically fights, the oppressed people he helps, and the lady he serves. Make up many verses, and send it to your teacher. If you like, you can set it to music, and record it for your teacher.

8. Finish reading *Tales of King Arthur.*

9. Continue gathering information for your research paper, it is due at the end of Lesson 24.

Day 5

During the Middle Ages, the people who lived in England were called the Anglo-Saxons. Like the barbarian Franks who migrated into present-day France, the Anglo-Saxons were descendents of different barbarian Germanic tribes called the Angles, Jutes, and Saxons. They came to Britain, probably from Denmark, and eventually took it over from the Britons who were already living there, pushing the Britons into Wales and Scotland. They renamed Britain "land of the Angles," or England. The Anglo-Saxons led fairly simple lives of farming and hunting. They were great hunters, using dogs and falcons to help them. They also used horses for racing. Christians called them pagans because they worshipped many gods, but they eventually became Christian like much of Europe. The Christian custom of celebrating Christmas with a lighted Christmas tree is believed to have come from the pagan ritual of parading an entire tree, lit on fire, to celebrate the Winter Solstice.

England often had to defend itself against Viking invasions. There is a famous story involving the Anglo-Saxons, the Vikings, and the Normans (who are descendents of the Vikings). In the 1060's, England was ruled by an old king named Edward the Confessor who had no sons to take his throne at his death. Two men were believed to have a claim to the throne: an Anglo-Saxon nobleman named Harold Godwinson (a Viking name), and William of Normandy, who was a Norman (and therefor also descended from the Vikings). Both men were distantly related to Edward the Confessor, and it seems that they were friends as well. However, all that changed when Edward finally died, and Harold Godwinson was crowned King of England. Harold promptly defeated the last great Viking king, Harold Hardraade of Norway, who had been trying to take over England for himself. His victory only lasted two days, however, because William of Normandy was furious. He felt that his claim to England's throne was stronger than Howard Godwinson's. So in 1066, William had many ships built (looking much like Viking ships), and sailed across the English channel and invaded it, defeating Harold and the Anglo-Saxons at the Battle of Hastings. Each army had about 5000 men, but the Normans also had many horses. William was called William the Conqueror, and was crowned on Christmas Day. Under the rule of William, England became a monarchy, which is a nation where the king or queen has all the power to rule.

Scene from the Bayeux Tapestry

A well-known tapestry shows the story of the Norman Conquest and the Battle of Hastings in 1066. It is called the Bayeux (pronounced bah-YOO) Tapestry, and it was made by the ladies of the Norman court. It was done in embroidery, and is almost 200 feet long. It begins with the friendship between William and Harold, and a scene with Harold hunting with other nobles. It portrays the death of Edward, the crowning of Harold, the fury of William. It then shows William having numerous longboats built and prepared, including the many horses he brought. The battle scenes are shown complete with all the different kinds of weapons, beheaded knights, and an early wooden castle being burned to the ground. William is triumphantly crowned, and the Tapestry ends with a great Norman feast, including the blessings of the Bishop Odo, who happened to be William's half-brother. Every event and detail is laid out in one long piece like a modern cartoon strip. The edges show scenes of ordinary life going on, such as farmers plowing. During the battle scenes, scavengers are shown stealing weapons and armor from those slain in battle. There are also embroidered words telling us what is happening.

William the Conqueror demanded an "oath of fealty" or (promise of loyalty) from every lord, and took away the land and property of those who refused. He created a stable government in England, and was responsible for the beginning of the feudal system there. One of his methods for rule was to consult with the lords and others before making important decisions for the country, unlike many rulers who simply did as they pleased. In order to collect taxes from the Anglo-Saxons, he had his officials make lists of all the people and their property, including sheep, cattle, and land. This became the first English census, and was recorded in what was called the Domesday Book (pronounced DOOMZ-day). The word "doom" comes from the Anglo-Saxon word meaning judgment.

At first the Anglo-Saxons resisted the language and the culture of the Normans, and for a time the noblemen would speak Norman French and follow French customs, while the common people spoke their Germanic tongue. However, the two languages blended together over time into what we call English today.

The beginnings of the English legal system were established at this time, in a form called "common law." Much of the English common law is still used today, even in American courts. Common law tried to take some of the power to pass judgment from the Catholic Church. It established a royal court to decide such issues as property rights. Common law also kept track of what judges decided in past cases, and expected that the judges would apply the same decisions to the cases at hand. In this way people could argue in court for a fairer decision based on how a similar case had been decided in the past.

Europe was beginning to form into what is called nation-states. Instead of areas of land constantly changing hands from one head of an army to another, and various tribes of peoples fighting one another for wealth, people were beginning to settle into one area of Europe and create communities and states of government headed by kings. Now kings might still fight one another, but at least everyone in the nation-state would fight for the same king.

In the meantime, the Catholic Church had agreed to crown King Otto of Germany as the Holy Roman Emperor. Otto liked the idea of Charlemagne having been long-ago crowned the Emperor of the Romans, and felt this would help him keep Germany stable by showing he had the blessing of the Church and the authority of Rome. He was able to use the title to persuade the Netherlands to become part of his empire. He also hoped it would allow him to get the Italian provinces to agree to become part of his empire. It never quite worked, however, and there is a long history of struggles between the Pope, the Holy Roman Emperor, and Italy.

10. **Finish reading *Tales of King Arthur* if you have not already done so. Then choose one of these writing projects.**

a. **Summarize one of the stories using your own words.**

b. **Write a short biography of one of the characters, such as a Knight of the Round Table, or Morgan Le Fay, or another of the principle characters. Tell their life story, using your imagination to fill in the gaps, but remaining consistent with the character and the times.**

c. **Write a short essay on Sir Lancelot and chivalry. Did Lancelot live up to the ideal of chivalry as described in your studies? Describe how he did and did not in two or three full paragraphs.**

11. **Keep reading and taking notes for your research report.**

12. **Have your Home Teacher give you a spelling quiz. Review any words you miss and add them to your list for further study.**

Extra Book Ideas:

See Lesson 20 for a list of supplemental reading on the Middle Ages.

Extra Project Ideas:

- Study heraldry in more depth. Make a series of coats of arms for friends and family, using symbols you feel represent them well.

- Investigate the development of armor and the different styles that were used through the years by different kinds of warriors and knights.

- Build your own mini-castle out of wood scraps or clay. Construct it outside, complete with a moat. Alternatively, you could use cardboard boxes and empty paper towel rolls to make a lightweight cardboard castle.

- Make your own chess or checkers pieces. Carve them from wood or form them with clay or fimo. Make your own board and hand paint it.

- Learn to spin or weave.

- Learn about Hildegaard of Bingen and listen to modern recordings of her music.

- Using the book *Make Mine Music* by Tom Walther or any other good source, make your own lyre, harp, or other instrument that was used in the Middle Ages.

- Listen to a selection of Medieval music such as "A Medieval Tapestry: Instrumental and Vocal Music from the 12th through the 14th Centuries," by the Folger Consort; "The Pleasures of the Royal Court," "Music of the Crusades," and "Music of the Gothic Era," by David Munrow; "William Byrd: The Great Service" and "Thomas Tallis: Lamentations of Jeremiah," by Peter Phillips.

- Watch the video of the musical "Camelot," starring Richard Burton.

- Write a story about a young nobleman's boy being sent away to a castle to learn to be a knight.

The death of King Arthur

• Look at pictures of the Bayeux Tapestry and make your own tapestry using pieces of paper taped together in a long strip, and colored pencil, crayon or paint. Tell the story, showing as much detail as possible. Hang your tapestry on the walls around the top of your room.

• Study the feudal system in more depth.

• Attend a medieval fair. The Society for Creative Anachronism often holds such events.

Social Studies/Art/English~~~~~~Lesson 22

MIDDLE AGES

Vocabulary Words

Your vocabulary words relate to the material you are studying in Social Studies. Define each of them without using the root word, and use them in a sentence in a way that shows you understand the meaning. Try to think about them in the context of your Social Studies work. If you are unable to find a word in your best dictionary, look in an encyclopedia.

serf	**expiation**	**parliament**
represent	**renounce**	**manor**
leprosy		

Spelling

Select ten words from your written material this week for spelling words. Write each of these words correctly five times and use each word in a complete sentence. Practice your spelling words in preparation for a quiz.

Grammar

1. **Write a sentence for each of the following pronouns: he, his, him, she, her, hers, it, its, they, their, theirs, them, themselves, herself, himself.**

2. **You will be finishing reading your resource books and taking notes for your research paper this week. You should then outline your paper, organizing your ideas and main topics. Review "Outlining" in the *English Manual*.**

Day 1

Eleanor of Aquitane was both a queen of France and a queen of England in the 1100's. Her father was a very wealthy landowner, and she stood to inherit a very large piece of France as a result. When she was fifteen, she married Prince Louis of France, the heir to the French throne, and he soon became Louis VII, King of France. Eleanor found life in the French court quite dull, and although she knew a great deal about politics, Louis' advisers felt she was a bad influence on her husband. She was a bright, well-educated woman, and enjoyed attending lectures at Paris's schools of theology and philosophy. Women were allowed to listen to the lectures, but couldn't participate in any way - even the queen.

Eleanor began to dislike her husband and her life in the French court more and more. Louis was dismayed with her as well, because she didn't bear him a son and heir - only two daughters. Eventually she and King Louis divorced and she went home, leaving her two little girls behind. Within a year, she fell in love with and married Henry Plantagenet, who after two years took the throne as King Henry II of England. Life was happier for Eleanor as queen in the English court, where her intellect and ideas were somewhat more appreciated.

Over the next twelve years, Eleanor had seven children. She loved them all, but her favorite was Richard, her third son, who eventually became king of England. As king, Richard spent most of his time in the Holy Land fighting in the Third Crusade. (You will learn more about the Crusades in a later lesson.) He was an absent king, but a courageous warrior, and was nicknamed Richard the Lion-Hearted.

John, his youngest brother, ruled as king while Richard was away, and was officially crowned when Richard was killed in battle in 1199. Eleanor grieved long for Richard, especially when John turned away her offers of assistance. She remained a powerful influence in European politics, however, until she died at age 82, in the year 1204.

In England the power of the monarchy grew steadily. During King John's reign from 1199 to 1216 he was so tyrannical that he made many enemies among the nobles and religious leaders. One by one they secretly renounced their allegiance to him, and in 1215 the angry lords forced him to set his seal to the Magna Carta. Magna Carta means *Great Charter*. In this document, the King agreed to recognize the barons' rights and privileges, including that of fair trial. It focused specifically on the rights of nobles, but paid no attention to the common people. Nevertheless, it was important because it said that although the king is the absolute ruler, he still must obey the laws, and he cannot limit the freedom of the Church. It also said he must form a parliament of other people to help make some decisions.

There were three main principles in the Magna Carta that we remember today because they are part of our constitution as well. They are:

1. Taxation only with representation. This meant that the king could no longer tax the nobles without first getting approval from the parliament, which was made up of the lords representing their people.

2. Right to trial. At first this meant that every baron accused of a crime had the right to be tried in a court by his fellow barons, and not by the king. Later this has come to mean a jury trial made up of one's fellow citizens.

3. Limits to power. The idea here was that the king also had to obey the law and could no longer do just as he pleased. As time went on, this came to mean that kings had to seek advice from others before making important decisions for the country. This is how William the Conqueror had ruled.

Robin Hood and his men

Robin Hood was a legendary English outlaw who stole from the rich and gave to the poor during the time of King John. He and his merry men in green took justice into their own hands when they felt it had been misused by dastardly officials such as the Sheriff of Nottingham. The stories about Robin Hood date back to the 1300's, and were a popular topic for storytellers.

1. **See if you can find Nottinghamshire on a map of England.**

2. **Begin reading from *Robin Hood of Sherwood Forest*. Read as many of the tales as you can before the end of the week.**

3. **Write one full paragraph telling what you think about the principles of the Magna Carta.**

4. **You should be close to finishing the research for your report.**

Days 2 & 3

The Norman kings of England were feudal lords over sections of French land, and the French were angry when England's King Edward III said he was also the king of France. The French kings wanted the lands in France that were being ruled by England. The English and French fought in France for 100 years over this land. This war was called the Hundred Years War.

One advantage the English had over the French was the development of the longbow as a weapon of war. The longbow allowed arrows to be shot much farther than the traditional crossbow used by the French, and it changed medieval warfare. This allowed English foot soldiers to cause whole rows of French knights on horseback to be knocked down and left helpless because they could not move in their heavy armor.

In 1415, Henry V of England defeated the French in this manner in a famous battle at Avignon in France, even though he was badly outnumbered by the French. France was exhausted by the decades of fighting. Having so many battles on French land had caused a lot of hardship to the people there. Many townspeople and peasants had been killed, and crops were often destroyed. Henry V signed a treaty with France, which said he would marry the French king's daughter, Catherine, and take over the throne when the French king died. It seemed as if soon England and France would be one land.

Because of the treaty, the French king's son, known as the Dauphin (pronounced DAW-fin), would not get to be king of France. Many people in France were dismayed. However, a rescuer came to France. Here is the story of that rescuer.

THE HOPE OF FRANCE

by Patti Bosomworth

I want to tell you a story about an ordinary girl, an ordinary peasant girl, who lived in France over 500 years ago. At any rate, she seemed like any ordinary peasant girl until she grew a bit older. Her name was Jeannette, or Jeanne for short.

As a young girl she sewed, spun wool, and watched over the flocks. Her mother tended to the home and to her brothers, and her father worked in his fields. She had a simple home, one probably typical for peasants in the early 1400's, with a packed earth floor and only the simplest of furnishings, for there was no money to spare on unnecessary things.

Jeanne's mother taught her the things she needed to know. What was especially important to her was that her mother taught her about the Christian religion through stories. Although she loved to learn, Jeanne never did learn to read or to write. She had little or no use for reading or writing as a peasant, unlike the nobles. She sang and danced with the other children, and from time to time they would deck their special tree, the fairy tree, with garlands and wreaths made from flowers. When Jeanne and her friends were very young, the fairies would come and take the wreaths at night, although Jeanne was not among the few who had actually seen the fairies. When she grew older, she would go at night with some of the older children and participate in taking away some of the wreaths so the younger children might enjoy believing the fairies had delighted in their offerings.

As Jeanne grew, the church and her religious studies became more important to her than dancing and playing with her friends. She spent a great deal of time in the church praying. She prayed for many things, but not for things like a new dress to replace her worn and somewhat small one. Jeanne prayed most of all for her beloved country of France.

Although there were no newspapers such as we have today, the news spread of war, of the English invasions, of the uncrowned King Charles (the Dauphin, or oldest son of the King as he was called) being driven from his lands, and of the hopelessness of the French ever reclaiming their lost lands and making their country whole again. There were stories of the Dauphin's mother, Isabeau of Bavaria, who played a part in the destruction of France for her own personal gain. She gave her daughter's hand in marriage to King Henry of England, and what is more, she signed a treaty practically giving the crown of France to England. The treaty stated that the firstborn son of this union should be ruler of both England and France. She had betrayed both France and her son Charles.

Just as it was known by all that Isabeau of Bavaria had played a part in the downfall of France, it was commonly known that there was a prophesy of a maid from France who would play a part in its restoration. This was just a fairy tale to Jeanne and the children until one day in 1425, when Jeanne heard a voice as she beheld a great light in the direction of the church. The voice said that she was to be that maid, and that she had been born for this purpose. She was advised to be good and to continue to pray to God. What a shock it must have been for this thirteen year old girl to think of becoming the heroine in her own childhood fairy tale!

The first voice Jeanne heard was that, she came to realize, of Saint Michael; later she also heard the voices of Saints Catherine and Margarette. All of this Jeanne guarded in absolute secrecy, telling no one, not even her two closest friends. The voices were sweet and gentle, and they instructed her and guided her, assuring her that they were serving God's will. She was told that if she would act upon their guidance, God's purpose would be fulfilled. The voices guided Jeanne for the rest of her life, even in the battlefield.

How 17-year-old Jeanne came to travel three hundred and thirty miles on horseback from her home to the Dauphin in the middle of winter, through enemy occupied cities and countrysides, is a story all its own which is best left for another time. Suffice it to say that she learned to ride quickly, and was a capable girl with endurance and determination, if not a bit of temper as well.

Charles, the Dauphin, was the first person she told her story to in full, and it took a fair bit of convincing before he would believe her. But when she recited, word for word, his own private prayer for the restoration of France, he believed her immediately. That does not mean things moved swiftly, especially not for Jeanne, who was filled to the brim with certainty, purpose, and Divine guidance. For her, the delay was agony. Things dragged more slowly than ever as Charles's more suspicious advisors, especially one named La Tremoiulle , insisted upon intensive questioning to be certain the maid was not a witch. Even priests were brought in to question her and hear her confession. They were more than impressed by her simple and direct speech, her purity, and her piety.

She told Charles that she had been instructed by her voices to do four things by the end of one year: Raise the siege at Orleans, bring about the retreat of the English, see him crowned King Charles VII of France, and release the Duke of Orleans from the English. Troops were gathered, armor was made for her, and a special sword was delivered to her from the special hiding place where her voices indicated it could be found. Finally ready, she led her troops off to battle in April of 1429.

It is recorded that Jeanne's armor was made of white unpolished steel. She must have been quite a sight indeed! She carried a specially made banner, as well as her sword, which she never once used to kill anyone. The banner was made for her at the command of Saint Catherine and Saint Margarette, her voices. Pictured on this was God holding the world, with two angels kneeling on either side of him in a field sown with lilies. The words JESUS MARIA were inscribed upon it. The very sight of her struck a chord of great hope and courage in the hearts of the French, and simultaneously brought forth fear in the hearts of the English.

The troops spent their first night in the battlefield drinking and carrying on raucously. The next day (probably at dawn) she made them all confess, and ordered that there be no more of that sort of behavior. They immediately obeyed, changing years of habit in the wink of an eye. Such reform had never before been heard of in any army, especially in one of over four thousand men.

In city after city, Jeanne boldly led the troops to victory. She constantly coached them to take heart, be courageous, have no fear, and to spur their horses. In city after city, the English retreated. It was really unbelievable: Jeanne d'Arc, a peasant girl, was giving orders to war-worn men, many of whom were more than twice her age. The whole French-English situation began to turn around dramatically, almost at once. The English said she was a witch.

Joan of Arc

It was not all as easy as it sounds. Indeed, La Tremoiulle and others of the Dauphin's advisors had been personally profiting from private deals made with the enemy, and they stood to lose financially if certain cities were taken back by France. Their personal gain was more important to them than the gains that would benefit all the people of France. They advised Charles against Jeanne's plans, and they slowed things down at certain times when Jeanne was advised by her voices to get things moving more quickly.

Eventually, after much work, Charles was brought to his coronation. It was a holy and splendid gathering, with many nobles present and, of course, Jeanne. The same special holy oil that was used to anoint him had been used for hundreds of years, for the coronations of all the kings of France.

Jeanne had but one more battle, which was the siege of Paris . This was where the English were holding the Duke of Orleans prisoner. Her voices told her to move ahead immediately, but the king's advisors convinced him that Jeanne was proud and war hungry, and that there was plenty of time to spare. They advised rest and retreat, during which time treaties were drawn up and signed. All this stalling gave the English time to reinforce their troops in Paris, so that when Jeanne and her troops attacked, they failed. Not long after that she led her troops in another attack which also proved too much for them. On the 23rd of May, 1430, Jeanne d'Arc was captured by the enemy.

The rest is mostly a sad, sad story. King Charles, whom she had served so bravely, did not order her rescue, or offer money in exchange for her. Certain selfish and greedy individuals, such as an English bishop named Cauchon, wanted her dead. She was bought at a high price. Young, brave, devout Jeanne was now Joan in the hands of the English. Joan was imprisoned. The English made a public spectacle of her, and she was clad in heavy chains. After all, without chains she might fly away— such was the common belief regarding those thought to be witches. Cauchon made sure the people would think he thought she was a witch whether he really thought so or not. Joan was held in a cold, dark, tower, always in chains, for over four months. Conditions in the prison were enough to drive anyone mad. The guards were drunk and often noisy. She was supposed to have been allowed more comfortable prison quarters and by law should have had a woman tend her. She was allowed none of this.

Bishop Cauchon arranged an improper trial with as many as seventy questioners at a time who would endlessly fire questions at her for over twelve hours a day, trying to trick her by paraphrasing the same questions over and over in the hopes that they might find some admission of witchcraft. She answered the questions wisely, and considering her lack of formal education, it is said she answered in a most scholarly manner. Bishop Cauchon was confounded. He was quite certain that he would receive a promotion to archbishop if he could prove Joan to be a heretic, and this may indeed have been his sole reason for twisting Joan's words, torturing, and tricking her. Joan would not take the oath of the church, and this was considered a crime in itself. She would only take an oath to God. It was very hard, if not impossible, to find cold hard facts against Joan, so the Bishop contrived to twist her story of the childhood fairy tree to appear as pagan sorcery, and her voices were said to be from the devil. Her page's clothing was held to be sinful attire for a woman, the consecrated ring Joan wore in the presence of Saints Catherine and Margarette was labeled a magical amulet used for sorcery, and so it went.

Finally, Joan agreed to wear traditional women's clothing so that she might be granted permission to attend mass and confession. Afterward, back in her tower, she was so terrified of the drunken guards that she resumed her page's attire, only to be accused of backsliding. Eventually, through trickery and treachery, Joan was condemned and excommunicated as a heretic. Her sentence was that she was to be burned at the stake, in spite of her appeals to have her case taken to the Pope. Joan's voices spoke to her of the ill fate that would befall anyone involved in the scandal, and she warned her persecutors, but to no avail. On her way to the stake she uttered prayers that were filled with devotion to God and stated that she was not a witch as the English proclaimed her to be. Her last request was to have the cross from the altar of the nearby church brought before her and held where she could see it until her last breath. She died on May 30, 1431, at nineteen years of age.

But this is not quite the end of the story, for the spirit of Joan lived on. Many at her execution overheard her praying and calling to the saints and Jesus. Many of those who had questioned her were priests and learned men, and they were overheard saying that they would never be saved, for they had burned a holy woman; some even prayed that their souls would go where they believed her soul to be - with God in Heaven.

In the end, Bishop Cauchon never did become Archbishop. Suspected of foul play, he was sent to a small chapel of the Virgin in expiation of his sin against Joan. He died of a shaving wound. It is said that one of the other conspirators lived the rest of his short life as a leper, while still others met ill fate or fell into disrepute.

Joan's undying spirit moved the leaders of France's fighting forces. They returned to their efforts in order to complete what she had begun. They removed La Tremoiulle, the King's scheming advisor, and finally succeeded in restoring France in less than the seven years Joan predicted it might take.

Nearly twenty years after her execution, King Charles decided to try to get Joan's name cleared of the charges against her. The trial lasted nearly six years, and included nearly everyone who had ever known her, at least those who were still among the living. Whether he did this for her or for his own sake, as his crown would not have been considered legal if it had been gained through witchcraft, is left to question. On July 7, 1456, the previous verdict was annulled, and Joan of Arc was declared to be without sin.

Five hundred years later, Joan was declared to be a symbol of love and sacrifice throughout the world. The following was written in her honor:

> *Across the night of history's blackest pages*
> *One name is scrolled by a shaft of sun:*
> *Joan of Arc, the glory of the ages,*
> *Who battled hate, and lost—and, "losing, won."*

The fighting finally ended in 1453 when the French pushed the English out of France.

5. **Finish reading your research books. You should have all your information on 3" x 5" cards. As you start thinking about your outline, you can arrange your note cards in proper order to follow the outline.**

Days 4 & 5

During the Middle Ages, a village was actually a sort of big farm, called a manor. The manor included a big house, where the noble or knight lived, which was usually surrounded by woods and pasture. The man who held a manor directly from the king was known as the lord of that manor. The lord was expected to supply his king with goods and services from the manor. The land in the fields belonging to each manor was divided among the tenants. Tenants in turn might divide up their land amongst even lower down serfs, who only had a few acres on which to make a living. Some tenants had laborers who worked under them, while other people were almost like slaves. These "bottom of the ladder" people were the serfs, and they could be sold or given away, as could their children. They had to ask permission from their lord to marry, and could be hanged if they tried to run away. Even so, they still had to pay taxes to their lord, and when they died, their families were charged a death tax.

Ninety percent of the people in the Middle Ages were farmers and peasants who worked hard all their lives trying to scrape out a living. The lord gave the serfs a hut to live in, land to farm, and protection. In return the serfs tended the lord's land, looked after his animals and did other work on the estate. These communities included the village, the lord's castle, a church, and workshops. The serfs produced goods and services needed within the community. There were blacksmith shops, bakeries, millers, carpenters, coopers (barrel-makers), cart-makers, and brewers. Often the lord controlled the mill and the ovens. This meant a farmer was forced to grind his grain and bake his bread in the lord's mill and ovens, and pay for doing it! All of this meant that the community was *self-sufficient,* or able to produce everything it needed.

There were two inventions in the Middle Ages which made it easier to grind grain. These were the water mill and the windmill. Mills had been used in the past, such as in Ancient Rome, but not very extensively as there had always been plenty of slaves to do the hard work. But medieval people were interested in making life a little easier and peasants more productive, so they put this old technology to work. Farmers also had new and heavier plows. A new harness was made for horses so they could pull the plows. Horses now wore horseshoes, and the metal shoes protected their hooves. Farming became much more efficient.

Most peasants were free, but still lived a very difficult life. They did the work that supported everyone else, raising animals for wool, leather, and meat, and growing all the crops. They had barely enough to eat and almost no clothing or other possessions. This terrible inequity was simply accepted for a long time, and those in better circumstances said that the peasants were paying for the sin of Adam and Eve in the Garden of Eden. The lords tried to get as much work as possible out of the tenants, and the tenants tried to do as little as they could for the lord.

The lords controlled the peasants as much as they could, and the peasants began to resent this. There is even a story of tenants being forced to keep the frogs outside quiet at night so the lord's wife could sleep. Imagine how impossible that would be! Toward the end of the Middle Ages the common people began to demand their freedom, and there were peasant uprisings from time to time because of their anger. John Ball, who helped lead revolts against the nobles in the 1300's, said, "Why should the lords hold us in bondage? Are we not all come from the same parents, Adam and Eve? Why should our lords be clothed in velvets and furs while we are forced to wear rags?... It is by our labor that they live well."

Ordinary people in the Middle Ages ate dark, whole grain bread, cheese and eggs, and vegetables from their own gardens. Common vegetables were onions, peas, beans, cabbage, and parsley. Their usual drinks were mead, ale, and beer. Sometimes these were mixed with herbs and honey.

The kings and nobles liked rich, elaborate food. The wealthy could afford to eat plenty of meat and pastries as well as imported luxuries like sugar, raisins and wine. They ate birds such as starlings, vultures, storks, swans, and peacocks, as well as chickens, and seafoods such as porpoise and dolphin, seal, whale, salmon, and eels. Popular meats were venison, pork, and mutton. The church forbade eating horses. Raw fruit was not often eaten, because it was thought to be unhealthy, as were cucumbers. Tomatoes were considered poisonous. Oranges weren't shipped to England until toward the end of the 14th Century, and even then they were rare.

Because there was no refrigeration in those days, food often went bad. Spoiled meat has a strong, unpleasant flavor, and spices were used to disguise the bad taste. Spices such as pepper, garlic, mustard, cloves, and cinnamon improved many meals.

Instead of plates, people used large slices of stale bread called trenchers. At the end of the meal, these supplies of stale bread were gathered up and given to the poor along with the leftovers. Trenchers were usually slices of coarse, dark bread made with wheat, rye, and barley. The bread was baked into a flat loaf which was turned several times in the baking so it would remain flat on both sides. It was allowed to sit for several days to become hard, and then was cut into squares.

Two people would sit together and share one dish of food and one goblet of drink. The technique was to reach into the dish with one's fingers, take a piece of meat, put it on the trencher, and slurp it off into the mouth. Before drinking from the shared cup, they were to swallow all their food and wipe their mouths.

Children were told in the 1500's, " Lay a clean trencher before you, and when your pottage is brought, take your spoon and eat quietly... Heap not thy trencher high with many morsels, and from blackness always keep thy nails."

Infectious disease, armies, and accidents killed many children. Out of five or six children in a family, only two or three could be expected to survive. The average life expectancy was only thirty years old, and medical knowledge was limited. Herbal remedies were frequently used, however, and many of them are still used today. Wormwood, for instance, was used to get rid of worms in the digestive system and was also put in clothing to keep fleas away. Other kinds of medicine often did more harm than good. The most common form of surgery was bloodletting, often carried out by uneducated barbers with dirty instruments. It was believed that bloodletting helped restore the balance of fluids in the body, but it usually just made an already sickened person weaker. Dentistry was also very primitive, with rotting teeth merely being pulled out with a sort of pliers by tooth pullers working in the marketplace. Nobles were sometimes fitted with new teeth made out of bone.

One of the most feared illnesses was leprosy, and lepers were usually forced to live in houses built well away from the manors and towns. They got by with subsistence farming and by begging. Lepers were also forced to wear certain clothing that distinguished them, and were forbidden in church, mills, bakeries and taverns.

The Bubonic Plague, or Black Death, as it came to be called, had a much worse effect, however. It caused dark patches to appear all over the skin, where blood had clotted underneath. The tongue turned black, and sores appeared under the arms and between the legs. Some people survived, but most died within three days. The Black Plague killed approximately one third of the population of Europe between 1347 and 1351. Whole families and villages were wiped out. It was accidentally brought to Europe from the East by germs from fleas on rats that were on board a ship. People did not understand how disease spread. They thought that these attacks of the plague were a punishment sent by God for their wickedness, and they tried to live better lives. Some believed the world was coming to an end. Unfortunately, although cats might have helped to control the numbers of rats, people thought cats were agents of the devil, and killed them by the thousands. The Black Death continued on and off for 100 years, but was never again as bad as those few terrible years.

Death was often on the minds of people, and not just because of the Black Death. In the Middle Ages, it was believed that if one did not make a final confession to a priest before they died, they would go to hell, but so many priest died during the Black Plague that most people were buried without any ceremony or prayers. Mass burial pits were dug as there were not enough coffins to go around.

The figure of Death was sometimes even acted out. Men would put on skeleton costumes and perform the Dance of Death as being the great leveler of society. The figure of Death can be seen in many churches and manuscripts, often leading a poor soul off by a rope as it plays a drum or a fife.

Because so many people had been killed in the plague, labor was at a premium and peasants could afford to move to places where they received better treatment. This meant that many more people moved into towns and cities.

6. **Choose one of these projects:**

a. **It is interesting to know that self-sufficient communities existed in medieval times. Think about the following questions and write an answer responding to each one. Use what you have learned so far about civilization to come up with ideas.**

1) **What are all the different foods that can be grown or raised in your community?**

2) What are the raw materials found in your part of the country that would be needed to make the necessities of life such as clothing, tools, power, etc.?

3) What are the various skills that would be required to turn these raw materials into products or goods for the use of the community?

4) What items do you presently use in your life that would have to be given up in a self-sufficient community?

5) How would you like to live in a self-sufficient community? Name advantages and disadvantages.

b. Write one page in which you tell what you think about what Robin Hood did.

c. Compose your own adventure for Robin Hood and his band of merry men.

d. Write a story as if you or your family or friends were victims of leprosy or the Black Death in the Middle Ages. How does your life change with the onset of the disease?

Extra Credit: Make your own trenchers and have your family eat a whole meal from them. To be authentic, let the bread sit for a few days before cutting. Eat the meal without using forks, only spoons. No forks were used in medieval times.

Recipe:

- 6 c. whole grain flour
- 2 c. barley flour
- 1 1/2 tsp. salt
- 1/2 tsp. sugar
- 1/2 package dry yeast
- 3 c. warm water

Mix the yeast with warm water and 1/2 tsp. sugar. Separately, sift the flours and the salt together. When the yeast mixture is bubbly, work it into the flour until the dough is stiff. Knead it well, and let it rise 1/2 hour. Knead it again, and shape it into flat rectangles. Let it rise 1 hour, and bake at 400°. After 20 minutes, turn the trenchers over and bake another 20 - 30 minutes.

Cool the bread thoroughly so it doesn't "sweat" when wrapped. Wrap it in a cloth and store it for several days. Then cut it into squares and use the squares for plates.

7. Begin making the outline for your report. The outline should be done by the beginning of next week.

8. Have your Home Teacher give you a spelling quiz. Review any words that you missed and add them to your ongoing list.

Extra Book Ideas:

See Lesson 20 for a list of supplemental reading on the Middle Ages.

Extra Project Ideas:

• Make a diorama of a typical manor village.

• Find a cookbook with recipes from the Middle Ages and prepare a meal for your family. There are books on Medieval food in the list of supplemental books in Lesson 20.

• Compose your own set of tales for Robin Hood and his merry men. Write them into a play and perform it with your friends, complete with costumes and a simple set.

• Read a biography of Joan of Arc. Several are listed in the supplemental book choices at the end of Lesson 20.

• Write a dialogue between Joan and her voices, or Joan and her persecutors.

- Research more about the Hundred Years War and what the issues were between England and France. Find out more about the Battle at Avignon.

- Find out about other people who are said to be martyrs for their faith.

- Dramatize any aspect of Joan's life which is the most interesting or exciting to you. Create a mural that tells the story.

- Research the four humors, the growth of medicine, and the Black Death.

- Watch a video of Shakespeare's "Henry V," such as the recent version by Kenneth Braugham.

Social Studies/Art/English~~~~~~ Lesson 23

MIDDLE AGES

Vocabulary Words

Your vocabulary words relate to the material you are studying in Social Studies. Define each of them without using the root word, and use them in a sentence in a way that shows you understand the meaning. Try to think about them in the context of your Social Studies work. If you are unable to find a word in your best dictionary, look in an encyclopedia.

pillory	logic	vice
revival	slate	guild
commerce	fortress	morality

Spelling

Select ten words from your written material this week for spelling words. Write each of these words correctly five times and use each word in a complete sentence. Practice your spelling words in preparation for a quiz.

Grammar

1. **Write sentences in which you use the following prepositions. Refer to the "Prepositions" section in your *English Manual*.**

above	about	along	at	for
between	before	from	by	in

2. **This week you will be finishing your outline and working on the rough draft of your report. First compose a topic sentence for each major paragraph in your outline, and then start to fill in the paragraphs for a rough draft. Make at least one illustration for your report. Your report should be finished by the end of next week.**

Day 1

There are a number of reasons why people in the later half of the Middle Ages began to live in towns. One was to find work. The Black Plague meant that there was now a lot of opportunity for people to find other kinds of work besides the hard life of farming. The other reason was to get away from feudalism. The Germans had a proverb, "Town air makes (you) free." People in town owed their loyalty and obedience to the mayor and councilors instead of to a lord. The mayor and councilors were chosen from among the most wealthy merchants and craftsmen. Many people found such a system less oppressive than the feudal system.

All commercial work was controlled by craft *guilds* who made sure that their members produced high-quality goods and trained young men in the skills needed for each craft. Guilds were groups of men and women who organized themselves by their trade, or business, and occasionally by social interests. A man who worked hard and became respected within a guild had a chance of taking part in the government of his town.

Just as we saw with the self-sufficient manor village, medieval life taught the lesson that individual survival depended upon collective power. Guilds were another way for people to know their place in medieval society, and guilds also made life better for their members. Those who worked in the same trade usually lived in the same area of the city, and tended to associate mostly with each other. The social guilds were composed of people who were especially devoted to a particular saint, or who had something else of that kind, such as the running of a hospital, to bind them together.

The trade guilds were of two kinds: merchant guilds and craft guilds. Craft guilds were broken up into the different types of skilled craftsmen. There were goldsmiths, tailors, furriers, woodworkers, saddlers and so on. The merchant guilds were made up of retail tradespeople such as butchers, fishmongers, and grocers.

Within the craft guilds there were three important levels. The lowest was apprentice, next was journeyman, and the top was the master. The family of an apprentice paid the master to train him. The apprentice lived in the master's home from a young age and was practically a slave to his master until he rose to the level of journeyman. As a journeyman he would be an assistant to the master, and receive a wage. When the time came to prove that he was finally ready to be a master himself, he was required to produce a "master work" using his very best skills. These master works were true works of art.

Often special craft techniques were kept secret, especially in cloth making and leather tanning. Each step of the process might be done by a different person who was skilled in just that one area. Shoemakers were actually forbidden to tan their own leather, and had to take it to a tanner to get it done!

Retailers often tried to trick their customers by selling inferior goods. The punishments they received were usually a kind of public humiliation. A baker who sold loaves that were too small would be pulled through the streets in a cart, with loaves of bread strung around his neck. He would be taken to the pillory, where he'd be tied up for the day while his dissatisfied customers threw garbage at him.

Women had many more opportunities in the towns than in the country. They could now spin, weave, and dye cloth instead of working in the fields. Some women even worked as shoemakers, tailors, bakers or barbers. Women were thought to be the best brewers, too.

Life in town had its own problems. The streets were narrow and often steep, and were either paved with bumpy cobblestones or left as hard packed dirt which turned to mud in the rain. The houses were narrow and tall, with shops on the ground floor and two or three stories above for family living. The top levels of the houses stuck out on the sides, almost touching high above the street below. Most houses were built of wood, with thatched roofs. The windows were very small, and had wooden shutters that could be closed for safety from theft and weather. Fire was a real hazard because of the wood and thatch, and the proximity of the houses to each other.

Medieval cities were very dirty. Waste was just dumped out from the upstairs windows of the houses, and would flow down the streets. Pigs, chickens, dogs, and even cows wandered around where they pleased. In the bigger houses of the nobles, food scraps and bones were tossed onto the floor after meals, so the dogs could eat. Housekeeping in those days was very different than it is today!

Inside, the walls were often covered with canvas or carpets, for insulation. The ceilings were low, and the rooms were dark. Medieval people had very little furniture. Tables might just be boards across wooden supports, and there were usually a few benches and stools to sit on. These trestle tables could be easily taken apart to make more sleeping space. Their few possessions were stored in chests. They slept on mattresses stuffed with straw, or if they were wealthier, with wool. The parents as well as the two or three youngest children all slept together in a big bed. If they could afford it, the bed might be hung with curtains around it for warmth. Privacy such as we have today never occurred to anyone. Even large families usually lived together in a couple of rooms which were separated only by archways, not by doors that could be closed.

The husband and sons worked downstairs in the family's workshop or business, while the wife and daughters did housework, dried herbs, prepared simple medicines, made thread, and sewed clothing. By our standards, people in the Middle Ages owned very few clothes. Not only were clothes expensive, but they had to be made by hand. The spinning wheel wasn't commonly used until the end of the 14th Century, so even the thread making had to be done by hand, with something called a *distaff*. People expected their clothes to last for many years. As medieval houses were cold, people wore many layers to keep warm. Clothes were made from wool, linen, hemp, and silk.

Few people in the Middle Ages could afford to marry for love alone. Arranged marriages were common, and children were expected to obey their parents' wishes. The poor generally had greater freedom than the wealthy to choose who they married, because the wealthy had more property at stake. Most families had five or six children. Parents hoped that their children would look after them when they were too old or sick to work. Some rich people could afford to retire to monasteries and pay to be looked after in their old age.

1. **Finish your outline by writing topic sentences for each paragraph of your outline. Work on your illustration. If you are ready, start filling in the paragraphs with the information on your note cards.**

Day 2

The growth of European towns and the rise of the middle class encouraged the revival of learning. Now townspeople had money to pay for education. In addition, there was a greater need for educated people. Education was traditionally divided strictly to meet the needs of those who held different positions in society. This meant that the son of a noble received a very different education from the son of a laborer or one who was promised to the priesthood.

Young people often went to study with scholarly monks or priests, or to live in the home of another noble in order to learn the skills they would need in adulthood. We have already seen how boys from noble families became pages at age seven, and at about fourteen, squires. Girls from noble families were companions to ladies of other high born families, and learned to spin, weave, do beautiful embroidery, and manage a household. In the lower classes children were usually apprenticed to a trade or worked in the fields.

Monastery schools were mainly for boys who planned to become monks. A boy might enter a monastery school at age five, grow up to become a monk, and live in the monastery the rest of his life without ever seeing his parents again. In time, many monasteries also began operating schools for the children of the towns. Students had to sit on hard benches or on straw scattered on the floor. Candles were the only light for studying in the evening. Classrooms were often cold and damp. Books were very costly so the teacher read aloud while the students took notes on a slate.

Cathedrals also ran schools of higher learning. In 1088 one of the first universities was established in Bologna, Italy. By 1200, there were universities at Paris, France; Oxford, England; and Salerno, Italy. The basic curriculum in the university consisted of the "Seven Liberal Arts," which included Latin grammar, rhetoric, logic, arithmetic, geometry, astronomy and music. More advanced courses could be studied in religion, law and medicine. To receive a degree of "master," a student had to pass examinations and write a scholarly paper.

Only young men were educated in universities, not the women. The medieval university student's day was long and hard. A student had to get up before 5:00 in the morning so he could go to church until 6:00. Then he attended classes until 10:00, had lunch, and attended classes until 5:00 in the evening.

Even though there was a revival in learning, the majority of people could not read or write during the Middle Ages. Stories from the *Bible* and the lives of the saints were told in verse in religious pageants and plays.

There were many holidays celebrated in the towns, because the Catholic Church had such a full religious calendar. Work (and pay), would stop for the observance of these holidays, sometimes as many as fifty times a year! There would be a religious procession and then the celebrations would begin. Horse races, wrestling matches, and archery contests were popular. So were "Mystery" plays, a popular form of religious drama which took place on these days. Guilds would perform appropriate stories from the *Bible*, such as Noah's Ark being presented by the shipbuilders guild. (The word "mystery" comes from the French word for trade). Plays were often performed on a cart that could be moved from location to location. Another type of play was a "morality play" where the characters represented human virtues and vices such as pride, sloth, faith, goodness, or greed.

Some plays mixed some of the old pagan traditions with the newer Christian beliefs. A traditional method of drama called "mummers" began when countryfolk would put on masks and dance and sing traveling from door to door. Later the mummers took characters from pagan stories and used them to tell a Christian story. One story often performed was the tale of Saint George and the dragon. The story of St. George is about a famous English knight who rescued the King of Egypt's daughter by slaying the dragon who was keeping her captive. St. George was made a saint after jealous noblemen in Egypt put him through a series of tortures which he survives. This mummers play is still sometimes performed at Christmas, and ends when the herbalist doctor can't revive the slain Saint George, but Father Christmas, with the power of God, can.

In the Middle Ages there were no radios, no televisions, and no movies. People were always eager to hear news of the world and to be entertained by stories and songs. Every so often, a group of traveling entertainers would come through town with a sort of traveling circus. They were called *jongleurs*, and they were musicians, poets, actors, acrobats, jugglers, comedians, and dancers. They might even bring dancing bears and other trained animals with them.

Lute player

Jongleurs and minstrels were of less noble birth than the troubadours who entertained in the castles, but were just as welcomed by the townspeople. It was a very exciting day when they came to town! The Church condemned such activity, however, because the dancing and other wild behavior was considered improper. In one story, a group decided to dance in the churchyard on Christmas Eve. As a punishment, they were forced to dance there all year until the Archbishop released them.

St. George and the Dragon

As more people learned to read and education became more sophisticated, the need for traveling jongleurs decreased, and the quality of their performances went down. By the end of the 15th Century, they primarily entertained in taverns.

Many popular games from medieval days are still enjoyed today. Playing cards came into use at that time. So did gambling with dice. Nine Men's Morris is an ancient game that was played in different forms in ancient Egypt, Troy, and Norway. Part of a Nine Men's Morris board was found in the remains of an ancient Viking burial ship from about 900 A.D.

2.   Choose one or more of the activities below to do this week. You will be telling your teacher about your experience at the end of the week.

a. **Learn to play Nine Men's Morris. You need two players, each with nine pieces. Pennies and dimes work well. A simple board is shown below, draw yourself a larger one to play the game. Typical boards were decorated elaborately with designs appropriate to the culture of the people playing the game.**

Directions: Start with the board empty. There are two parts to the game.

Part 1:

1) **Each player takes turns putting his nine pieces, one at a time, onto any vacant point (any intersection or corner) on the board.**

2) **If a player forms a row of his own three men in a straight line (called a *mill*), he takes one of his opponent's men off the board. Any piece in a mill is safe from being taken.**

3) In Part 1, the pieces that are removed by the making of a mill are returned to the board one at a time during the owner's subsequent turns. When all the pieces have been put on the board, Part 2 begins.

Part 2:

1) Players keep taking turns moving one man per turn to an adjacent vacant point along any line, trying to make a mill in order to remove one of the opponent's pieces.

2) Mills are continuously made and broken as turns are taken and pieces are removed from the board. Pieces that are removed are not returned to play.

3) If one of the players makes a mill but all the other player's pieces are also in a mill, no pieces are removed from the board.

4) When one player has only three men left on the board and they're all in a mill, he must break the mill on his turn in order to play.

5) To win the game, a player must either reduce his opponent to two playing pieces OR block all his opponent's pieces so he cannot move.

b. Practice some skills of a jongleur. Select three oranges, tangerines, or other small fruits of equal size, and practice juggling. Old tennis balls can be used too. You might like to make three small beanbags for juggling, as they last longer than fruit and can stand being dropped a lot. Also practice standing or walking on your hands. The trick is to keep your body and legs straight and strong, and find the point of balance that is uniquely yours.

c. **Listen to any or all of the following instruments - bagpipe, harp, hurdy-gurdy, lute, lyre, mandolin, and recorder. List the pieces you hear, and describe your response.**

d. **Make your own tambourine. You can use a tin pie plate or a small margarine tub with a lid. Make several holes and attach bottle caps, metal washers, or little bells. String colorful ribbons through some of the holes. Put on some music and supply the rhythm. Make a tape for your teacher to hear.**

e. **Put on your own play using the virtues and the vices as characters. Think about how each character can be portrayed, and make masks for them if you like. Think about how they would interact, and how you would want the play to end. Some kind of divine intervention was the usual traditional ending, with the grace of God honoring the righteous, and condemning the bad. A person can play more than one character.**

3. **Start filling in the paragraphs to make a rough draft of your report. Use the information you have gathered from your research.**

Day 3

The growth of towns and the power of the guilds meant that commerce started to grow in importance as the Middle Ages wore on. As wealth and trade grew, the demand for goods from other parts of the world grew as well. As you may remember from an earlier lesson, the Muslim empire had developed trading routes all over Asia, Asia Minor (Turkey), Africa and into Europe. The Muslims were responsible for bringing in goods that did not exist in Europe, such as silk, jewels, gold, spices, and cane sugar.

Marco Polo was an Italian who helped Europeans learn more about the East, and subsequently Europeans began to trade for eastern goods as well. When Marco Polo was seventeen years old he left Italy for China with his father and uncle. He stayed in China 24 years and worked for the emperor, often taking care of his administrative duties in various parts of the Chinese empire. Everywhere he went, he learned more and more about the Chinese and their culture. When he returned to

Italy, he brought many beautiful things with him and wrote a book about his travels. His book was full of exciting tales and embellishments, many of which were made up. Still, it encouraged many people to become interested in China. It is said that the Italian love for pasta originated from China, which had long eaten rice noodles. Trade grew between Europe and the East along the Silk Road, a route through Asia that was established by the Muslim traders.

As commerce grew, the hold of kings over their people became less certain. Feudalism eventually ended because of the growth of cities and the people's desire for a better life. The Holy Roman Emperor in Germany was having a hard time seeing to affairs in Italy, Germany, and the Netherlands all at once. The local lords and barons pressured him from one side, and the Pope feared his power on the other. As the Holy Roman Empire weakened, the people

The Chinese Emperor welcomes the Polos

in the towns in those areas had to fend for themselves if they did not want to be controlled by a local duke or count. As merchants became wealthier, they became less interested in giving money to the local lord who used it to fund his armies and keep his power. Instead they became more interested in fighting for their own rights and buying their own protection. It became more and more clear that even if there was a ruler or a Pope nearby, they would have to get along with the people. Sometimes a guild would build battlements and towers on its meeting hall in order to protect its holdings and members. Great merchant cities grew, acting independently and often in competition with one another.

4. **Continue working on your activity from #2 yesterday.**

5. **Look up Marco Polo in an encyclopedia, and write one paragraph about him. If you need to, look in other resources as well, and list some of the things we enjoy now because of the Chinese.**

6. You should be working on the rough draft of your research paper today. Don't forget your illustration!

Days 4 & 5

While Europe was evolving into the Middle Ages after the fall of the Rome and the Western Empire, a whole other culture was developing in the Eastern Roman Empire. You may recall that before the end of the Roman Empire, in 330 A.D., Emperor Constantine had finished establishing the capital of the Eastern Roman Empire in Byzantium, and the city was renamed Constantinople. Emperor Constantine converted to Christianity, and encouraged Christians to live there and study. Constantinople became the center of the new Byzantine Empire that developed out of the Eastern Roman Empire. Its language and traditions were Greek, which is not too surprising, as it is actually not very far from Athens, and Byzantium had been built by and populated by the Greeks for centuries.

Constantinople was located on a peninsula, so it was surrounded by water. On the sea sides, it was protected by a wall. On the remaining land side it was protected by a moat and three walls. This made the city a fortress in itself.

The emperors in Constantinople considered themselves the successors of the Roman Empire, but often there was a lot of fighting because there was no real system for deciding who would be the next Emperor. Like the Roman Emperors, they considered themselves chosen by God to rule, and took charge of all aspects of life in the Eastern Empire, whether it be commerce, the navy, lawmaking or foreign affairs. They also gave themselves the right to name the "patriarch" or head of the church, thereby controlling that as well.

The first great Byzantine ruler was Justinian, who reigned from 527 to 565 A.D. He is remembered for the Justinian Code, a set of laws based on the laws of ancient Rome, which you saw in your studies on Ancient Rome. These laws were strict, but gave the same rights to everyone, whether rich or poor, and so were considered fair. Justinian, like Constantine, was a Christian, and wanted everyone in his empire to be Christian as well.

Justinian was married to a very strong woman named Theodora. He often asked her for advice, and she had a great amount of power in government. She was a former actress, and the daughter of a bear trainer in the circus. She had a sharp wit and, before her marriage, performed occasionally as a comedienne. Once there was a revolt from those who wanted a different ruler on the throne. The rioting crowds even burned part of the city down. However, Theodora is said to have encouraged Justinian to stand firm in the face of the rioting crowds at a time when he was thinking of going into hiding. With her support, he was able to restore order. Theodora used her power to make life better or worse for people, depending on whether they were her friends or enemies. She was especially interested in making life better for women, and helped to create laws that allowed women to own property.

Many people in Constantinople wanted to make the Roman Empire whole again after the barbarian Germanic tribes took over much of Europe. During his reign. Justinian led his army to conquer North Africa, Sicily, and Spain from the Goths and the Vandals. Later emperors were able to take back much of Italy. The Byzantine armies were considered very superior, particularly because they kept the army well-supplied during war, and because they were very good at using their horses to fight. They were the first to use stirrups, which enabled them to stay on the horse while keeping their arms free for fighting.

Byzantine icon in mosaic

The Byzantine Empire was often under attack from other peoples also trying to build empires. Persians attacked Syria, Palestine, and Egypt, which were part of the Empire. Central Asian peoples started taking over lands in what is now Eastern Europe. The Germanic tribes took back Spain and Italy. The biggest threat, however, was from the Arabs, who were busily building themselves an empire based on Islam. The Byzantines were able to develop an explosive liquid called "Greek fire" which could be blasted across the water and set ships on fire. Because the formula for this was considered so secret, it was never written down, and no one knows for sure what it was. Constantinople stood firm against the Muslims in the end, and because of this, many people believe Europe was prevented from becoming part of the Islamic world.

The Byzantine Christian Church was called the Eastern or Greek Orthodox Church. Over the centuries, the Christians in Byzantium and the Christians in Europe developed more and more disagreements about Christianity. In Rome it was felt that services and holy writings should be in Latin, whereas the Byzantine church used Greek. Different religious holidays were celebrated, and there were disagreements about that as well. There were also differences of opinion about whether the clergy could marry, and about the display of icons. The emperors in Constantinople felt that because they were the Roman Emperors, they had authority over the whole Christian Church, including the Pope in Rome, and refused to accept the authority of the Pope. Eventually the Christian Church split in 1054, becoming the Roman Catholic Church in the west and the Eastern Orthodox Church in the east.

Icon inside the Hagia

Byzantine churches had a very distinctive architecture. When Constantinople was partly burned to the ground during the riots against Justinian, he decided to start a huge rebuilding program that included new churches and monasteries. The most famous of his structures is the Hagia Sophia (pronounced (HA-jah so-FEE-ya). At the time it was the most magnificent cathedral around the Mediterranean Sea. While building it, the architects developed a way to put an onion-shaped dome on the top of a square structure, and later churches and buildings used this design, which spread throughout Greece, Eastern Europe, and Russia.

Merchants, churchmen, and pilgrims who visited Constantinople returned to Europe with many stories of the splendor of the capital. It had paved streets and magnificent buildings. It was also a center for art and culture, where scholars came together to learn and share ideas about religion, philosophy, and art. The population was better educated and their monetary systems more developed; it was a more advanced culture than the European feudalism that existed at the same time.

Basil II was the emperor in 976, and his reign started a period of time called the Byzantine Golden Age. The empire became even stronger, and was a place where music and art of all kinds thrived. Artists were influenced by both the classical Greco-Roman style and the artists of the ancient Middle East. Much of the art focused on the national religion. Icons were popular in Byzantium. An icon was a piece of wood with an image of Jesus, his mother Mary, or a saint painted on it. These icons were regarded as being holy, and were placed everywhere, creating shrines in many nooks and crannies and rooms throughout the city. Perhaps the art form the Byzantines are most famous for is mosaic, which they used on walls and floors, especially in the churches. The Byzantine artists were so brilliant at placing the many tiny pieces of ceramic that in some icons it looks as if there really is light coming from the halos of the saints depicted.

7. **Review the location of Istanbul, Turkey on your map. This is the location of the city of Constantinople.**

8. **Go to the library and look at pictures of Byzantine architecture and art, and the Hagia Sophia. Look for information on the Hagia Sophia, and write a paragraph about this famous church in Constantinople. Include information on its history, the meaning of its name, and the art work inside.**

Extra Credit: Choose one of these art projects to do (use the internet resources listed previously if you wish):

a. **Look at pictures of Byzantine icons. Find an attractive flat piece of wood and paint a picture of your choice on it. See if you can imitate the flat, stiff appearance of the style of art seen in icons.**

b. **Look at Byzantine mosaics. Dye or paint egg shells in different colors and break them into pieces. Make a mosaic with them. An alternative is to use small pieces of colored tile. You may be able to get samples at a tile supplier and break them into pieces with a hammer. If you like, you can set your mosaic in plaster or hardening clay. Otherwise, you can simply glue them in place on a sheet of paper.**

c. **Look at pictures of Byzantine churches, including the Hagia Sophia. Draw one of the onion-shaped domes sitting on its rectangular base. Be as detailed as you can.**

9. **Keep working on the rough draft of your report. You have one week to complete this entire project.**

10. **Have your Home Teacher give you a spelling quiz. Review any words that you missed and add them to your ongoing list.**

Extra Book Ideas:

See Lesson 20 for a list of supplemental reading on the Middle Ages.

Extra Project Ideas:

*   Research the life and discoveries of Marco Polo in depth. Plot his course on a map.

*   Find a version of a traditional Christmas Mummers play and put it on.

*   Research the badges of the medieval guilds. Draw pictures of them.

*   Find a book of games from the Middle Ages and learn to play several of them

*   Make your own wooden board for Nine Men's Morris. Paint it with elaborate designs you think would be appropriate.

*   Find out more about the Eastern (or Greek) Orthodox Church.

*   Find out more about Theodora, Justinian, or Basil II.

*   Find out more about the Turks, particularly the Ottomans.

Social Studies/Art/English~~~~~~Lesson 24

MIDDLE AGES

Vocabulary

Your vocabulary words relate to the material you are studying Social Studies. Define each of them without using the root word, and use them in a sentence in a way that shows you understand the meaning. Try to think about them in the context of your Social Studies work. If you are unable to find a word in your best dictionary, look in an encyclopedia.

tyranny	**monarchy**	**allegiance**
penance	**luxury**	**bazaar**
missionary	**heathen**	**allies**

Spelling

Select ten words from your written material this week for spelling words. Write each of these words correctly five times and use each word in a complete sentence. Practice your spelling words in preparation for a quiz.

Grammar

1. **In your writing this week, be sure to start with a paragraph that introduces your topic or opinion, and end with a paragraph that concludes the topic or paragraph. If your essay is only one paragraph long, then start and end with introducing and concluding sentences.**

2. **This week you will also finish your five-page report. When your rough draft is done, read it aloud and make any changes. Correct it for punctuation, spelling, and word usage. Refer to the section called "Bibliographies" in your *English Manual* for information on bibliographies. Then, in your best writing, make a final copy. Add a cover page and illustrations.**

Day 1

As you may remember from Lesson 18, Islam began in the Middle East in Arabia during the early part of the Middle Ages. Islam was a very rich culture and Muslims were great traders. Not only did they bring goods back and forth between the east and the west and amongst the different civilizations, they brought ideas with them. Muslim rulers fostered art, learning, poetry and music, and there were many inventions that came to Europe from the Muslim empire. Muslim scientists and doctors were particularly skilled, even performing delicate procedures such as eye surgery. The science of apothecary, using herbal remedies and medicines, was developed by Muslims. One Arab doctor wrote a medical encyclopedia that became the basis for all medicine in the Middle Ages. They also developed algebra and introduced the numeral system we still use today, called Arabic. The lute, a stringed instrument popular in the Middle Ages, was introduced by the Muslims, and even today is traditionally decorated with Arab patterns. The art of needlepoint and tapestry came from the Muslims. They also introduced papermaking, which they had gotten from the Chinese, and later, printing.

The city of Baghdad was the center of trade and government in the Muslim Empire. It was centrally located between Europe, and Asia, in the Middle East (in what is now Iraq). It was filled with bazaars, where those with money could buy from a huge selection of Persian and Indian rugs; African jewels, gold, and ivory, and Asian silks, spices, teas, and jewelry. Trains of camels called caravans streamed in daily, laden with goods they had brought over mountains and across deserts.

The Muslims conquered North Africa, Persia, the Middle East and Spain, and by the 10th century became the rulers of a large empire. They didn't force people to become Muslims, but anyone who wasn't a Muslim paid higher taxes and could not own any land. This had a way of helping people convert to Islam. Part of their empire included Palestine and the city of Jerusalem, which even today is considered the Holy Land by Jews, Christians, and Muslims. For many years the Muslims let the Christians go to Jerusalem to worship freely.

The Muslims who lived in North Africa and Spain were called Moors. While the rest of Europe was in hardship, there was a lot of prosperity in Spain due to the Moors. They introduced new farming and trade techniques, and the Catholic and Muslim cultures for the most part existed side-by-side. The city of Cordova in Spain became a center for arts and learning. However, there is also a long history of conflict

Inside the mosque of Cordova, Spain

between the Muslims and the Catholics who wanted to control Spain. Over the course of 500 years, the Catholics, led by religious orders of monks who were also knights, slowly captured parts of Spain from the Muslims, and finally Spain became a monarchy ruled by King Ferdinand and Queen Isabella.

1. **Find Baghdad and put it on your map. It is in present day Iraq.**

2. **Choose one of these topics and look it up in the encyclopedia. Then write one paragraph on any aspect of the topic you like. Be sure to follow the grammar instructions at the beginning of this lesson.**

   a. **The early history of the city of Baghdad.**

   b. **The early history of the city of Cordova (often spelled Cordoba), Spain.**

   c. **The Order of Santiago.**

3. **Finish writing the rough draft of your report. Don't forget your illustration, cover page and bibliography. If you are ready, begin proofreading your report in preparation for writing or typing the final draft.**

Days 2 & 3

In the course of your studies, you have seen how the three Semitic religions, Judaism, Christianity, and Islam, all have their roots in that part of the Middle East called the Holy Land. You have also seen how civilizations, based on these religions, have grown in Europe, the Middle East, and around the Mediterranean Sea. A good deal of the history and culture of the Middle Ages is centered around the conflicts that arose amongst these religions.

The people of Europe in the Middle Ages were very much influenced by the teachings of the Roman Catholic Church, and the authority of the Pope, who was considered the mouthpiece of God. Lords who lived a life of bloodshed often founded monasteries or even became monks themselves, in their older years, to try to make up for their sins and get into heaven. Knights, off to battle, usually asked for a blessing, and might be talked out of their mission if the Church did not grant it. Bishops were sometimes the closest advisors of kings and noblemen, who feared making a political move without knowing if it would send them to Hell or not.

The Catholic Church also sent missionaries to convert other people to Christianity. Sometimes it was done through peaceful teaching, but sometimes by force. The Teutonic Knights, a religious order who were also trained as knights, fought the people in Eastern Europe to try to convert them.

One of the ways the Church encouraged devoutness was to have Christians go on pilgrimages to holy places in order to get help from the saints. People of all kinds went on pilgrimages, from kings to the lowliest leper. Pilgrimages were a way to make up for one's sins. One popular pilgrimage was to Canterbury, in England, to the shrine of Thomas Becket. Becket was an archbishop who was murdered in his own cathedral by King Henry II in a dispute over whether the king's court could try and punish men of the Church. The king lived in penance for the rest of his life.

A far more dangerous but greater pilgrimage was to the city of Jerusalem, in the Holy Land, where Christ was crucified and buried. It was especially important to the Christians to be able to visit Jerusalem, and for a long time, the Muslims who controlled that part of the world allowed the Christians to come and go freely. Those who made it back home were honored.

Then the Turks conquered Palestine, and the Turks did not let the Christians go to Jerusalem. The Turks, who were originally from Central Asia, had converted to Islam, and had taken over the Holy Land, angering many Christians. The Turks considered their attacks part of their holy wars. The Turks were also attacking Constantinople, and the Emperor of Constantinople asked the Roman Catholic Church for help to fight them off. In 1095, Pope Urban II saw that he could make the Roman Catholic Church more powerful if he helped Constantinople. So he told the Europeans that they should come together and fight to free Palestine, or the Holy Land. In a famous speech, he painted a horrifying picture of Jerusalem being defiled by ungodly heathens. He told the European leaders they could make up for all their sins if they laid down their arms against each other and joined forces to rescue Jerusalem. He told them their reward on earth would be the riches of the city. The Christian Wars to capture Palestine were called the Crusades, and the Christian soldiers were called Crusaders. Over the next 200 years there were numerous Crusades, costing many lives and much effort, and it is because of the Crusades that much of Europe lived the way it did.

The murder of Thomas Becket

In the First Crusade, with the blessing of Pope Urban II, the Crusaders captured Jerusalem. The First Crusade is sometimes called the Pauper's Crusade, because most of those who went were peasants, many of them women and children who had grown weary of the feudal life, and were willing to risk their lives for a new hope. They spoke of Jerusalem as a land of milk and honey, and believed God was finally giving them their reward.

The way to Jerusalem meant going east to Constantinople first, and the Crusaders began their long march. There are dreadful tales of how the Crusaders treated the people in Europe as they went. Many Jews were robbed and killed, and were blamed for the crucifixion of Christ. Farmers had their cattle stolen to feed the hordes. Almost all the people in the Paupers' Crusade were wiped out in their first battle against the Turks.

In the meantime, about 20,000 knights, mostly French, also gathered for the First Crusade. Each of them had five or six assistants with them including servants, maids and archers. They too marched to Constantinople to join the Byzantines. In 1099, after recapturing much of the Byzantine Empire back from the Turks, they captured Jerusalem, killing every Muslim and Jew they could find in the city. They then prayed together, and ruled Jerusalem for 100 years. During that time, Europeans became more and more influenced by Muslim and Eastern ideas and culture.

The Turks eventually recaptured strategic parts of the Holy Land, and the rulers in Jerusalem became worried. The Second Crusade to recapture these parts of Palestine was led by the French King Louis VII, the first husband of Eleanor of Aquitane. Eleanor was determined to go with him, although it was unheard of to allow a woman to undertake such a daring journey. She convinced her husband to let her go with him on the grounds that he would more easily entice other soldiers to go if she set such an example of bravery. So Eleanor went on a Crusade, with a group of ladies to attend her. They shocked everyone by wearing breeches and the armor of Amazons, or female warriors. The trip was long, dangerous, dirty, and exhausting, and she had a miserable time. She refused to enter the city of Jerusalem, and King Louis, determined to win the argument, had her carried into the Holy City against her will. This enraged and humiliated her. The Second Crusade failed, but for the most part, the Muslims and the Christian rulers in Jerusalem kept an uneasy peace.

The Muslim Turks recaptured Jerusalem in 1187, led by a fierce and determined man named Saladin who had managed to unify the Muslims. Saladin was angry because Christians were attacking and robbing Arab traders and Muslim pilgrims on their way to Mecca. The Christian armies were virtually wiped out, and many Christians sold into slavery.

Although Europeans were horrified at the loss of Jerusalem, many of them did not have the heart at first to try to recapture it. Because of the splendors of the east and the luxuries that were being brought in, people had become more interested in trade and less interested in feudal wars amongst each other. The Third Crusade began when Pope Clement III started preaching that Christians were no longer faithful in the eyes of God, and that the loss of Jerusalem had been their punishment. By recapturing the city, they could restore their devotion to God. The three greatest European kings took up the challenge, their motives may really have been financial. To keep their monarchies strong, they needed money and the goods people were getting from merchants. The taxes levied on traders from the Middle East were a great source of income.

King Richard the Lion-Hearted, the third son of Eleanor of Aquitane, led the Third Crusade. He was a natural leader: large, handsome, strong, and yet also well-spoken and cultured. Richard used the sea as a means to help his Crusade, blocking the port with his fleet to prevent food and supplies from getting into Jerusalem. He also successfully captured caravans on their way to Jerusalem.

Saladin, the Muslim leader, and Richard the Lion-Hearted were considered the two greatest leaders of the Crusades. They had a mutual respect for each other, and the soldiers of each army also had respect for the leader of the other. Legend says that Richard was so well liked, even by his enemies, that Saladin said if he had to lose Jerusalem to someone, he would rather it be Richard than anyone else. Both sides fought for what they believed in, and for the most part, the fighting was considered honorable. The Third Crusade, now considered the last important one, ended with a truce in 1192 in which the Muslims kept Jerusalem, but Christians would be allowed free access to it. The Christians were also allowed to keep some of the surrounding lands.

There were other Crusades, but none with the same ideals as the first three. People in Europe at the time did not see it that way, however. Pope Innocent III wanted a crusade to reunite the entire Christian Church into one with the Roman Catholic Pope as the religious and political leader of the whole Christian world. At first the kings of Europe were not very interested. Eventually, in 1203, a Byzantine nobleman who had been denied the throne paid the European leaders to conquer Constantinople for him, in exchange for which he would put the Eastern Orthodox Church under the rule of the Pope in Rome. Italian merchant cities, happy at the prospect of controlling the ports of Asia Minor, gave them ships and money. The Pope did not know about any of this, and gave the Fourth Crusade his blessings. Everyone's plans went awry, however, when the Christian troops proved to be savage conquerors, destroying the city and slaughtering the populace. After this, there was no way the people in Constantinople were going to accept the Roman Catholic Church.

Constantinople, under European rule, was never quite the same again. It was eventually taken over by the Turks, who were originally from Central Asia. For a time, Constantinople was able to get its European allies to help in resisting the Turks. But eventually there was not much left of the Byzantine Empire. For a month, the Turks battered away at the walls with half ton cannon balls until the defenders were finally overwhelmed. The Byzantine Empire ended in 1453 after a thousand years of cultural influence. Its mark is still seen in Eastern Europe and Russia.

Richard the Lion-hearted

Another sad story during the Crusades was the Children's Crusade. In 1212, a shepherd boy named Stephen started preaching from the *Bible* to other children that "the meek .... shall inherit the earth," (Matthew 5:5). As a result, thousands of unarmed children started on the journey to the Holy Land. Many people believed that they might actually succeed, and that the previous methods had failed because there had been too much reliance on the strong, and not on the weak and the poor. Most of the children died of illness and starvation even before getting to the Holy Land, and the few remaining ones were captured and sold into slavery by the Muslims.

Even though there was a lot of fighting and killing, one of the good things that happened during the Crusades was that the various peoples learned from each other. The Crusaders learned from the Muslims, and brought food, cloth, and new ideas back to Europe. Trade routes were developed between Asia, Africa, the Middle East, and Europe. People and cities prospered, and the feudal way of life began to decline.

4. **On your map, trace the land route that the Crusaders took from Europe to Constantinople and then to Jerusalem. Then trace the route by sea.**

5. **Write a paragraph about the Crusades. What do you believe was good about the Crusades, and what do you think was bad?**

6. **Read the rough draft of your report aloud. Make any corrections, paying attention to spelling, punctuation and word usage. Do all your sentences make sense? Do they say what you want them to say? Are your paragraphs arranged properly? Do you need to break big blocks into more paragraphs? This is the time to make changes! Then begin writing or typing your final draft.**

Day 4

Central Asia had long been a place where wild nomadic tribes lived. The Huns, the barbarian tribe that had been the downfall of the Roman Empire, had come from Central Asia. The Turks were also from there. During the Middle Ages, there was another great conqueror at work. He was called Genghis Khan, meaning "mightiest king." In the 1200's, he and the Mongol tribe built a huge empire in Asia which included China and stretched all the way west as far as Kiev in what is now the Ukraine. The Mongols were considered unequalled in their savagery, reducing the whole city of Kiev to nothing.

Genghis Khan was a very resourceful military leader. He divided his armies into different parts called "hordes." Hordes rode on fast ponies, sweeping across the plains and deserts on their conquests. They were skilled at using bows while they rode. The bows they used were shorter than the traditional longbow used by Europeans. These bows were superior technologically, because they included several different kinds of materials that made them more flexible and therefore able to shoot faster and farther. The longbow was made from a single piece of wood, had to be used by someone on foot, and did not go as far or fast.

Genghis Khan was a brilliant administrator who understood the importance of communication. Within the lands he conquered he enforced order by giving the hordes different duties. Each land had a separate "Khan," who ruled as a local king but took orders from Genghis Khan. To keep in touch with the local kings, he used swift messengers on ponies, who would stop at regular stations to quickly switch to a fresh pony before continuing their journey. The tired pony would then be rested up for the next messenger who came along. Sometimes the messengers would be switched in the same way, to keep them from getting too tired. In this way, Genghis Khan knew what was going on all the time in his vast empire, unlike others in the Middle Ages who relied on the slow-moving caravans of camels, or a single rider on his horse.

The leaders in Europe hoped that Genghis Khan would help them with their Crusades. Some of the Mongols were Christians, although they did not look to Rome or Constantinople for guidance. They sent messengers to Genghis Khan to see if he would fight the Muslims too. Genghis Khan was very polite, and listened, but he simply was not interested. Eventually, in 1258, some of the Mongols attacked the rich city of Baghdad, destroying the schools, libraries, and palaces that had made it so glorious. The Muslim empire was never quite the same again. But by now the Mongol Empire was dividing up, with each area ruled by its own Khan.

The Khans were tolerant of Christianity, and the Eastern Orthodox Church was allowed to spread throughout much of Russia.

7. Make sure you have all the countries of Asia on your map, including Russia. Review the locations of China, Kiev and Baghdad.

8. Go to the library and look at pictures of Genghis Khan and his Mongolian hordes.

Extra Credit: Draw or paint a picture of a Mongolian warrior on horseback, with his specialized short bow.

9. Make sure the illustration is finished for your report. Make a cover page. Begin rewriting your thoroughly proofread and corrected first draft.

Day 5

There are several reasons why the Middle Ages ended. As you have seen, the ability for common people to make money changed the feudal way of life. The disastrous efforts of the Crusades were taking up too much energy and cost too much in human life, and people turned to a new way of life. The introduction of gunpowder from the Chinese meant that guns could be built. The old fighting methods of knights no longer worked, and people did not fear them as before. It may be that the biggest changes occurred when people began to lose confidence in the leaders of the Church. Although everyone was still devout in their beliefs as Christians, the Church leaders were beginning to behave badly. For example, in those days, although the position of the Pope was in Rome, most Popes actually lived in Avignon, France, because it was safer from all the violence that often took place between the rival cities of Italy. In 1378, the Pope went to Rome and died. A new one was elected in Rome, but in the meantime, a new one also took his place in Avignon. For a long time, both Popes argued back and forth about who was the true Pope. No one knew who to believe. It was a very difficult situation for a Church that claimed to be the only one and undivided Christian Church.

Medieval thinkers believed that politics, economic life, law, and facts of nature must be based on the *Bible*. To understand nature and society, they said one first needed to understand God's plan for humanity. Of course, because Europe was primarily Christian, this meant that they looked at life from a Christian perspective.

Many churchmen thought that the logic of the Greeks would lead people away from God, and so preached against reason and philosophy. Medieval philosophers, known as Scholastics, disagreed. They believed that reason could be used to explain the Christian teachings. The most brilliant of these Scholastics was Thomas Aquinas, a member of the Dominican Order of monks in the 1200's. According to him, both reason and Christian teachings came from God. Aquinas and many other medieval thinkers took an interest in studying the natural world.

John Wycliffe was a teacher at Oxford University. He challenged several major doctrines of the Roman Catholic Church. The Church taught that in the sacrament of the Mass, when words that Jesus said at the Last Supper were repeated, a miracle occurred in which the bread and wine actually became the body and blood of Christ. Wycliffe disagreed, and said that this communion was actually just an act of faith between the believer and God. Furthermore, he said that individuals didn't need the Church in order to receive salvation or to teach them about God. He said it was important for everyone to be able to read the Bible themselves. Wycliffe believed so strongly in this that he and his followers translated the Bible into English for the very first time. Now any literate person in England could actually read the Bible and think about its meaning for themselves. Today Christians take this for granted, but it was a revolutionary act at the time.

Roger Bacon was one of the greatest medieval scientists. He was also an English monk and philosopher. He lived from 1220 to 1292 in the late Middle Ages. Bacon predicted that one day ships would move without rowers, carts without animals to pull them, and machines would fly.

These were all new ideas in those days. You will learn more later about changes that occurred within the Church and its relationship to society.

As you have learned, the Middle Ages were the years between the fall of the Roman Empire in the 5th century until the Renaissance in the 16th century, a span of a thousand years. England, France, and Spain all became nations during the Middle Ages. The Byzantine Empire rose and fell. During this period of a thousand years there were wars, Crusades, peasant revolts, plagues, and great cultural contributions. Thousands of medieval buildings are still standing. Medieval people wrote books and letters about important events as they happened and many of these have survived for us to read.

Sailors were beginning to be interested in exploring farther from home. The printing press was invented. The universities that were started in the Middle Ages grew stronger and drew more students who were full of curiosity for more learning. Economic growth and intellectual achievements went hand in hand, and gave way to a new age of discovery which we call the Renaissance.

10. **In your best writing, make a final copy of your five-page research report. Attach the cover page, bibliography and illustration. You may bind it or put it in a report cover.**

11. **Ask your Home Teacher to give you a spelling quiz. Review any words you miss.**

Extra Book Ideas:

See Lesson 20 for a list of supplemental reading on the Middle Ages.

Extra Project Ideas:

- The story of Archbishop Thomas Becket and King Henry II is fascinating. Find out the story by watching the video, "Becket."

- Read a children's version of *The Canterbury Tales*, written by Geoffry Chaucer, about pilgrims going to Canterbury.

- Find out more about Saladin, the great Muslim Turk leader during the Crusades.

- Write a story from the point of view of either a crusading knight, a servant or squire accompanying the knight, a peasant member of the Pauper's Crusade, or a member of the Children's Crusade. Remember to include the beliefs of the Crusader.

- Research and write a brief biography of the life of King Richard the Lion-Hearted.

- Find out more about Muslim bazaars, and paint a large colorful picture of a scene from one. Alternatively, paint a picture of a caravan making its way across the plains or deserts.

- Find out more about the composite bow and the longbow. Draw pictures of them.

Social Studies/Art/English~~~~~~Lesson 25

RENAISSANCE

Vocabulary Words

The following words are taken from your Social Studies lessons. Write definitions for each one of them without using the root word or any other form of the vocabulary words. Consider each in the context of your Social Studies material, and write a sentence for each that shows you understand the meaning.

etch	assassinate	aristocrat
superstition	prosperous	lavish
sponsor	cardinal	fealty

Spelling

Select ten words from your written material this week for spelling words. Write each of these words correctly five times and use each word in a complete sentence. Practice your spelling words in preparation for a quiz.

Grammar

1. **Write a sentence for each of the following prepositions:**

across	after	among	around	behind
during	beside	except	into	near

Days 1, 2 & 3

To begin, find Italy on a map. This is where the Renaissance (the French word for "rebirth") began, and from there it spread quickly to Spain, France, and eventually throughout the rest of Europe. European civilization experienced a rebirth of ancient Greek and Roman ideas and art. These styles of art and architecture are also called "Classical."

For a long time, people had lived under the authority of the Catholic Church. Now they began to question what they had been told about the world around them, and began to experiment with art and science like never before. With new ideas about humankind and God, they began to change their views on religion. With newfound wealth from trade, they began to support and produce a rich and human-oriented art. With better technology, they also began to explore the world beyond their shores.

As you may recall from your studies on the Middle Ages, the Black Death in the 1300's cut the population of Europe by about a third. This lower population meant that people who survived were needed more than ever for their labor and for the goods they made. People could now get more money and goods for their work, thereby making their lives better. This higher standard of living for all did not mean, however, that everyone lived the same way. Peasant life was still very different from the lives of kings and nobles. And in between there were merchants, artists, scholars, bankers, landowners, and tradespeople of all kinds.

Isn't it interesting to consider how much we take for granted today? Just think, at one time in history much of what you do and have today did not exist. For example, people ate with their fingers for a long time. They did not have soft comfortable mattresses to sleep on such as you do today, only mats on the floor. Many civilizations did not have glass in their windows. People in colder climates had to wear several layers of clothing to keep warm. Central heating and air conditioning did not exist. Supermarkets and department stores did not exist, nor did motor vehicles. The everyday freedoms we take for granted today are rather new as well. People still owned other people during the Renaissance period. However, this trend began to change, and the feudal system was disappearing.

On the other hand, many things that existed in the past are fading away today. One example is the fine craftsmen. With today's technology, master craftspeople are fewer and fewer.

Peasant life was not actually that much different on a daily basis than it had been for centuries. Diet still consisted of grains and some vegetables people grew themselves, and some meat and dairy products. Even though all of Europe depended on the farmers to produce their food and textiles, farmers were often considered stupid and dishonest. Serfdom, where peasants were forced to stay on the land of the lord and work the fields for a tiny share of the benefits, still existed in parts of Europe, although by now many had been able to get out of this form of slavery. Some peasants became "free" laborers, migrating about the countryside looking for work, free to choose to work for whoever they wanted. Some peasants were able to save money to buy tools and rent land, or become sharecroppers where they would do the work and then share half of the harvest with the owner of the land. Peasants lived very simple lives in the thatched-roof huts of past centuries, wearing wooden clogs in the winter and going barefoot in the summer, and cooking in clay pots. There were also amusements, and peasants were free to go to the tavern, celebrate weddings and births, and, if they had any energy left after working in the fields all day, dance and play games.

Many still believed in and practiced witchcraft, consulting the local wisewoman for cures and advice. Sometimes this caused trouble with the local churchmen, who felt that the ways of magic and superstition were a threat to God. Witch burnings were a way for the Church to keep its control over the people. As you might remember, Joan of Arc was one victim of such witch burning, where the men of the Catholic Church used witchcraft as a way to explain her "voices."

The middle class was made up of people with more money than the peasants but less than the nobles. They often lived in the towns, and were sometimes masters of the trades. Tradesmen would take in boys as apprentices who worked hard to learn the trade and grow up to become masters themselves. There were two types of middle class, and they were divided by wealth. The poorer were the craftspeople; the blacksmith who owned his own tools and property, the shoemaker who catered to the lower classes, or the crude broadcloth weaver in the village. On the other hand, the artisan textile weaver who made fine silk cloth for lords in the city or the architect who built beautiful homes would fare much better, and these would be in the wealthier and more prosperous members of the middle class. They sometimes grew fat, retiring early and leaving the work to their employees. Examples of other well-to-do middle class members were fancy shop owners, overseas traders, those who owned lots of land in the countryside, and local church leaders.

The Guild system continued to exist in the Renaissance as it had in the Middle Ages. How well a craftsperson or tradesman prospered was usually determined by the Guild that oversaw that particular trade. By making the rules about how a person could pursue his trade, a Guild was able to make its members very wealthy. Often only Guild members could practice their trade in a given area, preventing anyone else who might want to set up shop from doing so. Those who were most powerful in the Guild could control who got in and who did not, choosing family members and friends over others. Some Guilds became so strong that they became active as patrons of the arts. We will be looking more at patrons in a later lesson on the Renaissance.

Most children in the 16th century were treated harshly. They were set to work at an early age, and they had to be respectful to their parents even when they were being mistreated. They were often beaten for small mistakes. If a boy did not go to school, he was sent to live with a local craftsman to learn a trade before the age of ten. Some children were sent out into the fields by age four or five to tend the sheep or pigs. Girls helped with the cooking and washing. Children were not allowed much time to play and enjoy growing up.

Although there were kings and queens of nations during the Renaissance, government was not centered in the capitals, as it is today. Italy, for example, did not have any kind of central government for a long time. Instead it was made up of different city-states, with the larger and richer merchant cities having more power. This is similar to the way ancient Greek civilization was organized; you may recall that Athens was one of the most powerful of the city-states at that time. Although the cities sometimes went to war against each other, none of them were powerful enough to conquer others. The cities simply ran themselves, collecting taxes and making rules for their own area. The most powerful cities in Italy during the Renaissance were Florence, Genoa, Venice, Rome, Mantua and Pisa.

There was a lot of competition between the most powerful citizens of the cities to become heads of their local governments. The Renaissance period is full of stories of how the various powerful families in a city would plot to take over power from each other. Assassination was a common way to resolve these conflicts. Church leaders were sometimes just as involved in the power struggles. Sometimes they tried to seize control for themselves, or actively sided with one family or another. Some churchmen, including the Pope, even plotted assassinations, especially if it was felt that a particular ruler was too dangerous to the Church.

The ruling families of Italy led lavish lives, living in well-appointed, well defended palaces, eating foods from far-off lands, building monuments to themselves, and wearing jewel-laden garments. Leaving their homes to venture into the city was a parade in itself, with bodyguards and servants in attendance, and often a crier to announce their presence and clear the way. People in the streets were expected to notice them, and a ruler could monitor his power and popularity by how well he was responded to in the street. Many of them sponsored events and celebrations to keep the people happy and supportive of their rule.

A processional through the streets of Florence, Italy

Women were generally not held in high regard, with few choices in the direction of their lives. The birth of a son was a far greater cause of celebration than the birth of a daughter. Being a good mother was considered a woman's foremost responsibility. Toward the end of the 15th century, a bookseller in Florence said there were two rules women should follow: "The first is that they bring up their children in the fear of God, and the second that they keep quiet in church, and I would add that they stop talking in other places as well." Men still treated women as pieces of property to be bought and sold in marriage.

Women of aristocratic families did gradually begin to receive more respect, and girls were sometimes educated right alongside their brothers. Many women were able to take advantage of education when members of the ruling classes began to see that they could hold onto their power more easily if their wives and daughters were educated as well. The ability to play politics to the advantage of the family was sometimes valued in a woman.

Isabella d'Este of the Italian city of Mantua was one such well-known woman who was better able to defend and negotiate for the welfare of the city than her husband, causing him much distress! She was famous for her singing and brilliant conversation. She had one of the finest collections of books, paintings, musical instruments, and sculpture in all of Italy. In 1509 her husband, Francesco, was captured in a war against Venice, and Mantua was being threatened. Isabella took over command of the soldiers and refused to let them surrender, even if it meant her husband would be killed. The city was successfully defended, and she peacefully negotiated for the release of her husband. In spite of this he felt it was "unwomanly" of her to care more for the city and its people than for him!

*Portrait of a noblewoman
with her son*

In the 1600's, the idea was introduced of a unified scheme of household decoration. Up until that time, people had not considered coordinating their home decorating. Madame de Rambouillet introduced this idea. She hung curtains to match the color of the painted walls and picked carpet to blend with the color of the walls and drapes. This added a touch of elegance to the homes of Europe that had not existed in the Middle Ages.

You might be interested in some of the views people had of animals during the Renaissance period:

In Rome in 1500, a cardinal paid a sailor 100 gold pieces for an African gray parrot that could recite the Apostles' Creed.

In France in 1516, the finest trees of a particular area suffered from an unusual parasite. The ecclesiastical judge from the city told the people to repent of their sins and then gave the parasites six days to leave the region, with the threat of excommunication.

In France in 1543, the elders of the city of Geneva asked that the slugs which were infesting their fields be excommunicated.

In Rome in 1567, the Pope threatened any man who organized a bull fight with excommunication. In addition, he decreed that any man killed in a bull fight could not have a Christian burial.

A painting by Jan Vansteen showing peasant life

In Lorraine, France in 1572, a pig was found eating a child. It was taken to prison and locked up under the name of its owner. It was declared that the pig was to be hanged and strangled. It was to be tied up with a rope, completely naked because it was only a rude beast!

When an area of France was infested with caterpillars, the head of the ecclesiastical court invoked solemn curses. They worked extremely well.

When a particular type of weevil was ruining the vineyards in France, the weevils were taken to court. They were assigned a lawyer and the case was heard properly. The judge decided that the villagers should set aside one field for the weevils to live in. They chose a field and drew up a lease. The weevils were given full rights in their own field.

1. **Review the location of Italy on your map, if you have not already done so.**

2. **Choose one of the following subjects: the role of women, the place of children, or the view of animals. Write one full paragraph where you compare this subject during Renaissance times with the way it is today. Are there differences? Are there similarities?**

3. Choose one of the following projects.

    a. Go to the library and look at pictures of paintings and block prints of people in the Renaissance. Look at portraits of kings and queens and others of the ruling class, as well as paintings by Breugel (sometimes spelled Breughel), Vansteen or Van Hemessem of peasant life. Use them as guides for making three drawings - one each of a person in the lower, middle and upper classes. You may choose men, women, or children. Show the detail in their clothing, and add color if you like.

    b. Write a story from the point of view of a person living during the Renaissance. In your story, describe what happens as that person goes through one day in their life. You can choose either a peasant, a successful tradesman in the city, or a member of the ruling class.

    c. Write a story about a woman who was born into the ruling class. In your story, show how she uses her wits to negotiate or otherwise settle differences between two ruling families, or two cities at war.

Day 4

Rules of behavior were important in the years of the Renaissance. A very influential book was *The Courtier* by Baldassare Castiglione. In it he describes how people should behave in court and in public to show off their refinement and education. It recommended certain behavior for anyone who wanted to be considered a gentleman. It suggested that some people were inferior by birth, and that a courtier could "cheapen" himself by associating with them. A gentleman was cautioned against fighting with a peasant unless "he is assured of getting the upper hand." Obviously, the issue of upper class versus lower class was still very important. No longer could nobles act like the coarse knights of the past. Instead, "gentleness is most impressive in a man who is a capable and courageous warrior." One was always to speak well and behave with courtesy, rather than "push one another downstairs ... (or) ...hurl the soup, or the sauce or the jelly, in one another's face." A woman was to "choose topics suitable for the kind of person she is addressing," and should not pretend "to know what she does not know, but should modestly seek to win credit for what she does."

This idea of being a gentleman meant that a lot of poetry was written to win the sentiments of the ladies. The idea of romantic love began in the Renaissance. Before there had been fraternal love, as between friends or family members, and during the Middle Ages you saw the idea of "courtly" love, where a knight would swear fealty to the honor of a lady. But now another kind of love between men and women began to be written about.

The *Book of Manners* was written by Giovanni della Casa. Here are a few examples:

"Everyone should dress well, according to his age and his position in society. If he does not, it will be taken as a mark of contempt for other people."

"Refrain as far as possible from making noises which grate upon the ear, such as grinding or sucking your teeth."

"Anyone whose legs are too thin, or exceptionally fat, or perhaps crooked, should not wear vivid or parti-colored hose, in order not to attract attention to his defects."

"A man... will take care not to get his fingers so greasy as to dirty his napkin with them, because the sight of it would be unsavory to others. Nor is it polite to wipe them on the bread."

The Renaissance also saw the introduction of the fork and napkins at the table.

Do you remember the public bath houses of Rome? Public bath houses were popular in Europe during the Renaissance as well. Personal cleanliness was considered important. Bathing money was a regular part of every man's budget.

Day 5

The invention of the printing press in the middle of the 1400's had a big impact on the lives of people. During the Middle Ages, all books had been made in monasteries, handwritten and copied one by one. Now the printing press meant that a book could be made faster and at a far less cost. A German named Johann Gutenberg is believed to have printed the first book using a printing press, and the first book he printed was the *Bible*. Gutenberg made individual blocks of metal on which a single letter was etched, and arranged them in rows. Because the letters could be rearranged for new books, it was called "movable" print. Once the type was set in the right order, numerous copies of the same book could be made over and over. Now suddenly lots of people could have access to books, whereas before only the churchmen and the nobles had books. Before, all books had been religious treatises, but now people could write books on all sorts of subjects and have a means of spreading their ideas to a lot of people.

People already knew how to make paper. The Arabs learned it from the Chinese and brought the technique to Europe in the 12th century. Papermaking was not commonly practiced until the 15th century, however, when the sudden interest in books made papermaking important.

With so much more access to the printed word, more and more people became interested in having their children educated. Universities were developed, and students would copy down what the teachers said. Then they would go and have their version of the lectures published. Public schools, theoretically open to all (meaning boys) were established in Italy, although the lower classes often did not see much reason for their sons to go to school when they could be learning a trade.

"Broadsides" were a popular pastime, with people printing up a single sheet of humor, gossip or opinion. These were often passed from person to person, and if there was a person in a village who could read, the townspeople would gather to hear it read aloud. Almanacs were printed up for country people, arranged like a

A printshop in Germany

calendar and full of advice on weather and crops and home remedies. Poetry, plays and romance stories were more of interest to the upper classes.

Printing became such a big business that one town in Germany had over forty print shops working full time.

4. Choose one of the following assignments.

a. Go to the library and find out how the Gutenberg printing press worked. Use the encyclopedia if you need to. Look at pictures and describe the process in one or more paragraphs. Draw a picture if you like.

b. How has the invention of the printing press impacted your life? Describe all the ways the printed word is used in your daily life. How would your life be different if there was no printing press? Write at least one page.

c. Write a "broadside" for your family, such as a piece of family news or an opinion on a family event. Try to be humorous! Then make your own "movable" print. Use potatoes or carrots or other root vegetables to carve out letters, one letter per vegetable. Do both capitals and lower case letters if you like. Then press each letter onto an ink pad, and print your broadside using your movable print. Make copies and distribute it.

5. Have your Home Teacher give you a spelling quiz. Review any words you miss.

Extra Book Ideas:

Life In The Renaissance, by Marzieh Gail, Chanticleer Press, Random
    House, NY
If You Were There In 1492, by Barbara Brenner, Bradbury Press, MacMillan
    Publishing Co., NY, 1991
Breaking Into Print; Before and After the Invention of the Printing Press, by
    Stephen Krensky, Little, Brown & Co., New York 1996.
The Story of Writing and Printing, by Anita Gaveri, from "Signs of the
    Times" series, Oxford University Press, New York, 1995.

Extra Project Ideas:

• Write a play or conversation between a knight of the Middle Ages and a
   courtly gentleman of the Renaissance having dinner together.

- Find out about some of the ruling-class ladies of the Renaissance such as Beatrice D'Este, Elizabeth I, Catherine of Aragon, Catherine De Medici.

- Try eating a meal without a fork or a napkin. Are any of Giovanni della Casa's rules for good manners still appropriate today?

- Find out more about the beautiful furniture that was made during the Renaissance. Design your own Renaissance room, sketching the furniture and designing drapes, walls and rugs.

- Stage your own mock parade down the street of Florence. Dress as a nobleman, and have a crier announcing the way, and attendants.

- Find out more about some of the ruling families in Italy, such as the Medici's.

- Find out more about witchcraft, and the Renaissance and medieval views on witches.

Social Studies/Art/English~~~~~~Lesson 26

RENAISSANCE

Vocabulary Words

The following words are taken from your Social Studies lessons. Write definitions for each one of them without using the root word or any other form of the vocabulary word. Consider each in the context of your Social Studies material, and write a sentence for each that shows you understand the meaning.

patron	chapel	taper
scaffolding	adorn	contemplate

Spelling

Select ten words from your written material this week for spelling words. Write each of these words correctly five times and use each word in a complete sentence. Practice your spelling words in preparation for a quiz.

Grammar

1. **This week you will be doing two short research assignments. You may want to read and choose your assignments ahead of time in order to plan your trip to the library. Your essays should each include an introduction, a conclusion, and a bibliography. Review "Paragraphs," "Paragraph Forms," and "Bibliographies," in the *English Manual*.**

Days 1 & 2

There was competition between the lords and noblemen and the wealthy merchants of the various cities of Italy. They all wanted to show off their wealth and gain popularity amongst the population by building monuments to themselves in the form of great works of art. Many of them were also trying to make up for profiting by less than wholly moral activities, such as banking or war, by doing something to benefit others. We have already seen how the Crusade which destroyed Constantinople was helped by the Italian merchants providing money for the soldiers and weapons. As a result, these people became "patrons," hiring artists and architects to build and paint and sculpt for them. Even Popes and other Church leaders became patrons. The high demand for painters and sculptors meant that they became valued and acclaimed for their work, and were no longer considered humble crafts people.

Italy was not only the most civilized country in Europe at the time, but was also the leading country economically. Merchants from all over Italy bought goods from the East and sold them to the countries of Northern Europe. In exchange, Italy took wool, timber, wheat and hides to regions in the south.

It was in Italy that the idea of coins which had a standard value was invented, and we still use it today. Before that, there were so many different kinds of coins being used that no one could be sure that what they were getting was actually worth the money they were using, so the coins were not used very much. By minting a "gold florin" or a "ducat" which had only one value, people could depend on it, and so would use it more. Until the 15th century, international traders carried such coins with them to pay for their goods. Then the Italians made a further invention called a "Bill of Exchange." This was a written document that was a promise from one person to pay another person a certain amount of money by a certain day. Bills of Exchange could then be traded around, used very much like the paper bills we use today.

Portrait of a merchant

The Italians also invented double entry bookkeeping to record their transactions. This is still the standard accounting practice used today. Another practice was the use of what were called "joint-stock-companies." A group of merchants would get together and combine their money to form a company, each getting a "share" in that company. Those who had a share were called shareholders. The money put into the company would be used to try to make a profit on a trade. The shareholders then each got a share of the profit.

Sometimes the period between 1400 and 1750 is called the Commercial Revolution. Trade in general was easier, and the systems mentioned above laid the foundation for modern commerce. Many of the ways of doing business that were developed during this time are still used all over the world today.

Some Italian merchant families became enormously wealthy. They supported many famous artists of the Renaissance, and were even rich enough to lend money to the kings of Europe. Wealthy citizens gave gifts of money for charitable work, so the sick and needy could be taken care of. Many Italian cities, particularly Florence, became famous for the magnificent art and buildings that resulted from these displays of wealth and generous support of artists. Even today, visiting these cities can be a very rich experience.

A gateway in Florence

One famous family of Florence was called the House of Medici. The Medicis were a powerful and wealthy family that ruled Florence for generations, and survived many plots by other wealthy families and even church leaders to have them assassinated. They were also great patrons of the arts. Lorenzo de' Medici, also known as Lorenzo the Magnificent, was one of the most famous patrons of Florence, as well as being a ruthless and cunning ruler of the city. He was also a scholar, and encouraged education and the development of the Italian language. He was also

The Medicis owned many palaces throughout Italy, including this one in Rome

determined to make the city of Florence the most beautiful and spectacular, and paid for the solid bronze bas-relief gates leading into the Florence Baptistry. He also loved to hold festivals, pageants, and parades which celebrated the glory of Florence.

The expectation for the wealthy citizens and patrons of the Italian merchant cities was to own a palace in the city in which to do business, have a private chapel, and also own an elegant villa with extensive gardens in the countryside in which to cool down from the hot city, rest, and relax. In addition, guilds, and sometimes even individual patrons, liked to build public buildings to show off their power. As a result, there was a high demand for architects and builders. Many of the Italian architects took their ideas from the old ruins of ancient Roman times that lay partially buried around the country. Sometimes architects would even dig beneath the streets of Rome to find the traces of ancient buildings from which they modeled their own creations.

Andrea Palladio was an architect who designed some of the most famous villas. He took many of his ideas from ancient Greek and Roman buildings such as the Pantheon in Rome. The style he developed became known as the "Palladian" style, and many of our own buildings today are built in this style.

Filippo Brunelleschi was a famous architect who was able to figure out how to build a huge dome on the Cathedral of Santa Maria del Fiore in Florence. Previously, domes were built by laying long wooden beams across the bottom. However, the dome Brunelleschi built was to be so big that there were no trees tall enough to provide the beams. For months, the Guild of Wool Merchants, which was paying for the project, tried to get Brunelleschi to tell them how he planned to do it, but he refused. In one meeting, he asked the committee members to stand an egg on its end. When none of them could do it, he then took the egg and smashed one end on the table, making it stand. When the committee members complained that anyone could do that, Brunelleschi replied that once he told how he would build the dome, anyone could do it too. The Guild finally let him go ahead and build the dome, even if he would not reveal the secret of how it would be done. What Brunelleschi did was to build each layer of the dome layer by layer, finishing each circle of the layer (or "course") before starting the next. As he built each layer, he pushed the stone blocks slightly inward, so the whole dome tapered in as it went up. Each course would be supported by the course below it. As he went, he also built stone supports like ribs, on the inside of the dome for strength. In this way no beams or scaffolding were needed on the inside to support the dome as it was being built.

Brunelleschi's dome

1. **Choose one of the following topics and do some research at the library. Write up to one page, using your best grammar skills.**

   a. **The Medici family**

   b. **The "Palladian" style of architecture:**

   c. **The Cathedral of Florence, Santa Maria del Fiore (also called the Duomo) and its Baptistry.**

Days 3, 4 & 5

Giotto was one of the earliest Renaissance artists. He was so confident of his abilities, that when as a young man his family wanted to apprentice him to study to be an artist, he merely grabbed a brush from a pot of red paint, painted a perfect circle with one flourish of his wrist, and sent it off to the agent in Rome responsible for finding talented people to become artists. He got the apprenticeship. He was also an architect and liked to put buildings in his paintings. He liked the idea of making his pictures realistic-looking by using light on objects to show shadows, and showing clothing as being draped around the body. He is thought to be the first artist to stop using the flat-looking, two-dimensional way of painting that was the way people painted in the Middle Ages. One well-known painting of his has a carefully detailed ordinary housefly resting on the headdress of a lady. It looks so real that people looking at the painting often think there really is a fly on the surface of the painting itself! Many of the subjects of his paintings were religious, but he liked to paint the ordinary as well.

Leonardo Da Vinci was another Italian Renaissance artist. He was not well known in his own time, but is now considered a genius. He is the painter of the *Mona Lisa,* probably the most well-known painting from the Renaissance. He was an inventor and engineer as well. He kept extensive notebooks sketching out such inventions as flying machines, bicycles, submarines, and parachutes, none of which were actually made until centuries later. He was also interested in working out problems such as how to measure the earth. He studied nature extensively, dissecting corpses and sketching animals at play in order to understand how muscles and bones were structured and to make his paintings more realistic. He is thought to be the first to try to come up with general rules about how nature was structured, which is what our modern scientific research still tries to do. He was a deeply curious and experimental man, trying new things all the time. He was considered an eccentric by his countrymen for many reasons, such as wearing robes that fell only to his knees, rather than full-length, as was the custom. The

Mona Lisa

people he chose to paint may not have been particularly beautiful, but he liked them because they had interesting or unusual faces. His paintings tend to have a very warm, soft look, with loving gazes and smiles on the figures. He developed the technique of using the pyramid as the structure for his portraits, such as using arms crossed or folded at the waist to form the base of the pyramid, and then using the line from the elbows up to the shoulders and then to the top of the head as the sides. Other painters, including Michelangelo and Raphael, also adopted and used this method.

Raphael was an artist who had a short but productive life, dying at age 37. He became famous at a very early age, after studying in Florence with Michelangelo and Da Vinci. In addition for being famous as an artist, he became known as an archeologist, as he liked to dig under the streets of Rome to unearth ancient monuments and sculptures from Classical times. He would study these old buildings and use them in his paintings. Most of his paintings were of religious subjects, grouping people in rooms or other structures he painted, often with a piece of the sky somewhere to remind us of heaven. His interest in architecture at times led him to put in details like a building in the process of being built. He also had a habit of painting onto the bodies of his figures the faces of other painters in Florence he knew and respected. He was well-liked, known to be helpful, unselfish and a gentleman.

In northern Europe, the center for Renaissance art was in the area known as Flanders, a part of what is now the Netherlands. Jan van Eyck, the discoverer of oil paint, was an important part of the northern influence. Flemish artists liked to paint the ordinary scenes of everyday life. One of the most fascinating of these artists was Bruegel, for he would paint entire scenes full of many, even hundreds, of people engaged in everyday activities. These paintings are a wonderful way of getting a view of what life was like during the Renaissance, particularly for working people and peasants. In one painting, one can count about eighty different games, including marbles, hockey, and ring-around-the-rosy - being played by well over one hundred people.

Rembrandt was another Flemish artist in the 1600's. (Flemish is the word for someone from Flanders.) He also painted ordinary things, focusing mostly on the indoors and single people as subjects. He is famous for using light from a window or open door to show a still and contemplative mood. He was brilliant at capturing the spirit and personality of an individual. He did some religious subjects as well.

Other famous painters from the northern part of Europe during the Renaissance are Jan Vermeer, Albrecht Durer and Hans Holbein.

Perhaps the most famous artist from the Renaissance was Michelangelo. He may be most remembered for his work on the ceiling of the Sistine Chapel in Rome. When he painted the Sistine Chapel, he had very little previous experience with this kind of painting, but was determined to do it anyway. He took nearly four years to complete the ceiling of the Sistine Chapel, lying on his back atop scaffolding, arms raised straight overhead, paint dripping on his face. He is also famous for his sculpture and painting, particularly of the human body. He considered sculpture to be the finest of all arts, because he liked being able to make the figures he carved out of stone so lifelike. It was as if they were "breathing alive," as he put it. Like many of the artists of his time, he was fiercely competitive and determined to succeed. He was also known to be difficult to work with; his nose was broken early on from a fist-fight with another student. There is a statue he made of St. Proculus when he was nineteen years old which some say could be a self-portrait. It shows a very resolved and determined looking young man, fists clenched and brow furrowed, looking as if he is charging into life ahead. The sculpture which made him instantly famous was called the *Pieta* (pronounced "py-AY-tah"), which showed Mary holding the body of Jesus after he was brought down off the cross. Many believe that the face of Mary was modeled after Michelangelo's own mother. He also did many self-portraits, mostly in painting, and as he aged, the expressions seem to get more and

A painting by Vermeer

more weary and troubled. He was also known as a poet and a philosopher, and despite his reputation of being competitive and difficult, he actually had a very bright and humorous outlook on the nature of humanity and life, and often poked fun at himself.

MICHELANGELO

Lynnae McConaha

Michelangelo was one of the most famous artists of his time. He lived in a very exciting moment in European history. Italy was the center of the arts, sciences, and literature. Its works greatly influenced the rest of Europe. We don't often realize it, but the great explorers such as Christopher Columbus, Amerigo Vespucci, John Cabot, and others were from Italy and lived during this time.

The name given to this era is the RENAISSANCE. The Renaissance was a time of rediscovering books and knowledge from ancient times, and also a time of great change. Michelangelo lived from about the middle to the end of this period, from 1475 - 1564. He became a major contributor to the arts, and was considered to be a genius. He learned and remembered easily - he seemed to remember everything. When you know some of his background, you can understand why many thought he was a genius.

Michelangelo was born in Florence, Italy. For the standards of that city his family was very poor. His father had been given a government position over a very small village before Michelangelo's birth, but this only lasted a few months. Michelangelo was taken to a stonecutter's wife as a baby because his mother was not healthy. She had suffered a bad fall and was unable to nurse him. It was an accepted practice to find a foster-mother to care for a baby, but Michelangelo was left in her care for an extra long time. He was often left on his own to run around with the children of the village, fending for himself. This is why he was so independent. At times he was prone to use his fists, and he had a terrible temper. He had to rely on his own talents to survive, and found that drawing set him apart and elevated his position among the local children.

His mother died after several more children were born, and his father remarried. Michelangelo's stepmother arranged for formal schooling for him when he was ten. This only lasted 3 years, but he mastered the basics and an interest in writing was awakened within him.

By then, Michelangelo had already become very good at drawing, and it was a special form of communication for him. An older friend was apprenticed to a master painter named Domenico Ghirlandaio. Michelangelo's friend brought him along when he went to Ghirlandaio, to sketch the ancient art pieces and ruins that were around the city. After Michelangelo showed much progress, and seemed to be able to learn draftsmanship very quickly, his work was shown to the master. Ghirlandaio readily accepted Michelangelo as an apprentice into his workshop when the young artist was only thirteen years old.

A year later, Michelangelo and his friend were admitted to the academy of Lorenzo de Medici, the ruler of the city-state of Florence. Here they studied sculpture under a student of the very famous sculptor, Donatello. Lorenzo took a special liking to Michelangelo, and later he offered to take him into his personal household. He recognized Michelangelo's genius and had him eat at his own table.

Some pagan works of art which had recently been rediscovered were constantly discussed by the scholars of Lorenzo's household. The scholars tried to reconcile the current Christian beliefs they had been raised with and the pagan thoughts they were studying. Religion was a very big part of just about everyone's life then, and this study of pagan works caused problems for Michelangelo. The art work of the time was mainly religious in nature, and the great churches commissioned frescoes, sculptures, and architecture. Part of the problem Michelangelo experienced was due to his great respect and love of the perfect human body. A main teaching of the church was asceticism, or the renouncing of all worldly pleasures. The artist was expected to render all art forms around purely religious themes, and the figures tended to be flat and lifeless. Michelangelo finally resolved the problem within himself and set himself to studying the human form, portraying its beauty and expressing the energy within. He decided he could create either Christian or pagan images.

When Lorenzo de Medici died, Michelangelo was asked to stay with the household. Lorenzo's brother was now in charge, but he proved to be a poor ruler. He caused much political turmoil and eventually lost his power to France. Michelangelo knew he could not live under the brother's rule. He fled to Bologna, which was in the city-state of Rome, as he was afraid the rebellious people of Florence would not spare friends or partisans of the Medici's. In Bologna he went to live with a nobleman, where he completed several sculptures for the tomb of St. Dominic. But he felt he was wasting his time here, and was eager to get back to his more important work, Hercules, which awaited him in Florence.

By then there was a new government in Florence, organized with democratic principles, which appealed to Michelangelo. He returned after his year of exile and was welcomed as an anti-Medicean. By this time, he was well recognized as a talented sculptor, and many works were commissioned. He traveled between Rome and Florence. Two of the major works he completed during this time are the Pietà (a marble sculpture which shows the Virgin Mary holding the dead Jesus after the crucifixion) and his famous statue of David. This brought him the fame he hoped to achieve in Rome. He then returned to his beloved city of Florence, and was commissioned to do several other sculptures. There were many other artists in the city at the time, including one named Leonardo da Vinci. He was 23 years older than Michelangelo, and the two artists were spitefully competitive. Nevertheless, that didn't stop them from cooperating on a work of art for the walls of the city hall. Working together became an opportunity for Michelangelo to learn something from Leonardo about how to show flowing but vibrant movement.

Pope Julius II summoned Michelangelo to come back to Rome to paint the Sistine Chapel in the Vatican. He argued that he was a sculptor, not a painter, but Julius II, as stubborn as Michelangelo, continued his petition. Finally Michelangelo realized he must do the work, but was not satisfied with the subject matter. Unbelievably, after explaining his vision for the ceiling, Michelangelo was given leave to "paint as he liked!" The Sistine Chapel pictures nine scenes from the Old Testament. It has three scenes each of creation, the story of Adam and Eve, and Noah and the flood. These scenes are surrounded by other paintings.

Once he started on the ceiling, it was an inspiration to finish it. The Pope kept urging him to finish and he was the only person that Michelangelo permitted to see the work until half the ceiling was finished. He did have assistants, of course. He couldn't have managed mixing the plaster and paint alone, because in a fresco the paint is applied to wet plaster. There is evidence that Michelangelo allowed his assistants to paint some parts of the ceiling, which was customary. What was unusual is that it took him four years to finish, lying on his back high up in the air on scaffolding. The Pope kept urging him to finish, as he wanted to see the monument completed before his death. It was almost as if it was his own vision he saw painted there on the ceiling above him.

Michelangelo lived a very long life of nearly ninety years, and continued to sculpt and paint to the very end. He also devoted time to his writing. We are able to interpret many of his works through his poems.

In Michelangelo's later life he turned to architecture, though he did continue to paint, sculpt, and write. He was the chief sculptor, painter, and architect of the Vatican. He also became the chief architect for St. Peter's Cathedral. The work on St. Peter's had been previously left undone, and this gave Michelangelo the opportunity to show what he could do in this medium. The dome of St. Peter's is known as the finest in the world. He was in his eighties's when he did this and many of his directions were carried out through messages carried from his home to the workers who were building the dome.

Michelangelo had seen a lot in his life. The expansion of the world by the discovery of the Western Hemisphere, Martin Luther's challenge to the old religion, the scientific discoveries of Copernicus which changed the way the world thought of the solar system - all of these happened during his lifetime.

He remained single throughout his life. He said his children were the works he left behind. When he was in his 60's, he met a woman he considered his equal intellectually. She influenced him in the way he viewed religion.

From the ceiling in the Sistine Chapel

His later works tended to look futuristic and modern. His forms took on irregular designs. He truly expressed the spirit of the times, as artists tend to do. He was in his 89th year when he died. His long life allowed him to develop his talents in many ways and show the changes that went on about him throughout his life.

2. **Choose one of these Renaissance artists and write a one page essay about him. Choose one of the topics below as the focus of your essay. Make a bibliography for your essay.**

Artists:

   Giotto, Raphael, Da Vinci, Rembrandt, Van Eyck, Vermeer, Bruegel, Boticelli, Donatello, Titian, and Durer

Topics:

   • **Look at pictures and/or sculptures by the artist and describe what you like and dislike about his works of art. Be specific.**

   • **Write a biography of the artist, mentioning at least two or three of his best known works.**

3. **Have your Home Teacher give you a spelling quiz. Review the ones you miss and put them on your ongoing list for the year.**

Extra Book Ideas:

"Art For Children" series, by Ernst Raboff, JB Lippincott Junior Series, New York, 1988. The series includes volumes on Michelangelo, Raphael and Leonardo Da Vinci.

A Weekend With Leonardo Da Vinci, by Rosabianca Skira-Venturi, Rizzoli International Publications, NY, 1993.

Leonardo Da Vinci, by Elizabeth Ripley, Oxford University Press, NY 1952. Also wrote biographies on Botticello, Michelangelo, Rembrandt, Titian, Durer, and Raphael.

"Portraits of Greatness" series, Enzo Orlandi, general editor, Curtis Publishing Company. Includes The Life and Times of ...(Michelangelo, Leonardo Da Vinci, etc.)

Great Painters, by Piero Ventura, G.P Putnam's Sons, New York, 1984

History of Art for Young People, by H.W Jansen, with Samuel Cauman, Harry N Abrams, American Book Co., New York, 1971.

The Rainbow Book of Art, by Thomas Craven, World Publishing Co., New York, 1956.

Leonardo and His World, by Marianne Sachs, Kingfisher Books, Silver Burdett Co., Morristown, NJ, 1980.

Extra Project Ideas:

- Watch the video, "The Agony and The Ecstasy." This is the story of Michelangelo.

- Research and build a model of an Italian Renaissance villa.

- Build a dome for a cathedral using Brunelleschi's secret technique.

- Look at pictures in the library of the Palladeon style of architecture, and see if there are buildings in your area that use the same style or have parts of the same style. Internet sites were given earlier in this lesson.

- Watch the video, "Florence: Cradle of The Renaissance."

- Find out about some of the other famous patrons of Rome and Italy.

Florence

Social Studies/Art/ English~~~~~~~Lesson 27

RENAISSANCE

Vocabulary Words

The following words relate to your Social Studies lesson. Write definitions for each of them without using the root word or any other form of the word. Think about them in the context of your Social Studies material. Use complete sentences to show you understand how to use each word.

perspective	dimension	improvise	stag
mecca	sonnet	commentary	

Spelling

Select ten words from your written material this week for spelling words. Write each of these words correctly five times and use each word in a complete sentence. Practice your spelling words in preparation for a quiz.

Grammar

1. **Write a sentence for each of the following homophones:**

to - too - two	by - buy - bye	your - you're - yore
blue - blew	ate - eight	here - hear
no - know	rode - road	be - bee
flour - flower	in - inn	there - their - they're

Day 1

During the Renaissance, artists started moving away from focusing only on the religious scenes which were so common during medieval times. Sometimes they got ideas from looking at ancient Greek and Roman architecture. Other times, their subjects were ordinary people, such as the famous people around the city who wanted to be memorialized. After a while, artists tried to make things look the way they actually looked through people's eyes. They discovered that one way to make things look more realistic was to use three dimensions, and not just two. Instead of just painting everything by its height and its width, they started painting in ways to show how deep things were, too. As a result, several discoveries were made during the Renaissance which allow us to take a flat two-dimensional surface such as a piece of paper or canvas, and depict a scene that looks as if it has depth. As one stands at the outside of such a painting looking in, it appears as if objects are disappearing into the distance.

In order to make a painting look as if it had three dimensional perspective, the artist would first choose a *horizon line* for his painting - a horizontal line somewhere across the surface of the painting. The horizon will always seem to be at the eye level of the person looking at the painting. If the artist chooses a horizon line that is high up in the picture, it will make the painting look as if you are high up in the air, as if in an airplane or on top of a building. If the horizon is low in the picture, then it will appear is if you are lying on the ground looking up at the objects in the painting. Most Renaissance artists chose a horizon line somewhere in the middle, as if you were merely standing or sitting in the room with the other people in the painting.

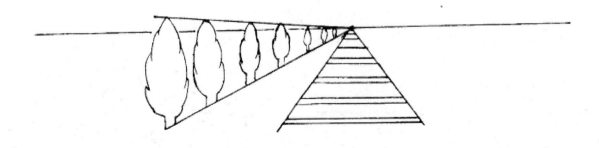

Objects appear smaller and smaller the farther away they are, and they seem to get closer and closer together as well. For example, if you look down a straight walkway lined with a row of trees all the same height, they seem to get shorter and shorter as they go off into the distance. The details of the trees also get fuzzier as they get farther and farther away, making it harder to see the individual leaves and branches. In the same way, if you were to stand on a straight stretch of railroad track and look into the distance, the two rails of the track would eventually seem to disappear into a single point way off on the horizon. Even though we know the rails of the track stay parallel and never actually meet, they look as if they do. For this reason, Renaissance artists would choose a *vanishing point* somewhere along the horizon. This vanishing

Can you see the vanishing point in this painting?

point would be the place where everything would "disappear." See if you can identify the vanishing point and the horizon line in the drawing above.

Many Renaissance artists painted buildings as part of their pictures. This was partly because there was a new interest in Classic architecture, but also because the nobles and other patrons who commissioned paintings liked to show off their villas, churches, and public buildings. In order to paint buildings in a way that looked realistic, artists used *two-point perspective*. For example, if you stand looking at the outside of a building from the corner of the building, you would see two surfaces of the building, perhaps the front and one side. Knowing that the top and bottom edges of the building are actually parallel, but look as if they are receding off into the distance, one would see that the front of the building would start to vanish off into one end of the horizon, and the side of the building would start to vanish off to the other end of the horizon. If one were to draw imaginary lines along the top and bottom edges of the building and extend those lines straight to the horizon, they would disappear into the vanishing point. This meant that the artist would choose not one, but two different vanishing points along the horizon line, one on one end for the front of the building, and one on the other end for the side of the building.

1. Choose one of the following assignments on perspective drawing.

   a. Choose a Renaissance painting you like that shows the use of three dimensions: height, width and depth. Copy one part of the painting that shows the use of these dimensions.

   b. Draw two pictures of a landscape using different horizon lines. Make one of the horizon lines high up, and the other one down low. Draw the same landscape in both pictures. Do you see how the horizon line can change how you see the landscape?

   c. Draw your own picture showing the use of either a single vanishing points or two vanishing points. Don't forget to select a horizon line first, even if you do not draw it in.

Days 2 & 3

Art in the Renaissance took many forms. Buildings were often adorned with *bas-relief*, a form of sculpture used on walls and the sides of buildings. Figures and objects in the foreground were sculpted right on to the wall, still attached, but made to look as if they were rising off of the surface of the wall. Sometimes deeper recesses in the background would be carved out of the wall itself.

Bas-relief

Fresco was a kind of watercolor painted directly onto fresh plaster. It was the major technique used to decorate inside buildings and walls. One of the most famous frescoes is on ceiling of the Sistine Chapel in Rome, painted by Michelangelo. Over time, frescoes become difficult to preserve, as watercolor is so thin and weak in pigment, and the plaster soaks up humidity, which causes it to crack and crumble as it dries. Plaster on walls can also get very dirty with time. Recently when the ceiling in the Sistine Chapel was "restored" by cleaning off the layers of grime that had accumulated over the centuries, it was discovered that the colors used on frescoes in the Renaissance were far brighter than had been previously thought.

Oil painting, which is still an important form of art today, was invented during the Renaissance. Previously tempera (a fast-drying pigment) had been used, but once it was on the picture, it was difficult to change anything. Jan van Eyck (pronounced "ike") from Flanders (what is now known as the Netherlands, or Holland) developed oil paint, which takes days to dry. This allows artists to take more time with their paintings, to change and even paint right over what had previously been painted.

After the printing press was invented, artists began to illustrate books by carving pictures onto wooden blocks. Ink was rolled on them, and the pictures pressed to the page of the book. Because it was such a relatively fast and easy way to show art, it quickly became a popular way in which many ordinary people or those living in rural areas could view art. Many everyday scenes from the Renaissance were shown in woodblock prints.

2. **Choose an artistic medium and work in it. Choices:**

   a. **Make a miniature Renaissance fresco wall. Start by using a pan as a mold for a small plaster slab. (Plaster in pre-mixed powder form can be obtained in art or crafts stores or through art catalogues, and sometimes even in hardware stores.) Use water color or tempera to paint your fresco. It is recommended that you use the "drypoint" technique for your painting: use as little water as possible to soften the paint, and then keep a paper towel handy to wipe off any excess moisture before applying the paint. This also helps keep the point of your brush sharp. The paint should not be too pasty, but dry enough to hold a lot of color and not run on the surface that you are painting.**

   b. **Make a bas-relief out of clay, starting with a smooth thick slab. Build it up on top and carve into it a scene which includes people and buildings. It can be fired or glazed if you have access to the equipment, or you can use the kind of clay which bakes in the oven. You may need to be resourceful with tools to get the kind of detail you want—try butter knives, chopsticks, shishkebab skewers and even toothpicks.**

c. Make a block print, using chisel and mallet. Make sure the block is very tightly secured, using clamps on a workbench, and that you push the chisel in the direction <u>away</u> from you. Wear goggles to prevent splinters from getting into your eyes. Use different-sized chisels for different details. Make a scene that depicts some aspect of Renaissance life, such as peasants working in a field, women weaving, or a merchant setting out his wares. Then roll ink or heavy paint onto the woodblock and carefully press it onto a piece of paper. Use an old towel and a rolling pin to press the block more securely onto the paper.

Days 4 & 5

Musicians and actors, much like artists, got by and made their living on the whims of those who would hire them. Sometimes noblemen would hire musicians as regular members of their household staff to provide entertainment for any number of events, such as having special guests in for dinner, holiday celebrations, or dances. Performing musicians wore elaborate costumes and masks. Acrobats performed even in formal gatherings at court. Trumpets sounded at dinner parties when the various dishes were carried in. Intermissions at plays included fireworks, and performers occasionally even set fire to the scenery, just to add to the excitement. Everyone joined in the fun, except religious fanatics who considered it a sin to enjoy themselves. Princes organized festivals of incredible splendor for their people, which would sometimes last for days.

More often, musicians would travel from place to place, trying to find work where they could, sometimes in troupes. Common instruments of the Renaissance were the recorder, lute, harpsichord, crumhorn, and the tambourine. Madrigal singing was also a very popular entertainment for the upper classes. Madrigals were written in four parts, usually about poetic subjects such as love, the beauty of the countryside, or death. They were always sung *a capella* (without instruments).

Most music from the Renaissance was still religious in nature, however, and some of the most beautiful sacred music comes from this time. Choral singing was usually accompanied by the church organ.

Dancing had a special philosophical meaning during the Renaissance. Many people believed that the harmony of skilled dance movements reflected harmony in government, nature, and the universe.

Hunting was considered "a true pastime for great lords." Large groups of nobles would set off together after a full grown stag or wild boar. Specially trained hunting dogs and falcons were a crucial part of every hunt.

Commedia dell'Arte, or "Comedy of Arts" was a form of entertainment that became very popular in Renaissance Italy, not only in the street for the common folk, but in the palaces for the noblemen. The actors traveled in groups about the country, willing to perform for any who would hire them, or for donations in the street. Often the shows were used to poke fun at particular well-known people or as political commentary. Wealthy people would hire a troupe to perform as a means of passing a message on to another citizen who might be a rival for power or prestige, or to get the people to see their point of view. Often the humor was very crude. We do not know much about what they actually performed, because they were usually improvised or made up as the actors went along, to go with the particular needs or interest of the audience.

Actors rarely found a permanent place in which to practice their trade. One exception was the area around London, in England. Under the rule of Elizabeth I, London became a mecca for permanent theaters and acting troupes. These were well-attended by an appreciative population from all classes.

Shakespeare

William Shakespeare is probably the most famous playwright to write in the English language. Even today actors find that being able to perform Shakespeare's plays is the best way to show their abilities. He wrote over seventy plays and numerous sonnets. Many of the ideas for his plays came from historical events, such as Henry V and the battle of Avignon in France, which you may remember from your studies of the Middle Ages, or Antony and Cleopatra, who were part of ancient Egyptian and Roman history. Sometimes his plays were from popular stories of the time. *The Tempest*, for example, was based on the discovery of the Bermuda Islands. Theater was very popular in London, where Shakespeare lived and wrote, with people of all classes crowding into the Globe Theater (where his troupe performed) to watch and comment aloud on what they were seeing. Some of Shakespeare's plays were written in honor of Queen Elizabeth I, or to entertain her. She had a particular fondness for his comedies.

3. **Choose one of the following projects.**

    a. **Listen to Renaissance music, such as Palestrina, Monteverdi and Josquin. Find out about several of the musical instruments of the Renaissance and draw pictures of them. Can you identify which ones you are hearing when you listen to the music? Describe in at least one paragraph.**

    b. **Present your own version of a Shakespeare scene. The argument between Titania and Oberon, or Titania falling in love with Bottom in** *A Midsummer Night's Dream* **are possibilities, but there are many others. Use your own words. Make appropriate costumes and props, and videotape your scene for your teacher.**

    c. **Perform your own Commedia dell'Arte scene with a live audience. Use no more than two or three characters. Start with an idea or situation you want to make fun of. Try improvising as you go, remembering that the more outrageous you get, the better. Remember however, that as you improvise, you need to keep track of how your audience is responding. Just because you think it's funny doesn't mean they will, and you may have to change what you are doing midstream in order to adjust to the mood of the audience. Videotape the scene for your teacher.**

    d. **Attend a Shakespeare play. If this is not possible, then rent a video of one of his plays, such as** *A Midsummer Night's Dream, Romeo and Juliet*, **or** *The Taming of the Shrew*. **Recently Kenneth Branaugh has come out with some good ones, such as** *Henry V*, **and** *Much Ado About Nothing*. **After seeing the play, write about your experience with Shakespeare and his use of language.**

4. **Have your Home Teacher give you a spelling quiz. Review the words you miss and put them on your ongoing list for the year.**

Extra Book Ideas:

Usborne Guide to Drawing, by Patience Foster, Usborne Publishing Ltd., London, 1981. Helpful section on drawing in perspective.

Shakespeare Stories, volumes I and II, by Leon Garfield, Illustrated by Michael Foreman, Schoken Books, NY, 1985.

Beautiful Stories from Shakespeare, by E. Nesbit, Weathervane Books, NY, 1952.

(There are several other writers who have written story versions of the plays Shakespeare wrote. Some of them may have more appropriate reading levels.)

"Men of Genius" series, volume on Shakespeare, Webster Division, McGraw-Hill Books, NY, 1968.

The Essential Theater, by Oscar Brockett. Useful sections and illustrations on theater.

An Elizabethan Songbook, arranged by Noah Greenberg, text by W.H. Auden, Norton Library, Doubleday Books, 1957

An Anthology of English, Medieval and Renaissance Vocal Music, ed. by Noah Greenberg, Norton Library, Doubleday Books, 1961.

The Oxford Junior Companion to Music, by Michael Hurd, Oxford University Press, London, 1979. Great resource on music throughout the ages.

Extra Project Ideas:

- Read some of Shakespeare's plays, or stories from Shakespeare, and summarize them. Or draw characters from Shakespeare, in their costumes.

- Read some of Shakespeare's sonnets, and find out about the structure of sonnets. Write your own.

- Attend a Renaissance festival. Internet resources to help you locate one in your area include:

- Find out about the seven laws of perspective, and do some drawings using them.

- Experiment with oil painting.

- Find out about the recent preservation of the frescoes in the Sistine Chapel.

- Find out about falconry.

- Study Commedia dell'Arte in more depth, such as the stock standard characters and what they were like.

- Make a Commedia dell'Arte mask.

Social Studies/Art/English~~~~~~Lesson 28

RENAISSANCE

Vocabulary Words

The following words are taken from your Social Studies lesson. Write definitions for each of them without using the root word or any other form of the vocabulary words. Consider them in the context of your Social Studies material, and write a sentence for each that shows you understand the meaning.

orbit	**ambitious**	**coronation**
humanism	**classical**	**geocentric**
anatomy		

Spelling

Select ten words from your written material this week for spelling words. Write each of these words correctly five times and use each word in a complete sentence. Practice your spelling words in preparation for a quiz.

Grammar

1. **Write six sentences which use the following synonyms. See the section called "Synonyms" in the *English Manual*.**

sad - glum	**frail - weak**	**quick - fast**
voyage - trip	**joyful - happy**	**love - adore**

2. **Write six sentences using the following antonyms. See the section called "Antonyms" in the *English Manual*.**

hard - soft	**good - bad**	**bright - dull**
sunny - rainy	**messy - tidy**	**fat - thin**

Days 1 & 2

A new movement known as the "New Learning" began in Italy during the 15th century, and from there spread to Spain, Portugal, France, Germany, England, areas of Austria, and the Netherlands. People started to read and study ancient Greek, and Roman scholars began to question the accepted authority of the Catholic Church. They started to ask "how" and "why" and wanted proof of what they were being told to believe.

Francisco Petrarch, an Italian poet born in 1304, is considered to be the "Father" of the Renaissance. Petrarch tried to understand the entire civilization of the ancient world. He was a pioneer in humanism. Humanism is a way of looking at our world which emphasizes the importance of human beings—their nature and their place in the universe. Humanism teaches that every person has dignity and worth. It focuses not just on facts and history, but on emotions and personalities. Humanists of the Renaissance also believed that people needed to understand the customs and ideas of ancient Greece and Rome in order to learn how they should behave in their own, more modern lives.

Medieval thinkers thought of earthly existence chiefly as preparation for the afterlife. In contrast, the people of the Renaissance believed that life on earth should be lived as fully as possible. They were interested in the unique qualities that made one person stand out from others. Like the ancient Romans, people of the Renaissance were ambitious for fame and worldly success. Like the ancient Greeks, they believed human beings could achieve great things. These attitudes encouraged a spirit of curiosity and adventure.

The Renaissance ideal, one which Petrarch fostered, was a well-rounded person, educated and creative. Both men and women were expected to develop their athletic abilities as well. While men still held the center stage in the fields of politics and business, women were expected to make use of their education and talents at home.

There are many writers and thinkers from the Renaissance who thought in humanistic terms. One was Rabelais, a French monk and scholar born in 1494, who promoted the benefits of living a purposeful, busy, thoughtful life. His best known novel was *Gargantua and Pantagruel*, which made fun of those who did not live from a humanist point of view. Chaucer wrote *The Canterbury Tales*, stories which humorously focused upon individuals from all walks of life in England as they made their ways on a pilgrimage to the cathedral in Canterbury. Although Chaucer actually lived and wrote closer to Medieval times, his writings are a good example of the early humanist vision. Part of the fun of reading his stories now is to see how much his characters are just like people we might know today.

Cervantes was a Spaniard who wrote a story called *Don Quixote*. His idea was to make fun of the old attitudes of the Middle Ages which revered chivalry and bloodlust. He used the character of an aging knight named Don Quixote, who went on an aimless quest to poke fun at knights. The expression "tilting at windmills," to describe putting a lot of effort into a pointless mission, comes from this story, and is still used today. It comes from a scene in the story where Don Quixote, because of his bad eyesight, is convinced that some windmills were actually giants, and charges at them with his lance.

Machiavelli was an Italian who wrote *The Prince*, a book about political theory. It is hard to say that Machiavelli was really a humanist, because although he, like other humanists, looked to Classical authorities, he encouraged some rather immoral and inhumane ways for a ruler to gain power and prestige. Nevertheless, he provided a good look at political behavior; some of his ideas are still relevant as we consider our own modern political figures.

Descartes

Descartes was a Frenchman who believed in scientific reason and thought that nothing existed without proof. He proved his own existence by stating, "I think, therefore I am." His method of scientific reasoning was to follow a clear, orderly progression from one place to the next. This method is still used today. Frances Bacon, from England, followed Descartes ideas about scientific reasoning, and promoted the use of science to help humanity conquer nature for the benefit of society. Pascal was a French philosopher who was also a scientist. He opposed Bacon by saying that the power of faith is important to human existence and there is a need to rely on God, even with science. He felt that faith and science could work together.

1. Choose one of the following, writing just a few sentences.

a. Do you believe nothing exists unless it is proved? Can you think of something that exists that can not be proven?

b. What humanism means to you. Do you disagree or agree with its principles? What do you suppose is meant by the term, "Renaissance Man?" How do you live your own life in regards to humanism?

Days 3, 4 & 5

As traditional opinions were questioned, people began to observe the world around them without reference to religious opinion. Everything was looked at with doubt, and then sometimes not accepted unless it could be proven. The period during the 1500's and 1600's became known as the Scientific Revolution, and it had its beginnings during the Renaissance.

During the Middle Ages, and well into the Renaissance, there were scientists known as alchemists and astrologers who were seeking secrets of the universe. The alchemists were early chemists who tried to change ordinary metals into gold and silver. They were also trying to find a cure that would allow people to live forever. They believed if they could make this "elixir of life" out of "liquid gold," they would have a universal cure for all ills. Alchemy is the basis for chemistry today, which still looks at the elements and tries to combine them for human uses.

Most people in the 1500's and 1600's continued to believe in astrology, witchcraft and magic. Daily life was often violent and dangerous, making the future uncertain. Astrology was used to explain the forces which might influence people or events on a daily basis. There were few people who did not believe that the movements of the stars and planets influenced human activity and natural events. Even the Popes used astrology to choose the time of their coronations. People did not have scientific laboratories to study the natural world like we have now, but instruments began to be invented in order to measure the world and prove new ideas. Inventions during the Renaissance included the microscope, the thermometer, and the barometer.

Leonardo Da Vinci was not only a wonderful painter during the Renaissance, he was an inventor as well. He understood and studied physics, sound, light, and sight. He made a machine for cutting threads into screws, a hydraulic saw, and a waterpump, all remarkable achievements for the times. He made improvements on the waterwheel, and designed the first machine gun. He was also fascinated with flying and alternative means of transportation, and was so fascinated and detailed in his drawings of the human and animal body that they were sometimes used by medical students.

During the 16th century in Italy, a man named Galileo Galilei noticed the chandelier as it swung back and forth in a cathedral. No matter whether the chandelier made a wide arc or a short arc, it seemed to take the same time to move from one end of its arc to the other. He reasoned that a big pendulum could be used to keep a clock ticking in time, and using this concept, he invented the pendulum clock. He also proved that all objects fall at the same speed, no matter how heavy each might be, unless a wind or other outside circumstances affect the objects.

Perhaps the most interesting story about science in the Renaissance was in the area of astronomy. Galileo Galilei was also an astronomer. He and another man named Nicolaus Copernicus questioned the Catholic Church's teaching that the earth was the center of the universe. They began to collect evidence that the earth moved around

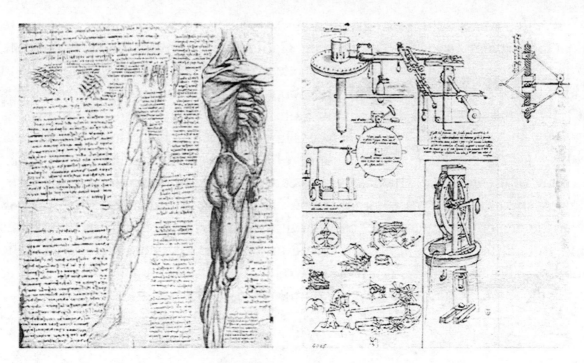

Drawings by Da Vinci

the sun. The Church thought that man was at the center of all creation and therefore the universe must revolve around the earth. The scholars of the "New Learning" attacked the whole basis of the medieval Church. They promoted the idea that men should be able to think for themselves and that each individual had a right to his own opinion, and were no longer willing to quietly accept whatever the Church taught at the time.

Copernicus was an astronomer who came up with the "heliocentric" theory. The heliocentric theory says that the earth and all the other planets revolve around the sun. This was a very new idea at the time. His theory debunked the Church's view that the planets and the sun revolved around the earth (which made man the center of the universe). The heliocentric theory not only said

Leonardo da Vinci

that the Church was wrong, but that the ancient Greeks and Romans had been wrong as well. The heliocentric theory got a lot more attention after Copernicus' death when Galileo was able to prove his theories.

Galileo was able to prove Copernicus was right when he used a telescope to look at the heavenly skies for the first time. Galileo did not invent the idea of putting two lenses together in a tube to make a telescope, but he had heard about it and decided to make one for himself. His telescope was good enough to see the valleys and hills of the moon and the rings on Saturn. He saw that the moon's glow was caused by the sun shining on its surface. He discovered that the moons of Jupiter revolved around it, which helped to support his observations that the earth was not the center of the universe. His discoveries caused a huge uproar amongst scientists, scholars, and especially the Church. People did not like the idea that they were no longer the center of the universe, but that they simply inhabited one of the planets going around the sun. Galileo was ordered to renounce his beliefs by the Catholic Church. He did so publicly in order to save his life, but the story is that as he was leaving the room, he muttered, "Yet it *does* move."

It was not until the early 1600's that the heliocentric theory was mathematically proven. This was done by a man named Kepler. At first he had a hard time making the theory fit with what was actually observed in the sky. However, he then realized that the orbits of the planets were not exact circles as had been previously thought, and he was able to show how the movements could be predicted. Other mathematicians of the Scientific Revolution were Descartes, who was not only a philosopher (the same one who said, "I think, therefore I am,") but also the founder of coordinate geometry; and a German, Gottfried Leibniz, who founded calculus.

In the early part of the Renaissance, medicine was not much better than it had been in the Middle Ages. If a person got sick, he could go to a physician, a surgeon or an herbalist. The physician was schooled in the classics and philosophy, and his diagnosis was based upon the study of the patient's urine. The surgeon might also be the dentist or the barber. He had little knowledge of what he was doing, and he did not use any anesthesia. Any knowledge he had about anatomy was based on studies done in ancient Greece by a doctor who dissected apes. The herbalist applied concoctions made from plants or animal parts. It was generally thought that the body was made up of four basic elements—earth, air, fire, water—and that medicine should attempt to restore the normal balance among these four elements. For many diseases the only known remedy was to reduce the blood pressure. This was done by letting leeches suck out the patient's blood.

Copernicus' solar system

Andreas Vesalius, who lived from 1514-1564, was fascinated by the structure of the human body. He did lots of experiments on muscles and tissues. He collected bones from graveyards and dissected the bodies of criminals executed at the gallows. He made many discoveries which older doctors thought were outrageous, such as the fact that the heart has no bone. Over time they came to respect him, and at one university there were so many people trying to watch him at his dissection work that the building collapsed.

Harvey was an English doctor who used laboratory experiments to describe circulation, the heart and blood vessels. Later anatomical discoveries during the early Scientific Revolution included the existence of cells and oxygen. The invention of the microscope in the 1500's enabled these discoveries. Slowly medical care began to improve.

When in the 1600's King Charles II of England and Louis XIV established national science academies, it was a time of triumph for science, for it now meant that people were free to continue to experiment and prove their observations without prosecution by the Church. Science "orders," (such as the Accademia dei Lincei, to which Galileo belonged, established in Rome in 1603) were created all over Europe. This movement would directly lead to Isaac Newton and the beginning of the "Age of Enlightenment."

We can be grateful for the Renaissance as it paved the way for the world in which we live today. When people began to question and think for themselves; many things were discovered and achieved. Men began to discover the natural world. They found they were no longer the center of the universe. They learned how the body worked, and developed new tools to help them. As a part of all this change, people began to argue about the teachings of the Catholic Church. As a result, Protestantism arose, during a period in religious history known as the Reformation. You will learn more about the Reformation in Lesson 29.

2. **Explore gravity. Stand up on a high ladder or on the second floor of a building (make sure you do this safely) and drop two small, unbreakable items of different weights at the same time. Have someone below to see which lands first. Try this experiment with items of different sizes, weights, and shapes, from as many different heights as you can easily arrange. Record your findings. Don't be discouraged if they fall at different speeds. This experiment works perfectly only with no extraneous variables - in a vacuum.**

3. **Learn more about pendulums by making one. You will need a ball of string, a weight, and a watch with a second hand.**

   a. **Tie your weight to a length of string.**

   b. **Hang the weight from a high place (a light fixture, a doorway, etc.)**

c. Start the pendulum swinging. Hold it out and release it.

d. Count ten swings to the left. How long did it take?

e. Now start the pendulum again but do not hold it as far out. Time ten more swings to the left. Did both experiments take the same amount of time, or were they different?

f. Now shorten the string and try it again as you did in d. and e. above.

What difference did the shorter string make? Describe all your results.

4. Look up two of the following people, and write a paragraph about each one. Ptolemy (the ancient Greek astronomer), Andres Vesalius, Robert Hooke, Joseph Priestly, Johann Kepler, Antoine Lavoisier. List some of their discoveries.

5. Choose one of the following projects.

    a. Leonardo Da Vinci explored the idea of making flying machines. Make a series of gliders and paper airplanes by folding paper in various ways. Explore different styles and compare the way they fly. There are some good books available on different styles of paper airplanes. You might want to get one!

    b. Take a day to observe your environment with a keen eye. Try not to have any preconceptions about how things look. Sit quietly and examine a flower, a leaf, a shell or some other natural object. Do some drawings as if you were Leonardo Da Vinci, looking at the same object from many different angles and in different positions. You can put several drawings on the same page. Try drawing upside down - you might get interesting results!

6. Have your Home Teacher give you a spelling quiz. Review the words you miss, and add them to your ongoing list.

Extra Book Ideas:

Copernicus, by Henry Thomas, Julian Messner Inc., NY 1960.

Galileo, by Leonard Everett Fisher, MacMillan Publishing, NY, 1992.

How Things Began, by Mary Jean McNeil, Usborne Publishing, Ltd., London, 1975. In the USA, Hayes Books, Tulsa Oklahoma.

A Weekend with Leonardo Da Vinci, by Rosabianca Skira-Venturi, Rizzoli, NY, 1993.

Leonardo Da Vinci, by Elizabeth Ripley, Oxford University Press, New York 1952.

Leonardo and His World, by Marianne Sachs, Kingfisher Books, Silver Burdett Co., Morristown, NJ, 1980.

The Pantheon Story of Mathematics For Young People, by James T. Rogers, Pantheon Books, Random House, NY, 1966.

The Universe of Galileo & Newton, by Bixby

Copernicus. Titan of Modern Astronomy, by Knight

Galileo & Leonardo da Vinci, by Levinger

The Harmonious World of Johann Kepler, by Sidney Rosen. Also wrote *Galileo and the Magic of Numbers* and *Doctor Paracelcus*.

The Quest of Galileo, by Patricia Lauber, Garden City Books, Garden City, New Jersey, 1959

Extra Project Ideas:

- Hold a two or three-way discussion between Ptolemy (the ancient Greek astronomer), Copernicus, and Galileo.

- Make up a play showing Galileo's debate with the Inquisition, the organization in the Catholic Church responsible for stamping out the beliefs that were contrary to the Church. Perform and videotape your play.

- Visit a local observatory.

- Make a large picture, mural-sized if possible, putting the sun in the middle and showing the orbits of the planets around it. Label the distances from the sun and the length of time for each orbiting planet. Also include the moons of each planet. Try to keep the size of the planets and the distances from the sun as proportionate as possible. Make the mural beautiful!

- Use a microscope to look at bacteria (your own saliva is a good source), blood cells, and a bone. Draw pictures to show your discoveries.

- Make a simple telescope using two lenses and a tube (availability of supplies allowing!). If not, see if you can get access to a telescope from a friend or school. Look at some of the things Galileo saw for the first time, such as the surface of the moon and Jupiter's moons, if possible.

- Find out about the first microscope, the first thermometer, or the first barometer.

Social Studies/Art/English~~~~~~~Lesson 29

THE REFORMATION

Vocabulary

Your vocabulary words relate to the material you are studying in Social Studies. Define each of them without using the root word, and use them in a sentence in a way that shows you understand the meaning. Try to think about them in the context of your Social Studies work. If you are unable to find a word in your best dictionary, look in an encyclopedia.

heresy/heretic	**layman**	**repent/repentance**
persecution	**sovereign**	**obstinate**
devout		

Spelling

Select ten words from your written material this week for spelling words. Write each of these words correctly five times and use each word in a complete sentence. Practice your spelling words in preparation for a quiz.

Grammar

1. **This week you will be writing a play. Turn to the section called "Direct Quotations" in your *English Manual* and review the rules for enclosing a person's statements in quotation marks.**

   Note: Plays do not use quotation remarks or rules for dialogue. However, in this play, we would like you to use quotation marks for practice.

   Remember that you must start a new paragraph each time a different person speaks.

2. When you are finished with your play, proofread it to be sure you have capitalized all names, put all dialogue in quotes, and used complete sentences with correct ending punctuation.

Days 1 - 5

As you have learned, the Catholic Church was the dominant organization throughout Europe for many years. It retained its power through the many priests, bishops, and cardinals who advised the various rulers of Europe, offering favors to some and threatening others with the possibility of going to Hell. Common people also lived in fear of disobeying the Church. Because it was so powerful, the different countries of Europe were not entirely independent of each other, as everyone had to obey the Catholic Church. During the 14th and 15th centuries, the Renaissance brought a new, more independent way of thinking. Christians began to challenge the authority of the Catholic Church, which had become very rich as well as powerful. Those who challenged or protested came to be called Protestants. They began what is known as the Reformation: the movement to reform the Roman Catholic Church.

Everyone had to pay a tax called a tithe to the Church every year, and the tithe was ten percent of all one's belongings, money, and property. Some people did not like being forced to pay taxes to the Church. The Church also made a lot of money by selling what was called *indulgences*. An indulgence was a piece of paper blessed by a churchman that said that the owner of the paper was forgiven for their sins. At first, people had to pray and do good works to get an indulgence, but as time passed, churchmen saw they could get rich by allowing people to buy them outright, without taking any personal action to find faith. People believed these indulgences would help them get into heaven when they died, so the more they bought, the better they thought their chances were.

Martin Luther was a Catholic priest in Germany who did not believe in selling indulgences. He became the leader of the Reformation in 1517 when he preached against the indulgences. He said the forgiveness of sins could not be bought, but that it was received only through repentance and faith. Opposing the teachings of the Catholic Church, Luther said that good works - prayers, pilgrimages, and other religious activities - could not wipe away sin. For him, faith was the most important thing, and he said, "God our Father has made all things depend on faith so that whoever has faith will have everything, and whoever does not have faith will have nothing."

Woodcut of Martin Luther

He believed that each person faces God alone, and that nothing, even a priest who is specially trained to lead people to God through the sacraments, should stand in between. He believed that everyone was equal before God.

Luther's intention in the beginning was not to break away from the Catholic Church but merely to reform it. He had initially assumed the Pope would support him in his battle against selling indulgences, but he soon learned otherwise. Stunned, Luther stood steadfast on the authority of the *Bible* over the Pope's wishes. When he refused to bow to the Pope's authority, a decree was issued that excommunicated Luther and sentenced him to be punished as an obstinate heretic. The usual punishment for this was to be burned at the stake. Luther, in turn, publicly burned the decree - a fiery symbol of his absolute and final separation from the Roman Catholic Church. He was then declared to be an outlaw.

Luther was kept alive by sympathetic people in Germany who liked his ideas. For some time, a German prince kept him safely hidden. While he was in hiding as an outlaw, Martin Luther translated the *Bible* from Latin into German so the German people could read it for themselves, rather than having to rely on what the priests told them it said. Before this time, very few people who were not officials of the Catholic Church had ever read the *Bible*. Even Luther had never seen a whole *Bible* until he was twenty years old. Over 100,000 copies of Luther's translation of the *Bible* were sold during his lifetime, and eventually the Lutheran Church became the official church of Germany.

There was another area where Luther disagreed with the Catholic Church. For hundreds of years, the Church had taught that being part of the clergy, or being someone who had committed themselves to a religious life set apart from the world, such as a monk or a nun, was better than being a common person living a regular sort of life. Luther said that being a parent and raising a family was especially important, but that all occupations were holy, whether a baker, a blacksmith, or a carpenter. To make his point, he said with tongue in cheek, "Surely it must be wrong," when the New

Henry VIII

Anne Boleyn

Testament said the shepherds went back to their fields after seeing the infant Messiah. "We should correct the passage to read, 'They went and shaved their heads, fasted, told their rosaries, and put on cowls.' Instead, we read, 'The shepherds returned.' Where to? To their sheep. The sheep would have been in a sorry way if they had not." You can see he had very strong feelings about this issue.

Another leader in the Protestant movement was Henry VIII, who was the king of England. His reasons for breaking from the Catholic Church were personal, however, and not based on faith. Henry VIII had six different wives during his rule. Henry's first queen, Catherine of Aragon, did not bear an heir to the throne after twenty years of marriage. Henry tried to get Pope Clement VII to dissolve the marriage so he could marry another woman, Anne Boleyn, whom he had fallen in love with.

Catherine of Aragon

When the Pope refused, Henry was furious and withdrew England from the Catholic Church, and created the Church of England. The Church of England granted Henry his divorce. Henry VIII then went on to marry five more times, either divorcing or beheading all of his wives save the last. The Church of England is called Anglican.

Erasmus was a Dutch scholar who wrote *In Praise of Folly*, which ridiculed the clergy and ordinary Christians, pointing out their ignorance, superstitions, and hypocrisy. The more extreme the Catholics were in their worship, the more open they became to Erasmus' ridicule. Erasmus believed that the early Christians were closer to God than his contemporaries, and wanted to go back to a simpler way of worship.

Erasmus

Thomas More was an English believer in humanism. He wrote a book called *Utopia* in which he created an imaginary society where everyone was free, with no laws. Money and greed would be replaced with enough for all, and everyone would lead simple, ethical, religious lives. There are still books written today that try to describe such idealized "utopian" societies. The Pilgrims who became the first successful European settlers in North America hoped to establish such a Utopian society.

John Calvin was a well-respected young humanist scholar and writer in Switzerland who became a leader in the Reformation in 1533 when he wrote *Institutes of the Christian Religion.* Like Luther, Calvin regarded the *Bible* as the supreme authority over any man, including the Pope. His book was addressed to laymen as well as ministers. Calvin placed more emphasis on the sovereignty of God, and the necessity of "good works" in addition to faith in order to receive salvation. Unlike Luther, he said that church and state (religion and politics) should work together to build a Christian society. He believed that God had already chosen a specific group of people who would go heaven. This is known as the theory of "predestination." People who followed him became known as Calvinists. Calvin settled in Geneva, Switzerland, and Calvinism became Geneva's official religion. Calvin virtually ran the city, making laws against dancing and card-playing, for example, and developing a code of conduct under which all citizens had to live.

In France, a group called the Huguenots were also believers in Calvinism. They engaged in many bloody battles to defend the cities they ruled from Catholicism. The kings of France at the time were Catholic, and considered the Huguenots a threat. Finally King Henri IV of France issued the Edict of Nantes, which was intended to make peace between the Catholics and the Huguenots. He also cleaned up the abuse of "tax farming," a common practice at the time which allowed officials in the various parts of the country to collect as much as they could in taxes, often by brutal means. Henri IV eventually centralized the French government in Paris.

Protestant movements began in many different places in Europe at about the same time. There was often rivalry amongst the different parts of Europe, and war was a common way to resolve the conflicts. As religious views began to change, many areas of Europe went to war against each other; there were wars in Spain, France, Germany, Italy and England. King Phillip II of Spain was a devout Catholic. He ordered the Spanish Inquisition to stamp out heresy, using torture and death as a means to try to keep the people Catholic. He established Madrid as the center of government in Spain, but got so interested in making every little decision himself that he brought the administration of government to a standstill. He also ran the economy into the ground by using all the money the country had to wage war in the name of Catholicism. He fought France to try to prevent a Protestant from taking the throne there, and led a disastrous military campaign called the Armada against England because its ruler, Elizabeth I (daughter of Henry VIII), was a Protestant. He also lost control of the Netherlands because of his religious and economic oppression of the people there.

Queen Isabella and King Ferdinand were co-rulers of Spain who were known for their mutual respect for each other. Before their rule, Spain had been divided, with the Catholics fighting the Muslims for the land. Spain was united when Isabella and Ferdinand, each from powerful Catholic families, used the contract of their marriage to create a large and significant nation from the separate areas. They became known as the Catholic Sovereigns, and spearheaded the expulsion of the Jews and Moriscos (Muslims who had converted to Christianity) from Spain. They wanted to make Spain purely Catholic, and were intolerant of other beliefs.

In an attempt to keep Europe solidly Catholic and to prevent rivalry amongst nations and cities, the Church appointed a Holy Roman Emperor among the kings of Europe. The requirement to be the Holy Roman Emperor was usually a strong spiritual life as well as the ability to make war to defend the Roman Empire. Charles V was one such Holy Roman Emperor. He was from Flanders (which you may remember is now in the Netherlands). He was from the Hapsburg Family, and became King of Spain. He led the successful defense of Europe from the Muslim Turks, and later divided the Spanish Empire between his son Phillip II and his brother Ferdinand of Austria. Thus we have the Spanish Hapsburgs and the Austrian Hapsburgs, still well-known royal families today. Charles V was a devout Catholic and retired to monastery life after dividing up his kingdom.

The Reformation had a very strong impact upon the Roman Catholic Church and resulted in what is called the Counter-Reformation, an attempt to bolster the power of the Church. As a result of the protests, the sale of indulgences finally ceased and many policies were reexamined by a special meeting by the Catholic Church leaders - known as the Council of Trent. Pope Paul III was the leader of the Counter-Reformation. Although he instituted a more spiritual outlook for the Catholic Church in response to the Reformation, he also used brutal means to try to keep Catholics within the Church. Administrative, educational, and moral reforms were made, but the Council reaffirmed that the Pope was the head of the Catholic

St. Paul's Cathedral at the Vatican, the central governing place for the Catholic Church

Church, and had the exclusive right to interpret the *Bible*. Also, a list of books prohibited from Catholics eyes was made, obviously a recognition that books and reading now had a major impact on what people thought. The *Index of Prohibited Books* was kept as recently as 1966, when it was finally abandoned.

Because church and state were so closely linked in European society, persecutions were carried out by both Catholics and Protestants, as both sides fought to stamp out the heresy of the other's point of view. As part of the Counter-Reformation, Pope Paul III and the Catholic Church set up special courts called the Inquisition. These courts tried Protestants as criminals for not believing in the Catholic Church. They also tried Muslims and Jews. Guilty people were tortured or killed. The Church tried to stop the Reformation and the growth of Protestantism, but to no avail.

The Jesuits were a group within the Catholic Church which believed in the principles of the Counter-Reformation. They stressed education and discipline, and their aggressive missionary quests took them all over the world, including China and Japan. They founded many schools and universities to combine both humanist and religious values. They opposed violence as a means of stamping out religious disagreement, thinking it better to convert people of another faith into their own religion.

Ignatius of Loyola was the founder of the Jesuits. He had been a soldier in the Spanish army, and walked with a severe limp after becoming injured. Ignatius wrote the book, *Spiritual Exercises,* where he said that salvation came from tremendous self-discipline and copious amounts of good deeds. He believed in acting on spiritual ideals, not merely talking about them.

By the end of the 16th century, the *Bible* had been translated into just about every language in Europe. As the *Bible* became available to more and more of the "common people" in their native languages, new Protestant Churches were born. It became increasingly important for people to know how to read, as the *Bible* was the basis of all Protestant Churches.

The Reformation also brought many changes to the Catholic Church. It strengthened the middle class because Protestantism emphasized responsibility, hard work, and upright living. There was a great deal of upheaval, but eventually Protestants and Catholics managed to make peace.

1. **Write a short play based on the Reformation. (Check the grammar guidelines.) Your play should show something about the life and problems of the time. Include Martin Luther, the Pope, Henry VIII, one of the Spanish Catholic rulers, a Jesuit missionary and at least one ordinary citizen. You may also include or make reference to the other people and ideas of the Reformation in this lesson. What issues and concerns do each of your characters have? Feel free to do additional research if you like.**

2. **Have your Home Teacher give you a home spelling quiz. Review any words you miss.**

Extra Book Ideas:

The Hawk That Dare Not Hunt by Day, by Scott O'Dell
Spy for the Night Riders
The Queen's Smuggler
Morning Star of the Reformation
Queens of England, by Norah Lofts, Doubleday & Co., NY, 1977. Useful
    sections on the wives of Henry VIII.
Lives and Legends of the Saints, by Carole Armstrong, Simon & Schuster
    Books for Young Readers, New York, 1995

Extra Project Ideas:

*   Watch the video of *A Man for All Seasons* about Thomas More and Henry
    VIII. See if you can find and watch the PBS series on the six wives of
    Henry VIII.

*   Write and give a sermon as if you were one of the religious leaders of the
    Reformation. What kinds of things would you say to your congregation?

*   Write an essay describing the differences among the Catholic, Anglican,
    and Lutheran Churches.

*   Watch the video *Martin Luther* starring Academy Award nominee Niall
    MacGinnis.

*   Research the life of Ignatius, the founder of the Jesuits. Explore the
    travels and missionary efforts of the Jesuits.

*   Learn more about the life of Martin Luther. What were the 95 Theses
    posted on the church door in Wittenberg, and what was the Diet of
    Worms?

Social Studies/Art/English~~~~~~~Lesson 30

ANCIENT MAYA

Vocabulary Words

The following words are taken from your Social Studies lesson. Write definitions for each of them without using the root word or any other form of the vocabulary word. Consider them in the context of your Social Studies material, and write a sentence for each that shows you understand the meaning.

vaulted	**phenomena**	**stucco**
chisel	**glyph**	**terrain**
gruel	**elite**	**plantain**

Spelling

Select ten words from your written material this week for spelling words. Write each of these words correctly five times and use each word in a complete sentence. Practice your spelling words in preparation for a quiz.

Grammar

1. **On Days 3 and 4 this week, you will be writing an essay. Make an outline first, then write your paragraphs. Review the "Paragraphs," "Paragraph Forms," and "Outlining" sections in your *English Manual*.**

Day 1

The ancient civilization of the Maya encompassed an area of about 125,000 square miles and included parts of Mexico, Guatemala, Belize, Honduras and El Salvador. This civilization began around 3000 B.C.

Mayan territory covered many different kinds of terrain. In the north was the Yucatán Peninsula, a dry lowland area with poor soil. The central territory stretched from the Caribbean Sea in the east to the Gulf of Mexico in the west, including parts of Mexico, Belize, and northern Guatemala. It was full of jungle lowlands and lush, steamy rainforests, and was the true heart of the Mayan world. The southern area of the Mayan civilization included the beautiful highlands and plateaus of southern Guatemala, the Chiapas region of Mexico, and a little bit of northern Honduras and El Salvador.

1. **This week, make a large, detailed map of the North and South American continents on a piece of posterboard. Be sure to add the seas, gulfs, and large bays, and the countries of Central America and the Caribbean.**

2. **Select a book of your choice to read. You will have four weeks to complete it.**

Day 2

Early archaeologists who explored the land of the ancient Maya had very different things to say about the people they thought had lived there. One said the ruins were Roman or Phoenician, and another said they had been built by the Lost Tribes of Israel. In 1885 an American explorer, Edward Herbert Thompson, became fascinated with what he saw there, and went on to study the ruins for over thirty years.

In 1952 an archaeologist named Alberto Ruz L' Huillier made a fascinating find when he started digging beneath the Mayan Temple of Inscriptions at Palenque. He and his workers dug slowly over several years' time, and discovered a stairway leading down to a box about 60 feet down. Inside the box were six human skeletons. Then they discovered a low triangular doorway sealed by an enormous stone. Ruz squeezed behind it into a vaulted room which had been untouched for a thousand years.

This room was filled with a great carved stone slab in perfect condition. Human figures modeled in stucco relief, probably representing the gods of the underworld, paraded around the walls. A huge monument filled up most of the room - a beautifully carved 12-foot by 7-foot stone slab resting on another immense stone, which in turn was supported by six huge chiseled blocks. Ruz had a narrow hole drilled into the base stone, and when the bit reached a hollow space, he poked a wire through the opening. The particles of red paint that stuck to the wire told him that he had found a coffin. The only problem was that the five ton sculptured stone slab was on top.

Inch by inch Ruz and his men were able to lift the beautifully carved slab of stone. What they found was an incredible sight! Not only were there the remains of a man, but green jade ornaments, red-painted teeth and bones, and the fragments of a beautiful jade mosaic mask. A treasure of jade ornaments had been placed on the dead man, including a headdress, ear plugs, a bead collar, a breastplate, rings on every finger, bracelets, and sandal beads. A single bead had been placed in his mouth to make sure that the spirit of this king or high priest could buy food in the afterlife.

When the inscriptions on the carved slab were read, it became apparent that this was the tomb of a king. His name was Pacal, and he had ruled Palenque from 615 to 683 A.D. Ruz found a stone duct (hollow tube) that ran along the wall of the stairway all the way to the front of the temple so the priests could communicate with the spirit of the dead man below.

The complicated structure of the temple proves the skill of the Mayan architects. They were magnificent craftsmen and sculptors who glorified their gods and honored their rulers through art and architecture.

Mayan temple

Each temple was dedicated to the service of a particular god. Temples were usually built in the shape of a pyramid. Stucco cement was spread over the stone building blocks so the outside surface was smooth. Occasionally, the stones were carved, or the stucco was modeled into different shapes. Then the temple was painted in brilliant colors with paints made from minerals and plants. The Maya were known for a beautiful shade of blue, which they made by mixing indigo dye and a special type of clay. They made reds and pinks from iron oxide and brazilwood; yellow from ocher, urine and alum; brown from asphalt and bitumen, black from carbon; and green from avocado or by mixing blue and yellow.

The Maya were master potters who produced all kinds of beautifully decorated bowls, plates, and vases. They didn't use a potter's wheel, but shaped the clay by hand. They often took strands of clay and coiled it to form pots, jars, and vases. They also made three-footed bowls, and whistles in the shapes of different animals. Most of their clay pieces were decorated by being painted or carved.

Other Mayan art includes elaborately carved jade and items made with copper and gold. Magnificent murals have also been found. They show battle scenes, nobles, priests, dances, ceremonies, and human sacrifice. Many stylized drawings of birds and other creatures have been preserved. Paintings show examples of Mayan weaving and mosaics made of feathers. In these mosaics, many different colors of feathers were tied, pasted, or woven into cotton fabric. The gretzal was a rare bird whose beautiful feathers were prized. Mosaics made from these costly quetzal feathers could be worn as helmets or jackets only by priests, chiefs, and very important warriors.

Ceremonial masks for religious celebrations and entertainment were made from jade, feathers, and many other materials. Mayan actors wore fantastic wooden masks carved as the faces of animals, birds, and reptiles.

The ancient Maya played a ball game called pok-atok. It was a ceremonial game that was played for fun, for telling the future, and because they believed it was the favorite game of their gods. Only nobles were allowed to play, but everyone could watch and make bets about what would happen. Pok-atok was played on a court that was shaped like an upper case I. There were two teams. Players tried to hit a six inch round hard rubber ball against a stone marker in the middle of each of the side walls of the court. Some ball courts had stone hoops instead of markers, but unlike modern basketball, the holes in the hoops were set vertically instead of horizontally. Players wore leather pads on their knees, hips, forearms, elbows, and shoulders, and used only these parts of their bodies to get the ball through the hoop. The ball was not allowed to touch the ground. When the game ended, the spectators quickly ran away from the ball court, because the custom was for the winning team to take any jewelry, clothing, or other items they wanted from whatever the spectators had with them.

Life was hard for most Mayan families. The women got up at 4:00 a.m. to start the fire and cook cornmeal cakes called tortillas. The men and boys got up at 5:00 a.m., ate tortillas, and went out to the fields, taking lumps of cornmeal dough and gourds full of water. They mixed the dough and the water to make a gruel for lunch.

If the crops had already been harvested, the men served as soldiers and laborers, helping to build temples, ball courts, roads, and other construction projects. Nobles didn't do any of the regular work, so the common people had to help build the elite people's houses and work their fields.

Each day some corn was put into pottery jars to soak overnight in order to get soft. In the morning the women washed and cleaned the corn and then ground it into flour. All grinding was done by hand, with a grinding stone rubbed against a hollowed out stone slab. The women had many other household duties as well, such as caring for the children, taking care of the family's animals (ducks, turkeys, deer, and monkeys), gathering cotton, spinning, and weaving.

The two most important crops were corn and cotton, because they provided food and clothing. Corn was considered sacred, and there were religious rules about every step of its planting. The Maya believed that the souls of the corn plants would move to a clean, newly prepared field if weeds were allowed to grow in the old field. Therefore, old fields were abandoned to the jungle, and new ones readied for the next corn crop.

Beans and corn were planted together in the same hole, so the bean vine could wrap itself around the corn for support as it grew taller. Farmers also planted tobacco, sweet potato, cacao beans, squash, gourds, chili peppers, pumpkins, and jicama. Orchards were filled with avocado trees. Papayas, bananas, nuts, and plantain grew wild. Many people kept beehives in hollow logs in order to have easy access to the honey.

Corn was eaten at every meal, in both gruel and tortillas. The evening meal usually included tortillas, black beans, and vegetables that were seasonally available. When the men went hunting, there might be rabbit, deer, turkey, armadillo, or even turtle meat for dinner. Mayans also loved to drink hot chocolate made from cacao beans.

3. **Do one of the following art projects:**

   a. **In ancient times, masks were made out of the natural materials available, such as clay, sea shells, feathers, seeds, corn husks, pine cones, etc. Make a mask using the following directions:**

      1) **Choose some natural objects from your environment to decorate your mask.**

      2) **Choose the substance of your mask from papier mâché, cardstock, construction paper, a paper plate, or cardboard. (A papier mâché mask could be formed over a balloon, as in the directions for the calabash in Lesson 11.)**

      3) **Cut out a full-face mask. Cut holes for the eyes, nose and mouth.**

      4) **Decorate your mask, using the natural materials that you have gathered. Glue these materials onto your mask.**

   b. **Make a feather mosaic by gluing feathers to a piece of fabric or posterboard cut in whatever size and shape you select. You can buy bags of colored feathers at many craft stores. Cut bits of the feathers as needed, or use them whole, to carefully create any pattern or image you desire.**

   c. **Make a story picture using the stylized Mayan animal drawings shown on the next page. Use vivid colors in your picture. You may copy this page and cut out the figures, or draw them by hand.**

4. Choose one or both of the following activities.

**a. Make your own pok-atok game by making a hoop and mounting it
high against a wall outdoors. You could use a cardboard box with
most of the box cut away, leaving just a frame. It should point vertically
rather than horizontally. Use a small, hard rubber ball and see if you
can get the ball through the hoop without using your hands. Good
luck!**

**b. Make a Mayan meal for your family. Enjoy a cup of hot chocolate
with a bit of cinnamon in it for dessert!**

Tortillas:

- 2 c. masa harina (corn flour - available at grocery stores)
- 1 - 1 1/3 c. lukewarm water
- 1/2 - 1 tsp. salt (optional - it's not traditionally used)

Mix the masa harina and 1 c. water in a bowl to make a soft dough. Add the extra water only if necessary. The dough should be flexible and hold together well without being sticky. Divide the dough into balls the size of small eggs. You can either roll them out as you did with chapatis in Lesson 8, or like this:

Put a ball between two sheets of waxed paper and press it down very hard between two boards. Cook it on a moderately heated, ungreased griddle or cast iron pan about 1 minute, until the edges begin to curl. Flip and cook another minute or so until lightly brown flecked on both sides. Delicious eaten hot with a bit of butter! Keep some to serve with your frijoles.

Chile Picante:

- 1 lb. green chilies
- 5 medium tomatoes
- 2 small onions

Wash the chilies well. Cook them with tomatoes and onions for about 15 minutes. Grind the mixture and add a little salt. Serve with your frijoles.

Frijoles Negros (Black Beans):

- 1 lb. black beans
- 2 medium onions, chopped
- 4 garlic cloves, diced
- salt to taste
- vegetable oil

Wash and pick over the beans. Soak them in 2 quarts of water for 3 hours. Pour off the water, then add 2 more quarts of water, 1 chopped onion, and 2 diced garlic cloves. Bring the water to a boil, then cover and simmer for 3 hours or until tender. Check periodically to be sure there is still at least a little water.

When the beans are cooked, mash them up. Sauté remaining garlic and onion until tender, and mix with the mashed beans. Fry the mixture until it thickens, and serve with your tortillas and chile picante.

Days 3 & 4

The Mayan civilization had the highest intellectual achievement of any civilization existing in America before the coming of the Spanish.

Their method of keeping track of time was the most accurate of any calendar ever used in the ancient world. The secrets of mathematics and understanding time were carefully guarded by the priests. For them, time was a supernatural phenomena controlled by the gods, some of whom were good and some bad. Each god was associated with a specific number and was represented by a particular glyph in the written carvings. The day was the smallest unit into which they divided time. The Maya divided their year into 18 months, with 20 days in each month. They added 5 days which they considered bad luck days. You might remember that the Egyptians had 360 days, plus 5 days for celebration.

Using nothing more complicated than a pair of crossed sticks, the Maya plotted the movements of the sun, moon, and the planet Venus with amazing precision. They could even predict solar and lunar eclipses. Calculations as accurate as this had to be based on a sophisticated system of mathematics. Their math included the concept of zero, something most other civilizations (except the Babylonians and Hindus) had not yet invented.

Mayan engineers designed elaborate roads, drainage systems, aqueducts, and bridges. They built a new pyramid-temple every fifty-two years, often simply building a new one around the old one. Several pyramid-temples have been uncovered, but there are many more yet to be explored. It is amazing to consider that the Maya did all of their feats of engineering without wheeled vehicles, draft animals, or metal tools. They did all of this merely with manpower, stone tools, log rollers, and rope to help lift heavy objects.

5. If you found yourself without tools out in the wilderness and needed to survive, what have you learned from the civilizations you have studied so far that would help you? In your answer, include ideas for getting water and food, keeping warm, and protecting yourself from bad weather and wild animals. What might you do for fun? Be specific. Write at least one page.

Day 5

What did the Maya look like? The women were probably not more than 4' 8" tall, and the men about 5' 1". Their bodies were strong and sturdy. They had black hair, dark brown eyes, and dark skin. At the base of their spine was a small purplish spot that faded before the tenth birthday. This was characteristic of Indian groups that traced their prehistoric origins to Northeast Asia. The fold of skin at the corner of the eyes was another common characteristic.

The Maya thought crossed eyes were beautiful. Mothers hung small beads close to their babies between the eyes to encourage the eyes to focus inward. Because they found broad heads and big noses attractive, a mother bound the infant's head between two wooden boards in front and back in order to flatten the forehead and emphasize the long line of the nose, making it appear more beautiful. Young men often burned the hair off the front of their heads so their slanting foreheads would stand out even more.

The Maya loved jewelry. When children were older, their earlobes, septum, lips, and one nostril were pierced so they could wear a variety of ornaments. Adults sometimes filed their teeth to sharp points, and the wealthy inlaid their front teeth with bits of obsidian or jade. Tattooing was a common practice. Intricate designs were cut into the skin, and different colors of dyes were rubbed into the cuts. The patterns usually followed the natural curves of the face and body.

Men had very little facial hair, and what they did have, they pulled out. They wore their hair in braids wound around the top of their heads, with a "tail" hanging down the back. The women wore their hair long, braided in two or four braids or hanging down. Both men and women trimmed the hair in front into a fringe, like very short bangs.

The Maya had very little clothing unless they were part of the wealthy aristocracy. They lived in a tropical climate, so the weather was never extremely cold. The men wore a simple loincloth - a band of material that went around their waist and between their legs, and tucked back into the waist. Some wore deerskin moccasins and a cloak which was thrown over their shoulders.

Women wore two layers. The outer one was a piece of decorated cloth with holes cut for the head and arms, and the inner one was a lighter weight version of the same garment. They often wore a shawl over their shoulders, as well.

The Mayan number system was very advanced, as has already been stated. It was based on the number 20, instead of 10, as we are used to. Mathematics was an important part of studying astronomy. Unlike other people of their time, the Maya understood not only the concept of zero, but that of place-value. They used only three symbols for writing numbers: the picture of a shell for 0, a dot for 1, and a bar for 5. Placement of the three symbols was important in designating values higher than 19.

Each city had a chief who was chosen from among the upper classes. Priests made up the highest class along with the wealthy nobles. Then came the warriors, who captured many enemy prisoners. Below them were the common people.

Religion had something to say about every aspect of Mayan life. Often the ruling chief was also a priest. The priests were the only people who were allowed to know all of the gods and religious rituals. Common people couldn't even go into the temples, but followed the guidance of the priests during religious festivals.

The Maya believed that the earth had been destroyed and recreated several times by the gods. They believed the gods were all-powerful and that it was important to keep them happy. The gods were connected to nature, and people believed that it was only because the gods kept making the sun shine and the rain fall that life kept going from day to day. Natural occurrences of nature, such as flood or drought, made them worry that the gods were angry. The sun and moon gods were believed to be the father and mother of all the people, and there were many other gods with many different jobs.

Sacrifice was a regular part of Mayan worship. They knew that blood was a special part of life, so blood was also a special part of their religious ceremonies. Most ceremonies only required the sacrifice of dogs, birds, or other animals. When the people had a big problem, such as lack of rain, they made an extra big sacrifice - a person. One way they sacrificed people was to drop them into a deep limestone well which was believed to be the home of the gods who knew about rainfall. Both the priests and the victims prayed and purified themselves for sixty days before this kind of ceremony. Then the victims were dropped in, along with other valuable offerings for the gods. If the sacrifice victim was still alive at midday, he or she was pulled up out of the well. Everyone wanted to know what messages the gods had sent back for the people with the rescued victim.

The Pyramid of the Magician, also known as the Temple of the Dwarf, is in the beautiful Mayan city of Uxmal. It is a pyramidal shaped temple with two rounded ends. Here is a wonderful story about the temple:

There once was an old witch who was longing for a son. She was told to get an iguana egg and put it in her house. She did this, and after awhile it hatched. Out came a beautiful baby boy. The witch was overjoyed to have a son, and she was a loving and good mother to him. When he was 8 years old, he stopped growing. The witch was perplexed by this, but as he seemed healthy in every other way, she didn't worry.

When the dwarfed son grew older, he was wandering in the forest and found a mysterious musical instrument. Everyone said that whoever could play this instrument would become the next king of Uxmal. The dwarf began to play beautiful music on the mysterious instrument, and the people of the city heard it. They said that the dwarf should become king. The current king became angry, because he still wanted to be king. He wasn't about to give up his throne to the dwarf, so he issued a challenge. In one night, the dwarf had to build the tallest, most beautiful pyramid-temple in Uxmal. If by chance he could actually do this, then three bags of coconuts would be broken over his head. If the dwarf could survive this, then the king would have three bags of coconuts broken over his own head.

The day of the challenge came, and the dwarf built the tallest, most beautiful pyramid-temple that had ever been seen in Uxmal. The old witch was worried about the bags of coconuts that were to be broken on her son's head, and figured out a way to protect him. She made him a special stone cap and covered it with a wig. When the three bags of coconuts crashed down on the dwarf's head, he wasn't harmed at all. When the coconuts were broken over the king's head, he died immediately. Then the people rejoiced and welcomed their new king - the witch's dwarfed son, who they now respected as a magician. The dwarf-king ruled the people wisely for many years.

Nobody knows exactly why the Mayan civilization disappeared. There were great cities as old as 600 years, but over a period of 100 years they all crumbled and vanished as the jungle took over. One theory is that the population increased to the point where there just wasn't enough food. This meant that people became malnourished and less resistant to disease. Also, as the nobles grew in number and demanded more and more from the common people, it is likely that the peasants revolted, just as they did in medieval Europe. Of course, not all of the Maya disappeared, and their culture developed in other places as some of the survivors traveled to new areas and blended with other groups of people. Eventually a group of warriors called the Toltec invaded the Yucatán Peninsula, and before long, had full control of it. Thus was born a new civilization. When the Spanish invaded Guatemala in 1524, life in the old Mayan region changed dramatically.

6. **Choose one of the following:**

   a. **Draw a detailed picture of a Mayan man or woman from the description given.**

   b. **Using the chart of the Mayan number system as shown below, make up your own simple set of math problems. With the numbers given, you can't go above 19. Write down your problems and solve them.**

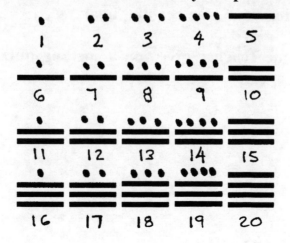

If you are interested in learning more about Mayan number systems so you can use bigger numbers, you will find information in the library under "Maya Vigesimal System of Mathematics."

c. You have read about some of the things that the ancient Maya believed made people beautiful. What are some customs and beliefs we have about beauty in our society?

d. Below is a picture of a wall painting of a fishing village. It was found in a temple. Compose your own story or poem to go with this mural, in keeping with the flavor of Mayan life.

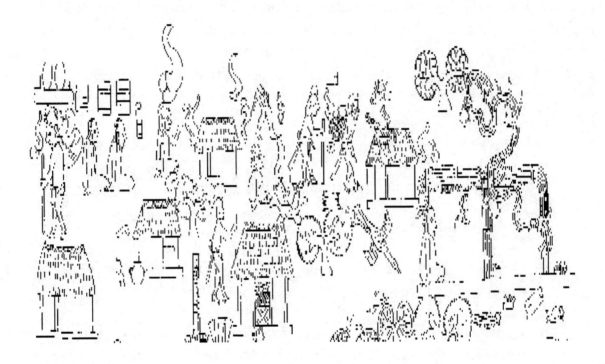

7. Continue reading your free reading book.

8. Have your Home Teacher give you a spelling quiz. Review any words you miss.

Extra Book Ideas:

The Maya, by Jacqueline Greene
The First Book of the Ancient Maya, by Barbara Beck
Everyday Life of the Maya, by Ralph Whitlock

Extra Project Ideas:

• Read a book of Mayan myths.

• Look at more pictures of Mayan art. Draw your own Mayan glyphs in the same style.

• Learn about Chichén Itzá, in the center of the Yucatán Peninsula.

• Find out about the Toltec and Olmec cultures.

Social Studies/Art/English~~~~~~Lesson 31

ANCIENT NORTH AMERICA

Vocabulary Words

The following words are taken from your Social Studies lesson. Write definitions for each of them without using the root word or any other form of the vocabulary word. Consider them in the context of your Social Studies material, and write a sentence for each that shows you understand the meaning.

ingenious	**millennium**
vanquish	**alliance**
kayak	**granary**

Spelling

Select ten words from your written material this week for spelling words. Write each of these words correctly five times and use each word in a complete sentence. Practice your spelling words in preparation for a quiz.

Grammar

1. **Make an outline of your speech on (see Day 5) before writing it. Then create paragraphs from your outline. Review the "Paragraphs," "Paragraph Forms," and "Outlining" sections in your *English Manual*.**

Day 1

During the 5th and 4th centuries B.C., a highly organized farming society developed in what is now the Ohio River Valley in the United States. This was the Hopewell culture, also known as *Mound Builders* because of the large earthworks they constructed. Some of these mounds were burial mounds and others were ceremonial. One, now called the Serpent Mound, was very long, and curled around in the shape of a serpent's head, body, and coiled tail. Many of the mounds contained objects of copper, pearls, mica, and other offerings. The Mound Builders included both the Adena and Hopewell cultures as well as several others, and their civilization is thought to have lasted for about 1,000 years.

1. Look in the encyclopedia under *Mound Builders* to see a picture of the mounds built by this civilization. Also use other resources if you have them. Write a short report about these early Mound Builders of North America. Mention both the Adena culture and the Hopewell culture in your report. If you find information on the Eastern Woodlands Mound Builders in Mississippi, you can include that as well.

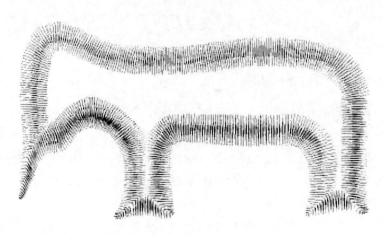

Elephant Mound in Wisconsin

Artifacts found in a mound in Missouri

2. Choose one of the following projects:

   a. Create mounds of dirt in the shape of animals as the Mound Builders did, only yours will be on a much smaller scale. Take a picture of your mounds to send to your teacher.

   b. Draw a picture of a mound you might build if you were living in an ancient American culture.

3. Continue reading your free reading book.

Day 2

By the 1st Century A.D. another group of people, the Anasazi, had created a farming culture in the dry lands of the American Southwest. Anasazi means "Strange Ancient Ones." The Navajo Indians named this group when they discovered their ruins.

The Anasazi built their houses of sun-baked clay called adobe. They built huge buildings resembling today's apartment buildings. The Spaniards who arrived several hundred years later called these huge buildings *pueblos,* which means "towns" in Spanish. The *pueblos* were built in canyons or on steep cliffs. There are several remaining today, mainly in Arizona. One of them has 650 rooms in it. Every *pueblo* had a *kiva* or central room which was used for ceremonies and religious rituals. The walls of the *kiva* were colorfully decorated with murals.

These people were farmers. They kept track of the seasons and cycles of nature with a sun clock. They asked the spirits of nature to bring them good hunting and abundant harvests. They were a peace loving group and only went to war when necessary. When the warriors returned from war, they did a ritual to cleanse themselves of the hatred that had been created by war.

The Anasazi women owned all of the houses and property, and had family clans. When a woman wanted to divorce her husband, she simply placed all of his belongings outside the house.

Schoolhouse Mound, just eighty miles from present-day Phoenix, Arizona, is the site of one of the largest archeological digs in the country. Archeologists have discovered a 300 foot long complex of 115 rooms and granaries which was built atop a ten foot high platform about 600 years ago. Approximately 2,000 acres of laboriously irrigated corn and bean fields were found there as well. The complex is filled with built-in granaries with big storage rooms, and other rooms with many large pots. The Salado Indians lived here 600 years ago.

Pueblo

Many Southwestern Indian Pueblo cultures abandoned their dwellings and apparently have vanished. Present day archeologists are asking why these ancient desert societies collapsed after a millennium of steady growth and ingenious adaptation. The name of one group - Sinagua - means "without water," which may provide an important clue.

4. **Choose one or both of the following projects:**

   a. **Pretend to be an archeologist setting out to uncover a secret of the past. You may not uncover an ancient civilization in your neighborhood, but you may find some arrowheads or evidence of some other past relic or event! Look around your environment with a detective's eye. Discover something from the past. It does not even have to be from the very distant past. What did you find? Perhaps it's a rock with an interesting shape; or an old rusty nail you found on a walk. Look at it as if you've never seen anything like it before. What could it possibly be used for? How important might it have been to an ancient culture? Use your imagination! Draw your find and describe its possibilities.**

   b. **Look at pictures of cliff dwellings at Mesa Verde and Canyon de Chelly. Draw a picture of a typical cliff dwelling.**

5. **Add the states and provinces of North America to your map from Lesson 30.**

Day 3

The Northwest Coastal Indians lived by fishing in the rivers and the oceans, gathering berries and hunting wild animals for food and furs. They made their dugout canoes, houses, and ceremonial masks with cedar from the forests. The Northwest Coast Indians were unusual in that they valued wealth and possessions. The natural environment was rich in resources, and food was never scarce. This allowed them to focus on more elaborate material goods, instead of basic survival. Their communities were divided into strict social classes, and they captured slaves in their raids.

The potlatch ceremony was practiced in this society. This involved very complicated, expensive gift giving in order to show that a person was wealthy enough to give away valuable items. Sometimes the potlatch gifts were simply destroyed - even slaves who were given as gifts - which demonstrated even greater wealth.

The Indians of the Northwest Coast loved wood carving. They made intricately carved boxes, boats, and masks. In front of their houses were tall wooden poles on which they carved totems which were symbols of their family or clan. These totems often included animals such as bears and owls, usually standing on top of each other's shoulders or heads. Some totems stood as high as thirty feet.

6. **Draw a totem using symbols that depict your family. Choose animals that you feel embody the spirit of your family or its members. If you would rather draw a separate totem for each member of the family, that would be fine. It might be fun to actually construct a small totem out of clay.**

Day 4

The Eskimos settled the northern most parts of North America. They created a way of life uniquely adapted to their Arctic environment. They fished and hunted walrus, whale, seal, and caribou for their food. They made practically everything they needed from these animals—harpoons, fishing hooks, knives, needles, sleds, kayaks, tents, warm clothing and oil. They carved bone and ivory. Their homes were made of snow and ice. Instead of being defeated by this challenging environment, they learned to use all its elements for survival.

7. Do one of the following writing assignments:

a. How did the Indians in your part of the country adapt themselves to the resources available? How did they make their homes? What did they eat? Which tribes were in your area?

b. Write a story about a person who wakes up one day to find themselves in an entirely different sort of environment from what they are used to. Describe what resources they find around them and how they adapt to life there.

c. Briefly read about the native people of the Arctic and write a paragraph about them.

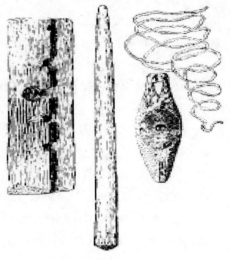

These are the only tools needed to make a fire in the Arctic

Day 5

Indians throughout North America were mainly peaceful and not interested in conquest. They had a fairly democratic organization in their villages and tribes. Respected elders usually formed a governing council. Most Indians had a strong sense of community, shared a feeling of harmony with nature, and did not believe in private ownership of land. Families were assigned a part of a field to use, but it was understood that the land really belonged to all.

The Indian boys and girls grew up sharing in daily work and learning the history and rituals of their people. Teenagers went through special ceremonies or "rites of passage" in order to be recognized as adults in the society.

By the early 1600's, Chief Powhatan from Virginia brought together many tribes into a confederacy. A confederacy was a loose alliance, but the tribes continued to govern themselves independently. The Iroquois League in what is now New York State was the longest active alliance. This was formed about 1580 and the leading women in each family clan chose a man to be a member of the League Council.

In 1854, Chief Seattle delivered a speech in which he spoke for peaceful Indians everywhere of all times. Here is his speech:

ALL THINGS ARE CONNECTED

Chief Seattle

"How can you buy or sell the sky, the warmth of the land? The idea is strange to us.

If we do not own the freshness of the air and the sparkle of the water, how can you buy them?

Every part of this earth is sacred to my people. Every shining pine needle, every sandy shore, every mist in the dark woods, every clearing and humming insect is holy in the memory and experience of my people. The sap which courses through the trees carries the memories of the red man.

The white man's dead forget the country of their birth when they go to walk among the stars. Our dead never forget this beautiful earth, for it is the mother of the red man. We are part of the earth and it is part of us. The perfumed flowers are our sisters; the deer, the horse, the great eagle, these are our brothers. The rocky crests, the juices in the meadows, the body heat of the pony, and man—all belong to the same family.

So, when the Great Chief in Washington sends word that he wishes to buy our land, he asks much of us. The Great Chief sends word he will reserve us a place so that we can live comfortably to ourselves. He will be our father and we will be his children.

So we will consider your offer to buy our land. But it will not be easy. For this land is sacred to us. This shining water that moves in the streams and rivers is not just water but the blood of our ancestors. If we sell you land, you must remember that it is sacred, and you must teach your children that it is sacred and that each ghostly reflection in the clear water of the lakes tells of events and memories in the life of my people. The water's murmur is the voice of my father's father.

The rivers are our brothers, they quench our thirst. The rivers carry our canoes, and feed our children. If we sell you our land, you must remember and teach your children that the rivers are our brothers and yours, and you must henceforth give the rivers the kindness you would give my brother.

We know that the white man does not understand our ways. One portion of land is the same to him as the next, for he is a stranger who comes in the night and takes from the land whatever he needs. The earth is not his brother, but his enemy, and when he has conquered it, he moves on. He leaves his father's grave behind, and he does not care. He kidnaps the earth from his children, and he does not care. His father's grave, and his children's birthright are forgotten. He treats his mother, the earth, and his brother, the sky, as things to be bought, plundered, sold like sheep or bright beads. His appetite will devour the earth and leave behind only a desert.

I do not know. Our ways are different from your ways. The sight of your cities pains the eyes of the red man. There is no quiet place in the white man's cities. No place to hear the unfurling of leaves in spring or the rustle of the insect's wings. The clatter only seems to insult the ears. And what is there to life if a man cannot hear the lonely cry of the whippoorwill or the arguments of the frogs around the ponds at night? I am a red man and do not understand. The Indian prefers the soft sound of the wind darting over the face of a pond and the smell of the wind itself, cleansed by a midday rain, or scented with pinyon pine.

The air is precious to the red man for all things share the same breath, the beast, the tree, the man, they all share the same breath. The white man does not seem to notice the air he breathes. Like a man dying for many days he is numb to the stench. But if we sell you our land, you must remember that the air is precious to us, that the air shares its spirit with all the life it supports.

The wind that gave our grandfather his first breath also receives his last sigh. And if we sell you our land, you must keep it apart and sacred as a place where even the white man can go to taste the wind that is sweetened by the meadow's flowers.

You must teach your children that the ground beneath their feet is the ashes of our grandfathers. So that they will respect the land, tell your children that the earth is rich with the lives of our kin. Teach your children that we have taught our children that the earth is our mother. Whatever befalls the earth befalls the sons of the earth. If men spit upon the ground, they spit upon themselves.

This we know, the earth does not belong to man; man belongs to the earth. All things are connected. We may be brothers after all. We shall see. One thing we know which the white man may someday discover: our god is the same god.

You may think now that you own him as you wish to own our land; but you cannot. He is the god of man, and the compassion is equal for the red man and the white. This earth is precious to him, and to harm the earth is to heap contempt on its creator. The whites too shall pass; perhaps sooner than all other tribes. Contaminate your bed and you will one night suffocate in your own waste.

But in your perishing you will shine brightly fired by the strength of the god who brought you to this land and for some special purpose gave you dominion over this land and over the red man.

That destiny is a mystery to us, for we do not understand when the buffalo are all slaughtered, the wild horses are tame, the secret corners of the forest heavy with the scent of many men and the view of the ripe hills blotted by talking wires.

Where is the thicket? Gone. Where is the eagle? Gone.

The end of living and the beginning of survival.

8. **Write a speech in which you speak to your fellow humans about their responsibility to the earth and each other. Write a speech for the 20th century. It is up to you whether it follows similar themes as Chief Seattle's speech or not. You may want to focus specifically on very modern issues that may or may not be different from the concerns of Chief Seattle. It should be at least one page long. If you can, present your speech and tape it for your teacher to hear. Send both the written and taped speech to your teacher.**

9. **Continue reading your free reading book.**

10. **Have your Home Teacher give you a spelling quiz. Review any words you miss and add them to your list for further review.**

Extra Book Ideas:

Island of the Blue Dolphins, by Scott O'Dell
In the Beginning, by Virginia Hamilton
Seven Arrows, by Hyemyohsts Storm

Extra Project Ideas:

• Investigate Native American Indian use of plants, both in the past and present. Can you locate any of these plants near your home?

• Research in depth a group of either ancient or recent North American Indians. There are many choices, including: Tlingit, Yurok, Anasazi, Iroquois, Hopi, Navaho, Apache, Cheyenne, Seminole, Cherokee - and many others. Which Indians of today are descended from the ancient tribes you have learned about?

• Compare housing of three different Indian tribes and build models of them.

- Read a variety of North American Indian myths, and compare creation myths of different tribes.

- Look at North American Indian art. Try painting your own similar designs.

- On a beading loom, make a beaded bracelet or strip with a traditional Indian design of your choice.

- Learn about the system of ancient towns in Chaco Canyon, New Mexico.

- Investigate the myth of Kokopelli, and draw a picture of him.

- Make your own basket. To make it like the baskets of the Pomo Indians, weave feathers as you're making it, and decorate the rim with beads or little shells.

- Try your own potlatch ceremony within your family or a group of friends. Each person should bring to the potlatch something that is of value to them personally and give it away to someone else, making sure everyone gets something from someone else.

Social Studies/Art/ English~~~~~~~Lesson 32

AZTECS

Vocabulary Words

The following words are taken from your Social Studies lesson. Write definitions for each of them without using the root word or any other form of the vocabulary word. Consider them in the context of your Social Studies material, and write a sentence for each that shows you understand the meaning.

spindle	**soothsayer**
midwife	**matchmaker**
humble	

Spelling

Select ten words from your written material this week for spelling words. Write each of these words correctly five times and use each word in a complete sentence. Practice your spelling words in preparation for a quiz.

Grammar

1. **Review the assignments in this lesson before you begin. During the week, you will write a diary for Social Studies. Write it in the first person in the present tense. Refer to "Writing a Short Story" in your *English Manual*.**

Days 1 - 5

The Aztecs occupied a huge empire in central and southern Mexico between the 1300's and early 1500's. Their greatest city was called Tenochtitlán, and it was located where Mexico City is now. This great city, which at its height was the home of over 100,000 people, was in the middle of Lake Texcoco. The lake was shallow and swampy, and the people took mud from the bottom of it and piled it up on reed mats to make little islands. These islands grew in number until they became a city in the lake.

The Aztecs were ruled by an emperor. The emperor, with the help of an important official called the Snake Woman (who was actually a man) ran the empire along with a Council of Chief Officials who acted as advisors and chose the emperor from within the royal family.

In addition to the emperor, Snake Woman, and the Council of Chief Officials, the empire was controlled by numerous governors who ruled specific territories outside the city of Tenochtitlán. These governors often inherited their jobs from their fathers, but some of them were filled by nobles or those who were singled out for this special honor because of their bravery in war or unusual level of service to the emperor. Being a good warrior was considered a duty for an Aztec man, and those who captured many prisoners were rewarded well.

Governing the empire made an enormous amount of paper work. The paper work was done by priests trained as scribes. The paper was made from the bark of the wild fig tree, soaked and beaten into sheets. It was coated with a chalky varnish and stuck together in strips as long as thirty feet in length. Occasionally deerskin was used. When finished, these "books" were folded much as we fold maps today.

The Aztecs had no alphabet. They wrote in pictures, or glyphs, which are sometimes called pictographs. If they wanted to show something as being far away, they drew the picture near the top of the page. Closer items were drawn at the bottom. If one man was drawn bigger than another, it meant he was more important. Human figures were only shown in profile. Blue, green, bright red, and yellow were used to indicate the different ranks of people. If they wanted to show a man speaking, they drew blue scrolls coming out of his mouth. A shield and arrows meant war, and a corpse wrapped for burial meant death. Old people were shown by lines on the face for wrinkles, and priests were identified by their black face, long hair, and red ear lobe. A black sky and a close eye meant it was night. A line of foot prints meant that a person was traveling far away.

The main square was the center of city life. Nine times each day the sound of conch shells boomed out from the temple platforms to mark the divisions of the day. Every four days a market was held in the square, and every twenty days the people gathered to sing, dance and offer sacrifices to the gods at one of their many festivals.

Within the city there were several clans. Each clan lived in its own district around its temple and school. Peasants built their huts around the edge of the city. They kept turkeys and rabbits. Craftsmen lived nearer the center in mud-brick houses.

Aztec city

Each room led out to a central courtyard. The nobles' palaces, made of white-washed stone and with over 100 rooms, were built around the main plaza. The patios and flat roofs were covered with flower gardens. Inside the houses, the rooms were very simple, with woven sleeping mats on the floor and reed chests and baskets for storing the family's possessions. People painted and embroidered beautiful hangings to cover their walls. Wooden torches on the wall provided light, and instead of doors, cloths were hung with copper bells.

The peasants lived mainly on corn, or maize, and beans unless they were lucky enough to trap a crow or duck, or if they chose to eat one of their rabbits. Every morning the women ground the corn into flour and boiled it into a porridge which was served with sage. Sometimes they had steamed pancakes stuffed with tadpoles, cactus worms or fish.

Richer people enjoyed turtles and crabs. Montezuma, one of the last Aztec emperors, chose from 100 different dishes every day, including wild pig and pheasant. Turkeys and dogs were raised for meat. Everybody ate with their fingers. It was considered polite to wash the hands and face both before and after eating.

The Aztecs loved children and took their duties as parents very seriously. A midwife came to help with the birth of a baby. If the newborn was a boy, the midwife explained him that he must be a great warrior, feeding the sun god with the blood of his enemies. She told the girls that they must stay at home and look after the family.

The relatives would bring presents and more advice for the baby. The Aztecs believed that a person's character was affected by their birth date. An astrologer came to choose a lucky naming day and to foretell the baby's future. On the chosen naming day, four small boys were invited to the house. The midwife made offerings to the gods as she laid the baby on a mat on the floor. If the baby was a boy, the midwife would put tiny copies of his father's tools and a shield by him. A girl received a little work basket, a spindle and a broom. The midwife showed the baby how to use them and told the baby its name. The four boys would then run off shouting the baby's new name throughout the streets. Relatives enjoyed feasting on honey cakes and making long speeches about the hardships of life.

Girls married at about sixteen and boys at twenty. The men could have as many wives as they wished, but they usually settled for just one. The parents of the boy picked a bride for their son. After a simple ceremony, people sang, danced and feasted all night. Lots of people took the opportunity to give long speeches of advice for the new couple. The clan gave every young couple some land to farm and build a house on.

During her younger years, a woman raised her children and ran her household, which kept her busy. But after the children were grown, she might become a midwife, matchmaker or a healer. A healer had to use magic to find out whether an illness was caused by an enemy or by the gods as punishment. She had to know the right prayers and spells to say and the herbal medicine for each disease. The Aztecs used 1200 different herbs to cure illness.

Clothes showed how well each person had served the empire and what his specific rank was. If anyone dressed above his rank, he could be put to death. An ordinary citizen's loincloth and cloak had to be of plain undyed cloth. If a common man was caught wearing sandals in the palace he was put to death. Nobles wore cotton cloaks with borders of precious stones, or woven feather cloaks. The farmers dressed in a loincloth and used a blanket as a cape. Farmers did not shave or pluck their hair. Peasant women wove cloth and sewed up the sides leaving a hole for the head - this became a blouse. They wound another piece of cloth around their waists and secured it with an embroidered belt. They had to take tiny steps so the skirt wouldn't flap open and expose their knees.

Clothing was woven from the fibers of the agave cactus, cotton, and palm leaves, and was then embroidered. In their spinning and weaving, people sometimes added rabbit hair and feathers for decoration. They made dyes from plants, insects, and a special snail that was found at the seashore. Craftsmen dyed the raw cotton green, blue, yellow and black with dye made from leaves and bark. Red was made with crushed insects, and purple with the froth of a sea snail. Skilled weavers wove the yarn into geometrical patterns and designs of birds and flowers. For winter, rabbit fur was woven into the cotton cloth.

The craftsmen made most of their goods for the emperor. They passed on their skills only to their children. Many items were used in daily life, such as knives and pottery. Bows and arrows made from wood and stone were useful for hunting and for war, along with colorful shields, and ornate wooden headdresses in the shapes of eagles and jaguars. Some Aztec headdresses were made from feathers instead of wood.

Featherworking was a popular family business and one of the most important crafts. The most valuable feathers were those from the quetzal, a bird with brilliant green feathers. Other feathers were gathered from eagles, parrots, and even hummingbirds. The children prepared glue from bat dung, the wife sorted and dyed the feathers, and the husband drew the design and made a stencil. He transferred this onto a piece of cloth glued to cactus fibers. He cut the dyed feathers to the shape he wanted, and stuck them onto the cloth. He then glued the cloth to a board backing. When this was dried, he applied the final layer of feathers. He outlined the design with thin strips of gold.

Goldworking was another important craft. First a model was made in clay. Then it was covered with beeswax and coated with more clay. The model was then heated to make the wax run out through a hole in the bottom. The craftsmen then poured in molten gold, let it cool and broke open the clay shell to reveal the final product.

The Aztecs loved jewelry. The people enjoyed wearing ear, nose, and lip plugs, pendants, rings for both fingers and noses, and hair ornaments, but there were strict laws about who could wear what kind of jewelry. If a person wore a crystal noseplug when he was not entitled to it, he was put to death. Most people pierced their ears to hold plugs of shell or polished stones. Nobles were allowed to wear gold and carved precious stones in their lower lips to show their high rank.

Jewelry and art objects were decorated with turquoise, gems, gold, silver, copper, and feathers. Other materials commonly used included jade, rock crystal, obsidian, amethyst, amber, blood stone, carnelian, emeralds, and shells. The Aztecs were skilled enough to make small gold and silver objects with moving parts, such as a bird or monkey with movable head, hands, wings, and feet. They also made beautiful mosaics using the various stones and gems mentioned above.

Netball and basketball come from the ancient Aztec game of tlachtli, which was nearly identical to the Maya's pok-atok. The Indians made rubber sap into bouncing balls. Like all games, the ball game had a religious meaning. The stone court was a copy of the heavens where they believed the gods played ball with the stars. Only nobles were allowed to play ball. The object of the game was to hit the ball through the opponent's stone ring, which was just wide enough for the ball to go through. This was a very difficult feat. The winner had the right to demand clothes and other possessions from the audience, so people left quickly after the game.

Another game was to scramble up a greasy pole to reach the sweet dough figure of a god at the top.

Aztecs enjoyed music, singing and plays. The rich households had their own orchestra and entertainers. They also loved gambling. They would first offer their prayers to Five Flower, the god of gambling, in the hopes of being lucky. Some people gambled away all of their possessions including their clothes, and were forced to sell themselves as slaves.

The cleverest boys went to the priests' school at the age of eight. They lived on tortillas and water, slept on the bare floor, and sometimes fasted for days. Every morning the boys had to prick their ears and tongue with thorns to please the gods, and sacrifice a quail to offer its beating heart to the sun. Each night the boys got up twice to pray. At night they collected insects to make black body paint that was worn by the priests. The priests taught the boys to write and read, to make herbal medicine, and to foretell eclipses, droughts, and famines by watching the stars. They also learned the right songs and prayers for each of the many gods. When a boy was 20, he could leave to marry. Then he might work as a palace scribe, a doctor or a soothsayer. One of his tasks was to choose the luckiest day to name a new baby and to foretell its future.

Boys who didn't go to the temple to train as a priest were sent to a boarding school to train as warriors. These boys led a tough life. They learned to be humble and obedient by doing lowly jobs like digging canals and sweeping the temples. Peasant boys were allowed to go home for a few hours each day to help their fathers. The boys had to learn the songs and dances of their religion, along with the city's laws. Lazy boys were punished with thorns. They learned to fight with wooden weapons. The boys would carry food into battle for the warriors. Every young warrior tried to capture three enemies alive and become a "master of cuts." He could then tie up his hair.

The Aztecs' main weapon was a wooden club edged with a razor-sharp blade of volcanic glass called obsidian. They also used wooden spears. They used an atlatl or wooden thrower to give their spears greater thrust. Their shields were decorated with feathers and mosaics, and they wore a sort of padded armor to protect themselves. Their purpose was not to kill those they attacked, but to take as many prisoners as possible. Prisoners either became slaves or were sacrificed to the gods.

The Aztecs created their huge empire by waging war. When they wanted to take over a city, they first sent ambassadors who stated their demands. They wanted the city to trade with them, worship their god, Blue Hummingbird, and send gifts to emperor every year. They gave the city three chances. Every twenty days they would return to repeat their demands. Every time a city refused to give in, the Aztecs gave the people a gift of spears and shields so they would not be helpless in the war which was to follow. If the city still held out, the priest chose a lucky day and the two armies met at noon. The battle was always short and fierce. When the Aztec army reached the enemy's temple the battle was over. The people then knew that the Aztec god was stronger than their own. The Aztecs bargained with their captives to decide how much tribute the city should send to them each year.

The Aztecs built their temples from huge blocks of stone. On the walls, craftsmen carved images of serpents' heads and eager warriors. The temples were raised as high as possible so they could be nearer to their sky gods. Every 52 years the Aztecs built a new temple to thank their gods for not ending the world. Instead of destroying their old temple, they built the new temple over the old one.

Aztec priests and priestesses wore dark clothes and painted their skin black. They let their hair grow long and matted, and they often wore cloaks embroidered with pictures of human skulls.

Religion was deeply important to the Aztec way of life. It affected everyone, because the Aztecs believed the gods governed every part of their lives. The gods had great power, but people believed that sometimes they could convince the gods to be kinder, by giving them gifts and sacrifices. There were numerous ceremonies and rituals throughout the year, many of which were devoted to Tlaloc, the rain god, and the goddesses of water and corn. Other important gods were Xipetotec, the fertility god who made plants grow; Coutlicue, the moon goddess; Xiuhtecuhtli, the god of fire; and Coyolxauhqui, the goddess of childbirth.

Because the Aztecs conquered so many other peoples who became part their empire, their religion developed into a complicated mix which included aspects of many of these cultures. They also worshipped numerous gods of other, earlier cultures, such as the Maya and the Toltec. They believed that the world had gone through four major periods called "suns" - each of which had been destroyed by the gods (the first by jaguars, the second by a hurricane, the third by fire, and the fourth by a flood) - and that they were now living in the fifth "sun," which would one day be destroyed by a huge earthquake.

Aztecs believed that if they did not offer a gift of blood to the sun every single day, the sun would not come up. The daily offering was a quail, but for other celebrations, bigger sacrifices were necessary. People thought that if their gods and goddesses weren't fed often with human blood, they would die. If the gods died, then the earth would also die. If someone wanted special forgiveness they would prick their skin with cactus spines in order to draw their own blood as an offering. At very important ceremonies when the people wanted to make the gods very happy, they sacrificed people at the temple, using special tools reserved for this important ritual. Usually the human sacrifice victims were prisoners of war or criminals. Those who were to be sacrificed were treated well before their death - the Aztecs considered it a big honor to be a human sacrifice, although their victims may not have agreed.

People who died by human sacrifice were thought to live a very happy life after death; they were believed to be reborn on earth as a butterfly or a hummingbird or to live in a place called Tonatiuhichan. Those who died in battle or childbirth, or who drowned were also believed to live a good and happy afterlife. Nearly everyone else would have a long journey to a place called Mictlan, a place of great emptiness. When they got there, they would disappear.

Those who died as heroes were buried; others were cremated. When people were cremated, their ashes were put into urns that were made in the shape of animals, and the urns were buried. The more respected a person was, the more decorative was the urn. The person's treasures were buried next to the urn, because it was believed that the spirit would need these things on the journey to Mictlan. Offerings of flowers, tobacco, rabbits, birds, and butterflies were also left at the burial site.

The Aztecs predicted the end of their civilization. The astrologers saw disaster approaching, and the old men and women had terrible dreams in which they saw the stones of their temple falling one by one, until it was completely destroyed. Here is a verse of poetry by Netzahualcoyotl, a poet-king of Texcoco:

> *Even jade is shattered,*
> *Even gold is crushed,*
> *Even quetzal plumes are torn...*
> *One does not live forever on this earth:*
> *We endure only for an instant!*

In 1519, Hernando Cortés reached the Valleys of Mexico with eleven ships which carried 600 men and sixteen horses. They came to find gold and treasures, and to convert the people to Christianity. He and his men completely destroyed the Aztec civilization.

1. **Find the location of Tenochtitlán on a map.**

2. **Make up several picture sentences that convey a message with Aztec glyphs. Include a translation for your teacher. Some glyphs are shown on the next page.**

3. **Imagine that you are an Aztec child. Write a diary for one week of your life. Describe your feelings and your activities. Include plenty of adverbs and adjectives to paint "word pictures" in your writing. Decorate the borders of your diary pages with Aztec glyphs.**

Extra Credit: Look at illustrated books about the way of life of the Aztecs. Include extra drawings with your diary. Show typical Aztec designs on pottery, common hairstyles on the people, and other aspects of Aztec life.

4. **The Aztecs played a game called *patolli* that was very similar to Parcheesi, a game originating in ancient India. You might enjoy playing Parcheesi this week.**

5. **Keep reading your free reading book this week. You should be finished with it by the end of next week.**

6. **Have your Home Teacher give you a spelling quiz. Review any words you miss.**

Extra Book Ideas:

The Aztecs, by Jacqueline Dineen
The Aztecs, by Frances B. Berdan
The Aztecs, by Barbara Beck
Growing Up in Aztec Times, by Marion Wood

Extra Project Ideas:

• Make a pottery bowl and paint it with Aztec designs.

• Make your own Parcheesi board, adapting the board you see in *Growing Up in Aztec Times*.

• Build a diorama of an Aztec city built on a swamp. You could use a cardboard box to show an underwater lake scene below (inside the box), and the city above.

• Read about the famous ruins found under Mexico City.

• Look at pictures of Aztec glyphs and compare them with the glyphs of the Maya.

• Read a selection of Aztec myths and then write your own, using Aztec sounding names.

• Write a report about Aztec gods, priests, and religious practices.

• Learn about Aztec burial techniques, and their beliefs about the journey after death.

Social Studies/Art/English~~~~~~~Lesson 33

SOUTH AMERICAN INDIANS AND INCAS

Vocabulary Words

The following words are taken from your Social Studies lesson. Write definitions for each of them without using the root word or any other form of the word. Use complete sentences to show you understand the meaning and how to use each word.

breechcloth	**initiation**	**alpaca**
betrothal	**hemorrhage**	**purgative**
bowels	**puberty**	

Spelling

Select ten words from your written material this week for spelling words. Write each of these words correctly five times and use each word in a complete sentence. Practice your spelling words in preparation for a quiz.

Grammar

1. **Review the section called "Word Usage" in your *English Manual*. Use each of the words listed there correctly in a sentence.**

2. **Use each of the following homophones correctly in a sentence. Refer to the section called "Homophones" in your *English Manual*.**

one - won	**son - sun**	**so - sew**
its - it's	**our - hour**	**see - sea**

Day 1

1. **Fill in the countries of South America on your map from Lesson 30. Include the Andes mountains, which extend from the Caribbean shores of Colombia in the north to Cape Horn at the southern tip of the continent.**

2. This week, finish reading your free reading book, and write a one-page book review.

Very little is known about the Indians of the Andean region of South America. They were under the rule of the Incas (a group of Indians who established an empire in the mountains of Peru) until the Incas were conquered by the Spaniards in the 16th century.

The Andean Indians lived in the valleys and plains in the area which you have just drawn. In the 15th century this land was ruled by the Incas, who were famous for their agricultural and engineering achievements.

One group of Indians in this area were the Quechua. Most of them lived in Peru, Bolivia, and Ecuador. Another group were the Aymara, who built their homes around the shores of Lake Titicaca on the border of Peru and Bolivia. These Indians are still in existence today. The Quechua tell of bearded white men who came to their land, taught them to sow seeds and harvest corn, and then went away.

The Aymara Indians believe their principal god, Viracocha, rose from the cold waters of Lake Titicaca to create a world of darkness and giants. When the giants angered their god, he turned them to stone. Then he created a new world with sun, moon, stars, and people of normal size. Viracocha's symbol is a rainbow, promising rain and sun for his creation. Near Lake Titicaca are the ruins of Tiwanaku (or Tiahuanaco). It is a mass of huge stone blocks which may have been a temple or a ceremonial center. There are stone figures of men and some carvings. The Aymara believe these huge stone blocks, called megaliths, are the giants which were turned into stone by Viracocha. Included there is a "gateway of the sun" with an Inca god wearing a short tunic and thick belt. There are tears in his eyes. The tears of the sun were the original source of gold, according to Inca legends.

3. Go to your library and find a picture of these huge stone blocks at Tiwanaku. Draw a picture of them. (If you can't find them, do the extra credit assignment.)

Extra Credit: Write a paragraph, poem, or short story about what it might be like to wander in the mountains and find giant stone blocks such as these. What do you imagine you might think about what they were and how they got there? What sort of story might you make up about them?

Days 2 & 3

There is an ancient Indian legend that tells how the people decided to burn down the trees to make a clearing. The legend says that the "fire blazed ferociously and smoke rose so high that it polluted the ice kingdom of Khuno." (Khuno was the god of snow and storm.) He was so angry that he sent down thunder and lightning and hail. The Indians had to take cover in caves. When the storm was over, the Indians emerged from their caves and found a single plant had survived. It was the coca plant. Since that day, the Indians have chewed the coca plant to relieve them of hunger and pain. Today, many Indians of South America chew this plant daily. It is used in medicine and in certain ceremonies to foretell the future. Sacrifices of the leaves are made to Mother Earth throughout the year and they are burned to bring good luck when a new house is built. The cocoa plant is also used to make the drug cocaine.

The Incas were one of the many groups of people living in the Peruvian Andes. Their empire was huge, encompassing many other tribes. Incas were very superstitious. They believed that all disease had a supernatural cause, and therefore must be cured by magic or by the gods. They used many herbal remedies as well as rituals. There were particular tribes who specialized in healing, and they acted as doctors for the other Andean people.

Typical remedies involved boiling bark, roots, or leaves, and applying the solution to the wound or inflamed joint to heal sores or dull pain. Other common treatments were *purging* and *bleeding*. Purging meant that the person was made to empty out his or her body by vomiting or emptying the bowels. This was done by giving special purgative herbs. Bleeding meant that a cut was made in the vein closest to where the pain was felt in the body. It was thought that allowing the blood to flow out would relieve the problem. For example, a headache might be treated by making a small cut between the eyebrows, above the bridge of the nose.

Twigs were used for cleaning the teeth and gums. Urine came in handy for bathing an infant with a fever. Tobacco was ground to a powder and inhaled, which was supposed to clear the head. As mentioned, coca leaves were used as a hunger suppressant and pain killer. Additionally, it was used as a stimulant, and it helped stop diarrhea and dry up ulcers. Leaves of the yucca plant helped eliminate joint pain, and various animal fats and herbs were mixed together for massage oil.

Many of these herbal remedies worked well and are still in use today. However, there were many superstitious cures that were more questionable. Umbilical cords were saved from birth so a sick baby could suck the illness from its body by sucking on the cord. Sacrifices and rituals were carried out to make sure that the illness wasn't caused by neglecting religious duties or ignoring long-dead ancestors. A special cleansing cure required that the sick person go to the juncture of two rivers and wash themselves with water and white maize flour. If a person broke a bone, it was thought to be caused by the spirits in the area where the accident happened, so a sacrifice was made in this spot.

The Incas were ruled by an emperor who was believed to be descended from the sun god, Inti. Every tribe in the empire had to build a temple to the sun god. The chief sun temple was in the capital city of Cuzco. The Inca New Year was celebrated on the day when the sun passed directly over this temple at noon. This celebration was called the great Sun Festival.

On this day, anyone in the city who wasn't an Inca left to go camp in the fields. Everyone else gathered in the main square by the temple. The emperor, also called the Sapa Inca, removed his crown and prayed to the sun all night. In the morning, when the rays of rising sun filled the temple, he came out. The people brought him a pure white llama. He welcomed it and gave it a special message to deliver to the gods. Then it was sent out into the mountains to deliver its message to the sun.

The people celebrated for the rest of the day with music, dancing, and beer made from maize. They honored the Sapa Inca, because he was the child of the sun. Just as the sun made their plants grow, the Sapa Inca cared for them and ruled them for their own good.

Inca society was very well organized. It had a place for everyone and work for everyone. The people lived in communities which were either family groups or groups formed for administrative purposes.

Administrative groups consisted of military officials, descendants of previous Sapa Incas, judges, chief civil servants, and lower level officials. There were also groups of specialist craftsmen. Family groups usually consisted of farmers and peasants.

Inca land was divided into three parts. The first part was for the gods, and it provided food for the priests and offerings for sacrifices. The second part produced crops for the emperor and his noblemen, and for the sick and needy. The third part was for the peasants.

Very few people suffered real hardship under Inca rule. However, the rules of society were strict. The intent of the government was for everyone to help everyone else. Everyone worked, except the very sick, the very old, and the very young. There was a tax system that allowed workers to be paid not in money, but in a percentage of what they produced. Everyone contributed taxes as described above, and the extra food was kept in special storehouses where it would be available to needy people and for emergencies.

Children were very much wanted in the Inca society. Women helped other women with the birthing. Most women preferred a helper who had herself given birth to twins, because twins were considered a sign of a god's favor, and mothers of twins were thought to have special powers.

Portrait of an Inca ruler

After the baby was born, the mother got up and bathed herself and her baby. In a very short time she was doing her house chores again. If twins were born or the baby had some defect, special rituals were performed.

When the baby was four days old, it was placed on a low cradleboard. The cradleboard stood on the floor, supported on four legs. Two hoops were fixed to the board, one at the head and one at the foot. The mother put a shawl on the board and placed her baby on it. The baby was tied to the board with straps of cloth. Then another shawl was thrown over the hoops of the cradleboard so the mother could strap the cradleboard on her back. In this way, the baby went everywhere with its mother. When the baby cried or needed anything, the mother could easily nurse it and tend to it without taking it out of the cradleboard. Inca mothers thought that taking the baby out of the cradleboard to hold it and rock it might encourage a baby to be a crybaby. A baby was nursed in the morning, afternoon, and evening, and not at other times, even if it cried. Mothers were afraid that sucking more than that would lead to vomiting and diarrhea, or result in the baby growing up to be a greedy person.

Even tiny babies were exposed to night air and bathed in cold water. This was said to strengthen the baby's limbs. If a mother wanted to pamper her baby, she took the bath water into her own mouth to warm it and then dribbled it all over the baby, washing everything except the top of the head, which was never washed.

A baby was not named until a year or two after birth, when it was weaned. The naming day was a big celebration which included cutting the hair of the child. After feasting, the most important male relative cut the first lock of hair and gave the child a gift. Everyone else joined in, and at the end, the hair was carefully preserved. The first name a child had was a "baby name." Then when the child reached maturity he was renamed, sometimes for one of his parents or for a certain quality his parents admired.

Young Inca children, like children everywhere, played games. The little boys had toy bows and arrows, toy spades, and digging sticks. Little girls played with dolls made of grass or molded of clay. At seven or eight years of age, children were expected to help their parents. Boys began to herd the llamas and alpacas, and girls ran errands for their mothers and helping with household tasks. Between the ages of ten and thirteen, a boy began to work with his father in the fields and at fourteen he was taxed as an adult. At fifteen he had to contribute his share of labor to the village. Through helping and imitating their parents, the children learned all the skills they needed for life.

4. **Choose one of the following:**

a. **You have read about many different approaches to medicine this year. Imagine that you are sick, and that doctors and healers from many different cultures through history arrive to treat you. Write about your illness and your experience with these various physicians. Write at least one page.**

b. What skills are you learning that are preparing you for your life? Consider very carefully everything you do. Think about the things you're learning in school and the things you're learning in other parts of your life. Do you have any special skills that you feel might open up some kind of career opportunity for you in the future? Write at least one page, addressing all of these questions.

Day 4

When an Inca girl reached puberty, there was a ceremony to introduce her to womanhood. The girl remained shut up in her home during the ceremony. She fasted for three days, and on the third day she chewed a few kernels of corn. On the fourth day her mother bathed her, and washed, combed, and braided her long hair. The girl put on a new dress, a shawl, and white woolen sandals. Then a feast was held for her. She waited on her relatives who had come to the feast, and her most important uncle gave her a permanent name.

Boys had an initiation ceremony at about the age of fourteen. This was a collective ceremony held once a year. The mothers of the boys wove a breechcloth for them. At the initiation ceremony, each boy received a man's name and put on the breechcloth his mother had made. He then joined the men of the village at a simple feast. After the feast there was plenty of celebrating with dancing, athletic competitions, wrestling, and mock battle games. These celebrations were a sort of endurance test for the boys, so they could demonstrate their courage, their ability to withstand pain, and their skill in making weapons in an emergency.

Once a year the village governors lined up the young men who wanted to get married. The girl whom the parents had chosen was placed behind the man she was to marry. Very often the young couple had fallen in love first and the man had asked his parents to speak for him to the parents of the girl of his choice.

After the public betrothal, the families paired off to arrange the wedding feasts for their sons and daughters. The groom and his parents went to the bride's home to meet her family. When the groom arrived, he knelt before his bride and put a sandal on her right foot. This signified that he was ready to serve her.

The families then went to the groom's house where the bride presented the groom with a metal pin for his cape, and a fine wool shirt and headband she had woven. The groom put on the new shirt and headband and sat down next to his bride to listen to instructions on marital behavior. The teachers were either relatives or wisemen. While all the talking was going on, the groom's mother and any other women present helped to prepare the marriage feast. When the talk was finished, everyone ate and then they drank. People always ate first and drank afterwards. No one drank anything while eating. After the feast, the bride went to live with the groom's family at a new home which the groom and his relatives had built.

The Incas took good care of elderly and handicapped people. When someone could no longer work and provide for themselves, he or she was supported from the community storehouses. He was still expected to do whatever level of work he could, as were any people who were disabled, deformed, or sick in any way. By law, anyone with a physical handicap could only marry another person with the same handicap. Blind people only married other blind people, and so on.

The Incas did not have a written language. Instead, they used a "quipu," which was a long piece of string to which a number of other colored pieces of string were attached, with knots tied in them. The colors represented specific information and the knots showed numbers. It was a complicated system, only understood by the quipu keepers, who were called quipumayocs.

Yellow strings stood for gold, white for silver, green for coca, red for soldiers, and so on. By looking at a quipu, officials could tell how many warriors they could expect from any village, the food available to feed them, and where it was stored. If there was a poor harvest in one province, they knew at a glance how much help its members could send. Knots representing births and deaths were constantly being tied and untied; quipus even recorded the ages of the population and the number of people following each occupation.

The ruins of Machu Picchu, one of the last strongholds of the Incas, sits high in the Andes mountains in the midst of rocky crags with precipitous drops of 2,000 feet behind them. It was discovered by an explorer in 1911 - a spectacular sanctuary of the Inca Empire. The entire town was discovered nearly intact, having been abandoned long in the past.

The Incas carved big blocks of stone. Every important town had a huge carved stone called an Intihuatana. This stone marked the days on which the sun passed

Machu Picchu

overhead at noon, when the center, upright part of the stone cast no shadow. This was a great time of celebration. Chicha, or maize beer was offered to the sun, along with many prayers of thanksgiving. Then the people danced, sang, and drank chicha for the rest of the day. While many Intihuatanas have been destroyed, the one in Machu Picchu remains to this day.

Space was limited and houses were cleverly crowded together. Every inch of space in Machu Picchu was set aside for some use. Behind each house was a tiny garden plot only a few feet square. All the districts of the city of Machu Picchu were linked by a web of stairs, side streets, and tiny alleys. A narrow watercourse just 4" wide carried water from springs on Machu Picchu mountain along a terrace and through four stone basins, which then divided around a catch-basin. The water ran on through twelve more shallow fountains.

Remember that the Incas did not know about the wheel, and used only simple tools of wood, stone, and bronze, and had to use ropes to move stones to build structures. The stones were so finely carved that mortar was not needed to fill the gaps between them. This was truly a remarkable civilization.

Steps, walls and doorway in Machu Picchu

Inca artists produced fine weaving, metalworking, and pottery. Women spun and wove cloth on looms, using wool from the alpaca and llama. Cotton was used as well. They used a backstrap loom. One end was tied to a tree or post while the other end was tied to a band around the weaver's back. By moving back from the tree, the weaver could tighten the threads on the loom.

5. Choose one of the following projects:

   a. Make a quipu for your family. Get a long piece of thicker string (perhaps black) on which you can tie the thinner colored string.

   1) Include a yellow string to show the amount of paper money you have on hand today. Use a system of knots to count by ones. The gold can stand for dollars.

   2) Use a white string to show the amount of change (silver) you have on hand today. Use a system of knots to count by 10's.

   3) Use a green string to show the amount of food you have on hand today. Use a knot to show each day's supply of food. If you have two day's supply of food, you will tie two knots in your green string.

   4) Use a red string to show the duties you must perform today. Use one knot for each duty.

   5) Use a blue string to show the number of members in your family unit.

   b. Go to the library and look at pictures of the ruins of Machu Picchu and other fortresses and cities left by the Inca Empire. Look at examples of Incan art, also. Draw a ruin or a piece of art that interests you.

In 1532, a small band of Spanish soldiers led by explorer Francisco Pizarro captured the Incan ruler, Atahualpa, and overthrew his empire. When Pizarro captured Atahualpa, the Inca King offered a roomful of gold as ransom. Priceless works of art in gold and silver were gathered from all corners of the Incan empire. Unfortunately, this vast treasure was melted down and sent to Spain.

The early Spanish conquerors never found out about Machu Picchu, which was lost in the mountains for nearly 400 years. It has been restored for tourists to visit today.

Day 5

There is a legend of the "Flying Inca Boy" which tells of wars between the Incas and the Maya. The legend simply says that the boy hung over the enemy lines in some sort of flying machine.

The question is, "Did the Incas have balloons?" Some people believe they did and give as evidence the fact of the tight weave of their fabric. Not only was this cloth used to catch fish, but it could have been used to make balloons as well. A man named Jim Woodman decided to reconstruct a balloon using the tightly woven cloth of the Incas. Huge pieces of ancient cloth have been found; because it never rains in that part of Peru, the air is incredibly dry, the fragile pieces of cloth found there have been miraculously preserved for more than 2,000 years. Jim used these huge pieces of cloth to form the "pyramid." Beginning at the center, he sewed the pieces together, working his way out. This gave the cloth balloon a spiral shape. This spiral shape was one of the most common shapes in the drawings of the Incas. Woodman used pieces of wood and ropes tied in knots for all the rigging. Even the basket that was placed under the huge balloon was made by hand. It was made in the shape of a small reed boat called a gondola.

The first thing Jim had to do was "smoke the balloon." He passed smoke through and around the cloth balloon so it could hold hot air. This filled the holes with smoke and soot particles. Next, a great pit was dug to hold a great wood fire. He bored a small tunnel that would draw fire and smoke to the open end of the balloon. The heat from the bonfire of dry wood went through the tunnel and into the balloon. Gradually the balloon inflated with hot air and began to lift itself off. Finally, Jim climbed aboard his balloon. The balloon, named "The Condor," actually flew. Woodman believed that he was repeating the flight of ancient balloonists some 2,000 years ago. Ancient Incan drawings even show pictures that look like rockets and space machines. Could they have been flying machines? Many people doubt that Jim Woodman is correct, but you may decide for yourself.

6. **What do you think? Did the Incas fly in balloons?**

7. **Create a modern day legend. You may pick any topic. Perhaps you would like to create a legend around our modern day airplane, submarines, television, computers, video games, etc. Or perhaps it would have to do with environmental concerns or current energy issues. It's up to you! Your legend should be at least one page in length.**

8. **Finish writing your book review.**

9. **Have your Home Teacher give you a spelling quiz. Review any words you miss and add them to your ongoing list for further study.**

Extra Book Ideas:

The Everyday Life of the Incas, by Ann Kendall
The Incas: Peoples of the Past and *Finding Out About the Incas*, by C.A.
   Burland
The Incredible Incas and Their Timeless Land, by Loren McIntyre

Extra Project Ideas:

- Research the religious rituals and beliefs of the Incas in more depth. What role did magic play in their lives?

- Learn about modern day Indians of Peru.

- Find out about the agricultural practice, both ancient and modern, of terracing hillsides for planting.

- Investigate more about the quipus of the Incas, and their numbering system. Their record keeping was meticulous, and it appears that they could even predict eclipses by keeping track of time on their quipus.

- Explore the idea that Incan art shows pictures of rockets and space ships. Look at the pictures yourself and draw your own conclusion.

- Look at samples of Peruvian weaving, both ancient and modern. Weave your own creation.

- Do a report on the art of ancient Peru.

- Learn about the Indians of the Amazon.

- See if you can find information about the legendary city of Paititi.

- Look up information about the system of roads and bridges built by the Incas.

Social Studies/Art/English~~~~~~Lesson 34

EXPLORERS

Vocabulary Words

The following words are taken from your Social Studies lesson. Write definitions for each of them without using the root word or any other form of the vocabulary word. Consider them in the context of your Social Studies material, and write a sentence for each that shows you understand the meaning.

navigation	conquistador	plantation
decimate	circumnavigate	atoll
strait	scurvy	mutiny
pestilence	placid	

Spelling

Select ten words from your written material this week for spelling words. Write each of these words correctly five times and use each word in a complete sentence. Practice your spelling words in preparation for a quiz.

Grammar

1. **Write six sentences using the following antonyms. See the "Antonyms" section of the *English Manual*.**

wet - dry	stillness - motion	smooth - rough
freeze - boil	leave - remain	light - heavy

Day 1

It was for economic reasons that the countries of Europe began to explore the rest of the world during the Renaissance. In order to increase their own wealth and become more powerful, kings and queens would send men in ships to find resources such as gold, silver, spices, and silk in other lands. Although Marco Polo had long ago explored the "Silk Road," offering trade for Europe with the Asian countries, it was believed that going by ship could make you richer, because ships were faster than walking in a caravan. The nations which were the leaders in trade were those which expanded their ability to go by ship. Not only did this give them quicker access to the East, but it allowed them to expand their presence in Africa, India, and eventually the Americas.

There was a theory in Europe at the time called "Mercantilism." According to the theory, there was only a certain amount of wealth in the world. In order to get more wealth and become more powerful, a country had to take wealth away from another. Therefore countries became interested in finding resources such as gold and silver in far-off lands. If gold or silver could not be found, then other kinds of goods such as spices, sugar cane, and materials to make cloth were desirable. This led to the rise of "colonization," where a nation would claim far-off lands for itself and establish settlements there in order to gather the resources it wanted.

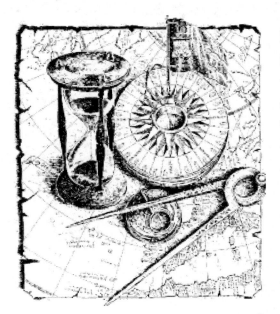

All this overseas exploration would not have happened without certain instruments and technologies being available. Navigation is the word used to describe finding one's way around on the water. Without navigation, it would have been impossibly scary to imagine taking off into the vast unknown ocean without any idea of where one was going or if one could get back. Indeed, even though some people were now aware that the earth was round, just about everybody still thought the world was flat and that there was a danger of suddenly sailing off the edge. It was during the 1400's that most navigational techniques were developed in Europe to the point that people felt comfortable enough to try longer ocean explorations. Even if they did not know where they were going, at least they could find their way back again.

The magnetic compass was first invented by the Chinese, but was used in Europe and Arabia not long after. It was discovered that a needle made of lodestone, which is an iron mineral, would always float north and south if sitting on a splinter of wood floating in a bowl of water. Once north was known, the other directions could be easily determined.

The first astrolabe was used by the Greeks, and it was used to calculate the movements of the planets, sun and moon, and the brightest stars. During the explorations of the 15th and 16th centuries, the astrolabe was used as a mechanical model of how the heavenly bodies moved. By pointing the needle across the astrolabe to line up with the sun or other bright stars, one could then tell one's approximate location. Mariners could then tell their latitude. "Latitude" is the word used to describe the imaginary lines that run east or west around the globe. These lines are used to measure where one is going when one travels north or south across the latitudinal lines. We will be looking more at this in the next lesson.

The hourglass was an instrument for telling time. It had been around for a long time as a sort of clock, but people figured out it could also be used to measure the speed one was going. Sailors would let out a rope (called a "line") on which there were knots at equal intervals. After a certain amount of time had gone by, measured by the hourglass, the line was pulled back in and the knots that were wet were counted. The modern nautical unit measurement of speed is still called a "knot," based on this early system

Making maps and charting the ocean became very important tasks as more and more explorers set off. Back in ancient Greek times, Ptolemy, an astronomer who described the movements of the planets as going around the earth, decided to take on the task of mapping the whole world. Of course at the time he did not know about America or Australia. However, he was a master at using "scale," a mapping technique in which a small measurement, such as the length of a thumb, can be used to represent a much longer measurement, such as 1,000 meters. By using scale, map makers can make a more accurate picture of what the world might look like.

The Jesuits made many maps during their missionary travels in China, India and Japan, traveling inland from the coast. They made the first accurate map of the whole of China.

The earliest known map which showed America was drawn by a Swiss monk about fifty years before Columbus sailed there. It shows a large island called Vinland which is now a small part of Canada. There were those who remembered that the Vikings had sailed across the northern part of the Atlantic to other lands, but most people did not believe such a place existed.

Maps made by traders traveling to other parts of the world were often kept secret in order to prevent rivals from using their trade routes. Eavesdropping, theft, and bribery were often used to gain access to maps and charts.

Ships have changed through the ages. It is very interesting to look at pictures of the early ships and compare them with other ships through the centuries. Perhaps the first ship was just a log floating in the water. There have also been different kinds of reed boats, skin boats, and kayaks. The oldest known boats are from Mesopotamia and Egypt.

Ships from the 1600's

The Minoans of Crete formed the first maritime empire which lasted until a volcanic eruption destroyed the Cretan harbors. The Greeks succeeded the Minoans as the major Mediterranean seafarers. The Phoenicians were another important seafaring nation. In the 10th century B.C., their ships carried the cedar timbers to build Solomon's Temple; they also brought him the ivory and gems of Ophir. The Vikings built ships that were effective for their raids and exploration. All of these ships required rowing to make them go. Up until the Middle Ages, steering had been done by means of oars lashed to the side of the ship near the stern, a rather slow way to get the ship to change its direction.

Better and faster ships were needed as the interest in exploration grew. The first major improvement was to develop sails for speed, rather than depending so heavily on oarsman to move the ship, as before. The first known ship to use a rudder at the stern of the ship for more accurate and quicker steering was a war ship first built by the English. A narrower hull - which increased speed - also began to be used. The French were the first to mount cannons on a ship, making it easier for Europeans to make war on far-off civilizations and trading ports.

Some of the types of ships that existed during the great time of overseas exploration were: the carrack (the kind Columbus used to sail across the Atlantic to the New World), the Great Harry, the Venetian Galley, the Elizabethan Galleon, the Merchantman, the Spanish Galleon, the Man O'War (used by English privateers), sloops and barks (small, fast ships used by pirates and privateers), and the nao, (used for Portuguese and Spanish exploration).

1. **Go to the library and choose one of the following topics to learn about:**

   a. **The ships of exploration. Draw a picture of one of the ships listed in the lesson. Color it beautifully, and write a sentence underneath describing the kind of ship it is and its place in history. Some good resources for looking at ships are listed under " Extra Book Ideas" at the end of the lesson.**

   b. **The astrolabe. Find out how it worked and draw a detailed picture of it.**

   c. **Old maps. It can be fun to compare what people during Renaissance times thought the world or continents looked like with how we see them now. Draw and color your own map of your country or state, taking liberty with its shape and size to make it look old. Use the colors and writing you see in the old maps to make your map look authentic.**

Days 2 & 3

As you may remember from Fifth Grade, Prince Henry the Navigator, a member of the Portuguese royal family, was one of the earliest rulers to become interested in exploration. In the 1400's, he made it his life's mission to find a way to use ships to take part in the African slave trade which the Muslims were controlling, and to trade with Asia. He set up a school of navigation and map making. He gathered together sea captains and shipbuilders to build the best ships. Then in 1433 he sent many of his most knowledgeable experts out to sea to explore the African coast. They only made it is as far as the other side of Cape Bojador, which was the name for the large "bump" coming out of the western part of Africa. It was farther south than any other European had gone before, as it was believed that the "Sea of Darkness" lay beyond, and that the equator was so hot one would burn up. The Portuguese continued to explore Africa even after Prince Henry's death, and in 1488, Bartolomeo Dias sailed around the Cape of Good Hope on the southern tip of the African continent. The Portuguese eventually colonized the Cape of Good Hope, and only recently have the native people in South Africa gained their independence back from white rule.

Prince Henry

The Portuguese took advantage of their access to the west African coast to set up sugar cane plantations using African slave labor to work them. Slave trading was begun on a large scale by the Portuguese at this time, using human life as barter with other nations. The Portuguese also traded in gold and ivory from Africa.

Vasco da Gama was a Portuguese who was determined to continue Prince Henry's mission to find a way to India and Asia by sea. In 1498 he rounded the Cape of Good Hope and sailed eastward to India, landing in Calicut (now Calcutta), a large trading port on the western coast of India. The Arabs, who already did lots of trading with the Indians, knew how to give gifts to the Hindu ruler, called the Zomarin, in order to gain favor and receive permission to trade. But Da Gama and his men were not so well prepared. They very much wanted to return home with a cargo of spices and jewels, but the Zomarin, possibly offended, would only sell them food. Nevertheless, Da Gama was considered a hero by his nation upon his return to Portugal, for now the Portuguese would no longer have to rely on the high prices set by Arab traders, or the slower overland trading roads with their high tolls.

Da Gama felt that the only way Portugal could have access to trade in the East was to use force. First the Portuguese sent ships and cannons and conquered the port of Cochin, south on the coast from Calicut, and built a trading post there. Da Gama himself went back to Calicut in about 1504 to bombard the city and get the Zomarin to agree to let the trading post in Cochin be left alone. Similar force was used to capture Malaysia and the Moluccas, or the Spice Islands. The Portuguese came to dominate much of India and Ceylon, and traded with China and Japan as well.

The Dutch and English later took over trade in India and Asia due to Portugal's weakening as a nation in the 1600's. The East India Dutch Company, a huge company owned by many wealthy Europeans, including royalty, was established to trade goods from the Spice Islands. The Dutch tended to be more successful as traders than the Portuguese had been, particularly in China and Japan. This is because they were not interested in converting other people to Christianity, but focussed on business only.

Queen Isabela and King Ferdinand, the monarchs of Spain, also became interested in searching for new trade routes. It was Isabela who had the sense of adventure, and Ferdinand who would find a way to finance the voyages Spain began in the late 1400's. Isabela and Ferdinand were a powerful couple, known for how they had united Spain and ruled it as equals. Devout Catholics, they also had little tolerance for other beliefs, and had little moral trouble with the notion of conquering and dominating peoples in other lands for financial gain. As you learned in Fifth Grade,

Columbus with Queen Isabela and King Ferdinand

they were the ones who sent Christopher Columbus off to find the New World.

As soon as Columbus came back from his first voyage to the New World, the Spanish and Portuguese realized there could be a lot of potential problems between them if they were to be exploring the same seas and claiming for themselves the land and gold they each found. They agreed to let Pope Alexander VI settle their disputes. Their agreement was called the Treaty of Tordesaillas. In 1493, a year after Columbus landed in the West Indies, and five years before Da Gama landed in India, a great global division was made from the North Pole to the South Pole, down through the Ocean Sea. Anything to the east of the line was Portugal's, and anything to the west was Spain's. Obviously, we know that with a round world, their land claims would eventually end up overlapping, but for the time the treaty worked well. (Of course the people who actually lived in all these places didn't necessarily agree!)

Pedro Alvares Cabral was a Portuguese sea captain who in 1500 was sailing for India, following Da Gama's route along the African coast. However, he ran into bad winds, and was completely thrown off course. He ended up on the coast of what we know now to be Brazil, and claimed it for Portugal. Ironically, although it was in the Western Hemisphere, it was also still east of the line fixed by the Treaty of Tordesaillas, and so the claim was honored for Portugal.

Amerigo Vespucci

Amerigo Vespucci was an Italian navigator who sailed on several voyages with the Portuguese across the Ocean Sea, which is what the Atlantic Ocean was known as then. It was during these trips that Vespucci became convinced that this was a "New World," and not islands off the coast of India. Vespucci was on a voyage which was expected to round the Cape of Catigara, just south of the equator, and sail on to India. (It was during these voyages to South America that European explorers saw the constellation of the Southern Cross for the first time, losing sight of the North Star over the northern horizon.) Vespucci and his party were using maps that the ancient Greek Ptolemy had made long ago. But Vespucci, while in the process of determining their longitude, suddenly realized the stars were not the ones that should be overhead at such a point. This confirmed his suspicion that this was a whole new continent. Vespucci went back to the Portuguese king with maps of the South American coastline and reported that he believed there must be even another ocean on the other side of this New World, which would lead to Asia and India. The name "America" comes from Vespucci's name - Amerigo.

The Spanish thirst for gold led to the invasion of the Aztec Empire in Mexico. Although the Aztecs were often willing to give gifts and trade for gold, the Spanish wanted more than this. Hernando Cortés led the capture and destruction of the wealthy and huge city of Tenochtitlan, well inland from the Gulf of Mexico. Horses and guns, never before seen by the Aztecs, played a large role in the conquest. Cortés also cut off the aqueducts that brought water to the city. The Aztecs fought for four months, but finally were defeated. The Spanish eventually built Mexico City on this site.

A map of the world according to Vespucci
(Notice the incomplete American continent)

The Spanish used a town on the Pacific coast of Central America as a base for exploring the southern part of the continent. Vasco Nunez de Balboa was a Spanish explorer who crossed Panama and discovered what he called the "South Sea." We know it now to be the Pacific Ocean. Another explorer, Francisco Pizarro, was a soldier who wanted to find fame and fortune as Cortés had. He had heard of a place called Peru that was said to be a land of gold. First he explored south by ship on the Pacific side of Central America until he came to a city called Tumbez, which was part of the Incan Empire. There he saw walls sheeted with gold, and met friendly people. He returned to Spain for ships, guns, horses, and men - and returned to Peru to conquer it for Spain. The Incan emperor soon realized that the Spanish wanted gold, and offered them a roomful of it in exchange for being left alone. The Spanish agreed, but soon decided that this was not enough, and Pizarro overthrew the Incas completely. Soon after this, Pizarro was killed by a rival group of conquistadors who had taken to fighting amongst themselves for rule over the new lands and riches.

Pizarro

Incan painting of the fighting between the Spanish and the Inca

The Spanish not only wanted gold, they wanted to conquer and rule. They set up colonial governments everywhere they went, and the governors of these colonies swore allegiance to the Spanish throne. The biggest business of the colonies was to reap the wealth of the land. Indians, as the native populations were called, were forced to build cities, and work the gold, silver, and gem mines. The mining of gold became so important that the carefully constructed irrigation systems which kept the land green and fruitful were neglected. Christian missionaries traveled to South America to preach the Catholic faith. They often forced the Indians to wear western style clothing, and they destroyed temples, statues and other Incan religious sites and artifacts. One bishop in the Yucatan ordered the mass burning of the beautifully painted Mayan books, which were the only evidence of a written Native American language. The Indians decided that the white Europeans must be gods to be so powerful, and often converted to Christianity willingly. In addition to their religion, the Spanish also brought diseases with them, such as smallpox and syphilis. Between disease and the slave-like conditions, the native population of Mexico was decimated to about a twentieth of what it had been before the arrival of Cortés.

The Portuguese and the Spanish continued the practice of using the slave trade to establish their wealth in the Americas. Slaves were used to work on sugar cane, tobacco, and tropical fruit plantations in South America. However, the Portuguese gradually realized that they could also get rich by providing other nations with slave labor to spread their own colonization efforts. Later the Portuguese lost their grip as a world power, when they were taken over by Spain in 1580.

Then the English and French became heavily involved in the slave trade. They set up what has become known as the "triangular trade." The first stage of this was when merchants in Europe would ship goods and weapons to Africa in exchange for African natives to be used as slaves. Slavery had been practiced in Africa from the earliest times, and it was often the African rulers themselves who traded goods for people who had

Converting Indians to Christianity

been captured from other tribes. However, the way African practiced slavery amongst themselves was very different from the way the Europeans used it. Children born of slave women were considered free, and usually an adult slave had opportunity to buy back their freedom. Slaves in African society often had a role and place in society. As practiced by the colonists, slaves were considered property. It was often thought to be good business to work slaves even to death. Chances are many of the African rulers did not know at first what they were subjecting their people to. Later, the slave trade had a disastrous effect on African societies. Tribes sometimes used the arms they had acquired through trading with the Europeans to do battle with other tribes, hoping to gain captives to trade away as slaves.

The "Middle Passage," or second part of the triangular trade was the worst of all, in which Africans were chained in extreme confinement, with little food or water or air, in the bottom of ships - and taken to the Americas. Many died before reaching shore. Those who survived were sold in open marketplaces and often subjected to brutal working conditions.

The third leg of the triangle was when products from American plantations were shipped to Europe and used to generate money to purchase more slaves from Africa. And so the cycle began again.

The Spanish ships full of gold, making their way routinely back across the Atlantic to Spain, were vulnerable to the hurricanes that raged through the Caribbean. There was another threat as well, from the many pirates who roamed just outside the West Indies and near the European coast. The area around the Caribbean Sea became known as the Spanish Main. Pirate crews were often made up of men of many nationalities - African, European and Indian - who were willing to attack any merchant ship. Some pirates also became slavers, capturing slave ships as they left the African shore, or raiding African slave ports. Runaway slaves sometimes took to pirating as well.

Another kind of pirate, called a "privateer," was someone who was given license by their king or queen to attack ships for the gain of the country. Elizabeth I of England with the help of Sir Walter Raleigh, used privateering to gain wealth for England. The French privateers, or "corsairs," in turn attacked English ships coming through the English Channel on their way to London. Often there were strict rules about privateering, where one could only attack ships belonging to countries that one's own country was at war with, and where those who were captured were treated well and allowed to go free.

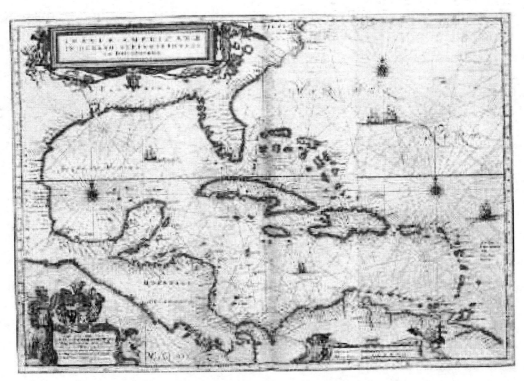

Old map of the Spanish Main

Later, under James I, such privateering licenses in England were withdrawn, and completely lawless "buccaneers" took over the privateering business on the Spanish Main. The buccaneers were often murderous and cruel.

As you may remember from your studies in Fifth Grade, the English, Dutch and French were the people who made the most inroads in North America. Although the Spanish claimed much of the southwestern part of North America for themselves, they soon realized they were not likely to find much gold there.

2. **Choose one of these research projects:**

a. **Read more about famous pirates of the Spanish Main and write at least one page. For extra credit, include a drawing of either one of your chosen pirates, or one of their ships. Ideas include Sir Francis Drake, Jean-David Nau (called L'Olonnois), Henry Morgan, Captain William Kidd, Edward Teach (called Blackbeard), Mary Read and Anne Bonney.**

b. **Choose one of these explorers to find out more about: James Cook, Hernando Cortés, Francisco Pizarro, Amerigo Vespucci, or Nunez de Balboa. Write at least one page about the voyages of your explorer and draw a map showing his routes.**

James Cook

Amerigo Vespucci

Fransico Pizarro

Hernando Cortés

Nunez de Balboa

Days 4 & 5

In 1519, Portuguese explorer Ferdinand Magellan began his voyage with five ships and about 250 men to find a western route to India and Asia. The Portuguese had established their route by the east, and Columbus had determined that another continent lay in between, in the west. But unlike the English (who would decades later look for the Northwest Passage through the North American continent), the Spanish believed that there must be a way through the South America continent.

Ferdinand Magellan was born in the year 1480 to a nobleman and his wife in the Portuguese mountain town of Sabrosa. When he was twelve years old, he left his home to apprentice at Queen Leonora's school for pages. A man named Duke Manuel supervised the pages, and took an instant dislike to Ferdinand. Despite this unfortunate circumstance, which Ferdinand's persistent efforts didn't change, he was happy as a page. He was taught music, dancing, etiquette, hunting, and swordsmanship. He was also instructed in map making, astronomy and navigation.

Ferdinand dreamed of the day when, as a ship's officer, he could sail in search of riches or new places. Unfortunately, by the time Ferdinand was old enough, Duke Manuel had become king and stood in the way of him going to sea. In those days not just anybody could go to sea. They had to have the blessing and support of the king in order to gain command of a ship.

Eventually Ferdinand was able to enlist as a lowly sailor. He worked his way up by determination and effort. He had many trials in his early life at sea and was seriously wounded twice in battle. He was left with a limp for the rest of his life, but this did not stop him. He was obsessed with a desire for adventure. Finally, in 1519, after breaking with King Manuel of Portugal and giving himself to the service of King Charles of Spain, Ferdinand Magellan took up the challenge to circumnavigate the world.

First, he hoped to find a waterway through the continent of South America. Next, he hoped to prove that it was possible to sail all the way around the world - either leaving from a certain place and arriving back at it by going all the way around, or by going first to a place by sailing east, and then going back to the place by sailing west. Either way would prove that you could sail all the way around. Nobody that he knew of had ever done that, and nobody knew if it could be done. As a sailor, he had once been on a ship that sailed east and discovered a group of islands called the Philippines. At the time, he had assumed they belonged to Spain, and had angered King Manuel of Portugal by saying so. He wondered if he would ever be able to find those islands again.

Now, Magellan did not have a shiny, clean boat for his voyage around the world. He had five old ships in need of repairs. The ship he would sail himself was the Trinidad, the second largest of the five. King Charles of Spain helped him prepare his tall, square-rigged ships for the long journey. For long distance ocean voyages, the food and drink had to be stored in barrels for long periods of time. Drying and salting were the only methods of preserving meat, fish, fruit and vegetables. Often the flour became infested with worms and weevils. The food was not nearly as appetizing as your food. Wine and water were taken to drink, but sometimes they went bad or ran out. Constant inspections were needed to check on how well the food and water were surviving the voyage. If anything was found to be going bad, the crew had to consume it immediately. The cooking was done by boiling on the deck, with a bucket of water kept nearby in case of fire. Meals were served on deck. Think what it must have been like for these explorers to be out of contact with their homeland for months, facing hunger and thirst, and possible death from storms and ship wrecks! Disease was rampant. Many sailors got scurvy from the lack of fresh fruit and vegetables, typhoid from bad water, food poisoning from rotten food, "rat-bite fever" from the rats that infested their ships, or typhus from lice.

Magellan and his men set sail on September 20, 1519, heading across the Atlantic to the coast of South America. They had many adventures, including bitter disappointments and arguments, especially when they found themselves facing part of the winter anchored in the icy waters of the Antarctic. They were weary and disheartened when on October 21, 1520, a year and a half after they had set sail, they achieved Magellan's goal of finding a waterway by going around the southern tip of what we now know to be South America. Rounding that tip meant negotiating amongst many tiny islands, now known as the Straits of Magellan. By then his five ships were down to three. He headed into the strait and spent the worst 38 days of his life. The winds were violent, the air freezing, and the strait narrow. The sea was rough. The waters were fast and dangerous, and so deep there was no way to anchor. They had to tie the ships to outlying rocks to get rest. It took them over a month, but finally they pressed through the strait and came out into the ocean.

As Magellan sailed out of the waterway he called "El Paso," and which we now call the "Strait of Magellan," into the calmer waters of the ocean, he displayed the flag of Spain. The priests who traveled with the expedition led the men in prayer and singing a hymn of thanksgiving. Then Magellan shouted victoriously, "We are about to stand into an ocean where no ship has ever sailed before! May the ocean be always as calm and benevolent as it is today. In this hope, I name it the Mar Pacifico!"

He had discovered and named the Pacific Ocean. "Pacifico" means "placid." He followed it north, along the coast of Chile, to a latitude near the equator. There he turned west, hoping to sail in just a few days to Asia. He thought it was now just a short distance to the Spice Islands. But where he thought the Spice Islands lay, four degrees south of the equator, was only more empty sea. He sailed for two months without seeing land, realizing daily that not only was the Pacific much bigger than he had imagined, but that the whole world was much bigger than he had dreamed.

The crew's food and drink began to go bad. Maggots covered everything, and the sailors had to hold their noses just to drink the water. They began to get sick, and by January of 1521, almost a third of them had died from scurvy. A month later, they found a tiny atoll, and stayed for a week to fish and rest. They replenished their drinking water by catching rain water in their sails. Then they sailed on.

By early March all their food was gone, and they knew that within a few days they would die. Two days went by. In the early morning, the lookout screamed, "Praise God! Land! Land!" They were greeted by hostile natives, so Magellan and his men fired their ships' guns to scare everyone away, and spent several hours feasting on any food they could find before sailing on. This island is now called Guam.

Nine days later they again reached land, and Magellan realized it was the same series of islands he had found in 1511, when he sailed eastward from Malacca. As Ian Cameron, one of Magellan's biographers wrote, "After 550 days of storm and mutiny, hunger, pestilence and death, he had circumnavigated the world." He had arrived at the Philippine Islands.

In addition, he proved that the world was round because he reached the Orient by sailing west from Europe. Here is the course Magellan took: Magellan put to sea from Seville, Spain and charted a course south towards South America. He continued southwards and at last arrived at the southern tip of the South American continent and found a strait running west between it and the islands just off shore.

The journal of one of the men who sailed with Magellan says this: "So noble a captain... he was more constant than anyone else in adversity. He endured hunger better than all the others, and better than any man in the world did he understand sea charts and navigation... The best proof of his genius is that he circumnavigated the world, none having preceded him."

When Magellan reached the Philippines, the ruler of a nearby island boarded the Trinidad to speak to him. He invited the sailors to come ashore. Magellan and his men developed cordial relationships with the native people. Many of them seemed to want to become Christians. An outdoor Catholic mass was held and thousands of the natives were baptized in the ceremony.

Magellan was so excited by this that he decided to try to spread the faith even further. One of the chiefs of one of the islands had let it be known that he had no intentions of bowing to Spain or the Spanish religion. Magellan proceeded despite the warning. The natives opened fire with bamboo lances, staves hardened in the fire, stones, and even darts. Magellan was struck in the leg by a poisoned arrow. Finally an angry islander succeeded in thrusting the end of his lance through the bars of Magellan's helmet, wounding him in the forehead. Magellan died in the Philippines.

The sailor's journal says of this moment, "Thus perished our guide, our light, and our support. On falling and seeing himself surrounded by the enemy, he turned toward us several times, as if to know whether we had been able to save ourselves. As there was not one of us who remained with him but was wounded, and as we were consequently in no condition either to afford him succor or revenge his death, we instantly made for our boats... To our Captain indeed did we owe our deliverance, as the instant he fell, all the islanders rushed toward the spot where he lay."

The remaining men left quickly for the long voyage home, escaping with only their lives. Six months later, after meandering about the Pacific, they managed to make it to the Spice Islands. After trading there, one ship from Magellan's original five made it back across the Indian Ocean and around the Cape of Good Hope. There was as much danger from the jealous Portuguese guarding their trade routes as from the weather. Some men were captured by the Portuguese and others died of scurvy. By the time the first voyage around the world landed in Spain, there were only eighteen left of the 250 men who had set sail. Where five ships sailed away, only one came back.

By the late 16th century, enough of the world had been explored for mapmakers to be able to show the continents of Europe, Asia, Africa, and the Americas quite accurately as we know them today. However, it was believed that there must be as much land mass in the southern hemisphere as there was in the north in order to keep the globe balanced as it rotated. Therefore it was believed that there was a "lost continent" somewhere below the tips of Africa and South America, and maps of the time showed a vast land mass covering a huge part of the lowest, or most southerly, part of the globe. When New Zealand and Australia were first discovered, it was believed they were tips of this "lost continent."

Drake's ship, "The Golden Hind"

The Spanish and the Portuguese had established themselves as masters of exploration and conquest of far-off lands. England was a relatively poor and small country by comparison, but it had a determined and ambitious ruler, Elizabeth I, who wanted to share in the world's wealth, and who wanted a hero of the sea as well. In 1577 she secretly sent Sir Francis Drake as a privateer to pass through the Strait of Magellan, plunder Spanish gold ships along the coast of Peru, and return. If he was caught, she planned to deny any involvement with an independent "pirate."

After rounding the Strait of Magellan, Drake was blown far south off-course. He soon realized there was no sixth "lost" continent in that part of the southern hemisphere as had always been thought, and which his maps showed. There was no need to go through the Strait, he could simply sail around further south in safer, open water.

Drake managed to capture Spanish ships laden with gold, that were making their way up the western coast of South America towards Central America. However, Drake had trouble finding a way back to England. He did not want to risk the Strait of

Magellan again as the Spanish were itching for a fight, and the eastern way back through was considered even more dangerous than the west. He could not go overland through Panama as the Spaniards did to bring their gold back to Spain, as it was heavily fortified by the Spanish. He explored the California coast and northwest Canada, trying to find the other end of the Northwest Passage, but to no avail. The only option left was across the open waters of the Pacific.

Drake reached the Spice Islands after stopping at the Philippines. The islanders had recently driven out the Portuguese and were interested in trading with the English. After returning to England, he led Elizabeth's conquests against the Spanish colonists in America, including the burning of their settlement, St. Augustine, in Florida. Finally, in 1588, Philip I of Spain assembled the "Armada," a group of 130 ships and 30,000 men, to attack and defeat England. The attempt was a disaster, as it was carried out as if the Spanish were taking over American land from native people, and not an established warfaring nation like its own. Drake led the defeat of the Armada, further earning him the respect of queen and his country. The English would eventually take control of the trading routes to the east and North America, becoming some of the richest and most successful colonists and merchants in the world. Drake is the man who inspired this era.

3. **Choose one of these:**

   a. **Write a journal as if you were a seaman on either Magellan's or Drake's circumnavigation of the world. How do you feel as you leave? What are your hopes and expectations? Do they change as the voyage goes on? What are the realities of the voyage? How do you feel when you return home? This can be done in pieces, writing journal entries that tell about the highlights of the trip.**

   b. **Make one of the earliest usable compasses. Magnetize a simple sewing needle by stroking a magnet along it, in one direction only, about fifty times. Then carefully balance the needle on a thin piece of cork and float the cork in a bowl of water. The needle will swing to the north. Use a modern compass to check. You can then label north on the edge of the bowl, and the other directions around the rest of the rim. Label NW, SW, SE and NE as well.**

4. **Have your Home Teacher give you a spelling quiz. If there are words you miss, then review them and put them on your study list for the year.**

Extra Book Ideas for Lessons 34 and 35:

Maps, Getting from Here to There, by Harvey Weiss, Houghton Mifflin Co., Boston, 1991

Maps and Mapping, by Barbara Taylor, Kingfisher Books, NY, 1993

The Book of Where, or How to Be Naturally Geographic, By Neill Bell, Yolla Bolly Press, Little, Brown and Co., 1982

The Story of Maps, by Lloyd A. Brown

All About Maps and Mapmaking, by Susan Marsh, Allabout Books, Random House, NY 1963

Geography; Landscape, Climates and People, by Dougal Dixon, Franklin Watts, New York, 1984

Children's Atlas of the World, by Stephen Attmore, World International Publishing, 1990

The Complete Geography Project and Activity Book, by Susan Julio, Scholastic Professional Books, New York, 1993

Sold! The Origins of Money and Trade, Runestone Press, Minneapolis, 1994

Atlas of Exploration, by Dinah Starkey, Scholastic, HarperCollins Publishers Ltd. NY, 1993

"Exploration and Conquest" series, by Betsy and Giulio Maestro, Lothrop, Lee and Shepard Books, NY, 1994. Includes *The Discovery of the Americas*, and *The Americas after Columbus: 1500-1620*

This Book is About Time, by Marilyn Burns

Explorers and Mapmakers, by Peter Ryan, Lodestar Books, E.P. Dutton, NY,1989

Oars, Sails and Steam, by Edward Tunis, The World Publishing Co., Cleveland and New York, 1952. Useful sections on the ships of the time.

Around the World in a Hundred Years, by Jean Fritz, G.P Putnam's Sons, New York, 1994

"Exploration Through the Ages" series, by Richard Humble, Franklin Watts, NY, 1992. Includes volumes *The Voyages of Jacques Cartier*, *The Voyages of Vasco Da Gama*, *The Voyage of Magellan*

Forgotten Voyager, The Story of Amerigo Vespucci, by Ann Fitzpatrick Alper, Carolrhoda Books, Minneapolis, 1991

Christopher Columbus, The Great Adventure and How We Know About It, by Delno and Jean West, Atheneum, NY, 1991

Discovering Christopher Columbus, How History is Invented, by Kathy Pelta, Lerner Publications, Minneapolis, 1991

Christopher Columbus; Voyager to the Unknown, by Nancy Smiler Levinson, Lodestar Books, Dutton Children's Books, 1990

The Sea King, Sir Francis Drake and His Times, by Albert Marrin, Atheneum Books for Young Readers, Simon and Schuster, NY, 1995

"Explorations and Encounters" series, by Peter Chrisp, Thomson Learning, NY, 1993. Includes volumes; *Voyages to the New World, The Search for a Northern Route, The Search for the East*, and *The Spanish Conquests in the New World.*

Aztecs and Spaniards; Cortés and the Conquest of Mexico, by Albert Marrin, Atheneum, NY, 1986

"The World's Great Explorers" series, by Jim Hargrove, Children's Press, Chicago, 1991. Includes volumes on Hernando Cortés, Ferdinand Magellan, Marco Polo, and Robert Cavelier, Sieur de la Salle.

Marco Polo, by Charles P. Graves, "Junior World Explorers" series

Ponce De Leon, by Wyatt Blassingame, Chelsea Juniors, Chelsea House Publishers, NY, 1991

The St. Lawrence, by Trudy J. Hanmer, Franklin Watts, NY 1984.

"World Leaders, Past and Present" series, ed. by William Hansen, Chelsea House Publishers, 1986. Includes volumes on Cortés and Queen Elizabeth I.

Pirates and Privateers, by Jeremy Pascall, Sampson Low, Theorem publishing, 1978

"Eyewitness Books" series, *Pirate*, by Richard Platt, Alfred A. Knopf, NY, 1994

16th Century Galleon: Inside Story, by Richard Humble and Mark Begin

Captain Cook, Pacific Explorer and *Vasco da Gama; Sailor Toward the Sunrise*, by Ronold Syme

Columbus by D'Aulaire

The World in 1492, by Jean Fritz and Katherine Paterson

The Usborne Book of Explorers: From Columbus to Armstrong, from Usborne Books

Balboa, by Jeanette Mirsky

Cortés and the Aztec Conquest, by Blacker

The Conquest of New Spain, by Bernal Diaz

Exploration: Great Lives, by Milton Lomask

First Around the World, by George Sunderlin

The Northeast Passage: Black Water, White Ice, by Helen Orlob

The Man Who Discovered the Amazon, by Ronald Syme
Pacific Voyages, by Gerhard F. Muller
Atlas of Discovery, by Gail Roberts
Great Adventures and Explorations, by Wilhjalmur Stefansson
The Great Voyages of Discovery: Circumnavigations & Scientists, 1764-1843, by Jacques Brosse
Great Adventures That Changed Our World, by Reader's Digest
Explorers of the World: The Story of Man's Conquest of his Planet, by William R. Clark
A Voyager Out: A Life of Mary Kingsley, by Katherine Frank
Mighty Mississippi: Biography of a River, by Marquis William Childs
Seafaring Women, by Linda Grant de Pauw
On Top of the World; Five Women Explorers in Tibet, by Luree Miller
Forging an Empire, Queen Elizabeth I, by Elizabeth Linington, Britannica Books, Encyclopedia
"Great Lives" series, *Queen Elizabeth I*, by Dorothy Turner, Bookwright Press, New York, 1987

Extra Project Ideas:

•   Study the life of Queen Isabela and King Ferdinand of Spain.

•   Write a discussion between Columbus, Ferdinand, and Isabela.

•   Draw maps of the travels of some explorers of your choice.

•   Discuss the impact of the explorers on the cultures they "discovered." What happened to the Aztecs after Cortés, and to the Incas after Pizarro? What about other cultures?

•   Write a dialogue between an Aztec and Cortés or between an Inca and Pizarro.

•   Be a soldier in the army of Cortés, and write a journal about his discovery and confrontation with the Aztecs. Consider the geography and climate as well as the culture.

- Find out about women who were explorers or adventurers in any time in history. (A few names: Beryl Markham, Amelia Earhart, Mary Kingsley, Mary Patten (and the ship, "Neptune's Car"). Female pirates include Madame Ching (Hsi Kai Ching Yih - a 19th Century Chinese pirate), 12th Century pirate princess Alvilda of Sweden, Mary Read, Anne Bonney. What about women explorers in space? In science? Climbing or sports?

- Watch the old movie "The Captain from Castille," about Cortés.

- Watch any of several 1990's movies about Columbus.

- Learn more about the history of maps and the process of mapping.

- Research more recent adventurers such as Lewis & Clarke, Livingstone & Stanley, Robert Peary, Roald Amundsen, William Beebe, Jacques Cousteau, Edmund Hillary, the Apollo 11 expedition - the list is endless!

- Research the history of the search for the Northwest Passage

- Find out more about the triangular slave trade, or slavery in South America in general.

- Find out more about Elizabeth I and Sir Francis Drake. Write a conversation between them, or a play about them.

Social Studies/Art/English~~~~~~~Lesson 35

AROUND THE WORLD

Vocabulary Words

The following words are taken from your Social Studies lesson. Write definitions for each of them without using the root word or any other form of the vocabulary word. Consider them in the context of your Social Studies material, and write a sentence for each that shows you understand the meaning.

sphere	proportion	turbulent
organism	extensive	interval
sophisticated	emitted	

Spelling

Select ten words from your written material this week for spelling words. Write each of these words correctly five times and use each word in a complete sentence. Practice your spelling words in preparation for a quiz.

Grammar

1. **Write six sentences using the following synonyms. See the "Synonyms" section in the *English Manual* for examples of other synonyms.**

fail - break	stop - halt	play - frolic
send - mail	steal - rob	thrive - prosper

Days 1, 2 & 3

For centuries, some of those who watched the stars and the movement of the planets found that the Earth was spherical, like a ball. Others looked around themselves and saw with their own eyes that the Earth was flat. Science has shown us over and over that the former view is correct, although there are still doubters! Perhaps the most telling evidence was when the first astronauts came back with photographs of the Earth taken from space, which showed that the Earth was round. These photos further show that the Earth is spherical because one can see the shadows of night traveling across the surface, in the same way from Earth we can see the shadow created by the sun as it travels across the surface of the moon over the course of a month.

Explorations during the Renaissance also demonstrated the roundness of the Earth, especially when Magellan's expedition was able to go around the whole world for the first time, ending up where it had started in Portugal. Before that, there had been many others who were able to see the roundness of the Earth in various ways. For example, it was seen that when one is on a ship out in the ocean, and sees another ship approaching, what one sees first is the top of the ship and its sails, and later the deck and the hull, and then finally the water beneath the ship. This is because before the ship gets close enough for one to see the whole thing, the rest of it is still below the other side of the horizon line.

The horizon line is the lowest spot of sky you can see anywhere around you. Turn slowly around in a full circle and look at the lowest spot where you see sky as you turn. Sometimes mountains will make the horizon very bumpy. Or perhaps you live in a place that is very flat. Either way, that full circle around you, the lowest point at which you can see the sky, is the horizon for that place. When the sun sets, we see it disappear down below the horizon line, and rise again from behind it in the morning.

The problem for explorers, including ourselves, is that it is impractical to carry around maps that are spherical in shape. Furthermore, very often we only want to travel in a relatively small part of the world at a time, and need more detail than we can get if we were to carry around a globe. Therefore, even though we know the Earth is round, we still like to show it as flat.

Trying to turn something round (like the Earth) into something flat (like a map), poses some problems. For example, imagine you are holding a grapefruit or an orange, and you are peeling it, starting at the dimple where it was once attached to the tree. Imagine pulling the peel away keeping it in one piece, so you can lay the whole peel flat on a surface. If you actually do this, you will see there are large gaps in the peel. This is the problem facing mapmakers who are trying to show the round Earth in a flat picture.

Now imagine there is a light bulb in the center of the Earth, and its light is shining out through the Earth's surface. Pretend you are wrapping a rectangular piece of paper around the outside of the globe, taping together only the opposite edges that meet. Then you imagine the light from inside reflecting the shapes of the continents onto the piece of paper.

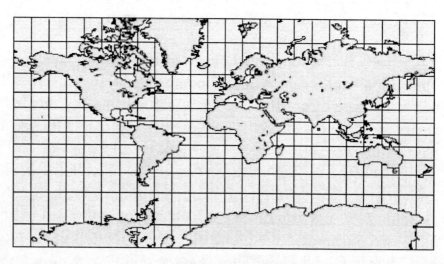

Mercator projection

This and other methods of showing the round Earth in a flat picture are called *projections*. It's a little like projecting the picture on a photographic slide onto a screen. Unfortunately, the shapes of the continents are distorted in all map projections. In the one described above, called the Mercator projection because it was developed by a Renaissance mapmaker in the 1500's named Gerhardus Mercator, the continents shown at the top and bottom areas of the globe are larger in proportion to the land forms in the middle than the real land is, however, with those closer to the top and the bottom of the globe being made larger in proportion to the landforms in the middle of the globe than the real land is. Because of this, mapmakers stretch certain parts of the world when they draw this type of map.

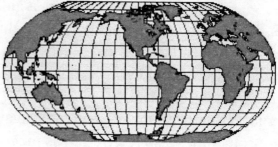

Other kinds of map projections

There are other kinds of projections you might see when looking at world maps. If you look in different atlases, you might see a landform such as Australia, which is closer to a pole, portrayed in several different sizes. Sometimes a landform will be shown the same size as another when in reality it is up to eight times smaller!

Now that we have a whole globe in mind, we need to have a way to organize it. Take a look at that grapefruit or orange again. (Go ahead, all this is a lot more fun - and a lot more clear - if you actually get one and try this out for real.) If you slice it right across the middle between those two dimples at the top and the bottom, you will have what we call the *equator*. Think of this word as splitting the earth into two "equal" portions. Each of those two halves is called a *hemisphere*. The top one is known as the Northern Hemisphere, the bottom as the Southern. Think of this word as being *half* of a *sphere*. The next term you will need to keep in mind is *pole*. We have two of these on the globe; the one at the top is the North Pole, the one at the bottom is the South Pole. These are the points on your grapefruit or orange we have been referring to as the dimples. Now there is one last division we have to make. With a knife, slice an orange in half from one "pole" to the other. This is how we divide up the Western Hemisphere and the Eastern Hemisphere. We will be looking more at these two hemispheres later.

The Ancient Greeks are responsible for the system of longitude and latitude that we still use today in mapping. It's a very useful system, because it gives us a way to make a map of something that is round. If the earth was square, it would be a simple matter to figure out the exact measurements from end to end, but it's an altogether different kind of problem with a round planet!

The only "fixed" points on a globe are the North and South Pole. Take a look at that orange again. Peel the whole thing carefully, keeping the fruit inside whole. What you see inside is the pieces of orange (or grapefruit) held together in wedge-like sections. The slightly indented lines you see between these sections are exactly like what we call the lines of *longitude*. They all run directly north and south from the poles, around the sphere, and meet again at the opposite pole. The lines of longitude are sometimes also referred to as the *meridians* of the earth.

The lines of longitude do not run parallel. As you have just read, they run north and south on the globe, meeting at the North and South Poles, just as spokes meet at the center of a wheel. This means that degrees of longitude are not the same width. Near the poles, the longitude lines are closer together. At the equator, they are as far apart as they can get. Lines of longitude are drawn in big circles through both poles and around the globe, and are all the same length.

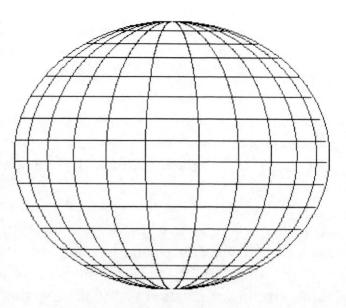

Lines of *latitude* may be a little easier to understand, although not easy to see on an orange! Latitudinal lines are imaginary lines that circle the globe in the opposite direction from lines of longitude. They go around the globe in the same way that the equator does, running parallel to it. The further away they go from the equator, the closer they get to the poles. As they get closer

Lines of longitude and latitude

and closer to the poles, the circles they make around the globe get smaller and smaller. However, they stay parallel to each other the whole time. Lines of latitude are also called *parallels* because they all run parallel—side by side— without crossing.

As you may remember, longitude lines are also called meridians. When the sun shines exactly on a meridian, it is 12 noon everywhere along this meridian. Meridian means "midday line." Just as we use the equator as our starting point to designate where the lines of latitude fall, we use what is called the *prime meridian* as a starting point from which the lines of longitude fall. Do you remember when you cut the

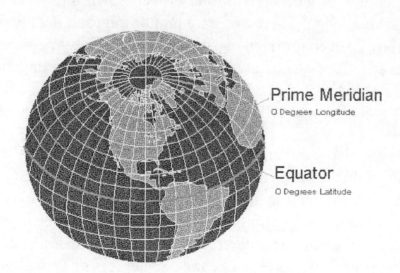

Prime Meridian
0 Degrees Longitude

Equator
0 Degrees Latitude

orange or grapefruit in half through the poles to demonstrate the Western and Eastern Hemispheres? One side of this cut is called the prime meridian. Long ago, early English mapmakers established the prime meridian as running straight through the small town of Greenwich, England, where the Royal Observatory happened to be located. Where that line appears on the opposite side of the globe is called the International Date Line. Together, this line and the prime meridian make a circle around the Earth. Because there are a total of 360 lines of longitude around the globe, the International Date Line falls on the 180th line. Everything to the west of the prime meridian all the way to the International Date Line is considered to be in the Western Hemisphere of the Earth. As you probably can guess, everything to the east of the prime meridian all the way to the International Date Line is said to be in the Eastern Hemisphere.

We now have the globe divided up into a grid, with all these lines crisscrossing each other. Navigators on the sea and travelers on the land can use this grid to figure out where they are on a map. However, we also need a system to keep track of where we are on the grid. Each of the lines of latitude and longitude is called a *degree*, symbolized by a notation that looks like this: ° Parallels of latitude are numbered beginning at the equator, which is 0°, moving upward in number as they progress toward the poles. The latitude of the North Pole itself is 90° N, and the South Pole is 90° S. This adds up to a total of 180 lines of latitude, 90 above and 90 below. As you remember, anything between the equator and the North Pole is in the Northern Hemisphere, and areas between the equator and the South Pole are in the Southern Hemisphere, and so each line of latitude is designated by "N" to show it is in the Northern Hemisphere, or "S" to show it is in the Southern.

Each degree of latitude and longitude can take up hundreds of square miles of space, so even this grid system is not really accurate enough to find your way around the globe, particularly if you are sailing from one side of the ocean to another, like an early explorer. Therefore, each line of latitude is further broken down into what is called *minutes*, symbolized with a ' sign. There are sixty minutes in each degree of latitude. Each minute is then broken even further down into sixty *seconds*, symbolized with a " sign. (These minutes and seconds are not to be confused with telling time on a clock!) The result is that the latitude of a place might be symbolized like this: 40° 17' 20"N.

The lines of longitude are also numbered using degrees. There are a total of 360 lines of longitude, starting with the prime meridian as 0°. If you were to stand on the prime meridian in Greenwich, England facing north, anything to the left of you would be to the Eastern Hemisphere, and anything to the right of you would be in the Western Hemisphere. As the lines of longitude progress to the west they are designated by °W, and to the east, °E. There are 180 degrees of E, and 180 degrees of W, making a total of 360. Where east runs into west, on the other side of the globe from the prime meridian, is the International Date Line. Using the even more precise terms of minutes and seconds, the longitude of a place might be symbolized like this: 72° 36' 10"W.

Using latitude and longitude together, in the form of degrees, minutes and seconds, you can pinpoint any spot on the Earth within just a few hundred feet.

1. **Do the grapefruit or orange experiments described in the text if you have not already done so. Use these fruits to find the poles, the equator, the four hemispheres, and longitudes.**

2. **Complete two of these projects:**

   a. **Go to the library or some other resource and look up photographs of the Earth taken from space. Look especially for ones that show the Earth passing from night into day or day into night, much like the phases of the moon. Can you see the spherical shape of the Earth? Now make your own picture of the Earth from the perspective of space. Use any art medium of your choice, and make it beautiful. Show the atmosphere of the Earth swirling above the oceans and continents, and the deep black of space in the background. Show Earth passing from night to day, with the shadow of night setting off the curve of the planet.**

   b. **Get a balloon, blow it up, and knot it. You will use this as the form to make a papier mâché Earth. Use a mixture of flour and water to dip small strips of torn-up newspaper and layer it smoothly over the balloon several times. Allow it to dry between layers. When it is all dry, paint the major landforms and oceans onto the globe. There is no need to get too involved, but you can add as much detail as you like. When the paint is dry, use a large permanent black marker to draw the equator, the prime meridian, the International Date Line, and the poles. Use a thin pointed black marker to make all the lines of latitude and all the lines of longitude. Refer to a good atlas or a globe to mark these. Then label all these lines, showing the degrees of latitude and longitude as well. (Suggestion: Use pencil first to mark out where you are going to draw. If there are mistakes, they can be covered with glue and newspaper and painted over before proceeding.)**

c. **If you do not already have one, see if you can borrow a globe. (If necessary, you can also use the one you just made.) Carefully tape sheets of tracing paper over the globe, one sheet for each of the seven continents of Australia, South America, North America, Europe, Africa, Asia, and Antarctica. You will also need to cover the oceans. Then use a pencil to trace the outline of each of the continents, making sure you also include all the areas where landforms are attached to each other. Then remove the tracing paper from the globe, and lay the sheets flat. Next, use tape to attach all the pieces of the continents together in the right places, so the areas where the landforms are attached meet as well. What is left? Are there any gaps in your map? You can see now that mapmakers must make choices as to how to fill those gaps when they turn a sphere into a flat map!**

d. **Go to the library and look in different atlases at maps of the world. Look at other maps of the world as well. How do they differ from one another? Different landforms will be shown in different sizes depending on the projection used. Sometimes the name of the projection will be printed somewhere in small print in the margin of the map. See if you can find an interrupted projection, the Mercator Projection (also known as cylindrical), an oval (or molleweide) projection, a conic projection, and an azimuthal projection. Describe the differences in distortion (or lack of), in each of the projections you are able to find.**

3. **Use a good atlas to do the following exercises on latitude and longitude, and list your results.**

    a. **On which continent is 20° N latitude and 20° E longitude?**

    b. **What U.S. state falls at 64° N and 156° W?**

    c. **What U.S. capital falls at 43°N and 89°W?**

    d. **What is at 180°E and 180°W?**

    e. **What is at 30°E and 30°S?**

f. Think of a place you have always wanted to visit. What is its location?

g. What is the location of where you live?

h. If you were to dig a hole straight through the center of the Earth from where you live, at what degree of longitude and latitude would you end up? What is the name of this place? Is it in China, like the expression, "digging a hole to China"?

Day 4

The North Pole is where we consider to be true north on the globe. However, there is also a very important location called *magnetic north*. Because the Earth spins at a slight tilt (as you can see on a globe), the needle on a compass will always be drawn to magnetic north. Magnetic north is fairly close to the North Pole, so it is convenient to use a compass to determine what direction one is going. Maps often indicate not only where north is, but also where magnetic north is.

Navigators have been measuring distances by latitude and longitude for at least 2,000 years. Airplane pilots need to know how high they are above the ground. To determine this, they measure altitude. For the pilot, altitude is the distance above the ground. But for astronomers or navigators who are already on the ground, altitude is the distance something is above the horizon. In order to determine where they are on the globe, they need to know where they are in relation to an object that is beyond the Earth itself.

Altitude is how high something is above the horizon. Once you know where the horizon is, it is easy to find the altitude of a star, sun, or other object in the sky. Try this: go outside, and point one arm at the horizon, and the other arm at the sun. (Be careful not to look directly at the sun.) Hold both arms stiff and have someone mark off the angle between your two arms onto a big piece of paper. Now you can use a protractor to measure the angle. This angle is the altitude of the sun at the time you measured it.

If we stand and watch the North Star long enough, it seems as if the whole sky turns around this star, while it stands still in the middle. For this reason it is very special, and has been a guiding light for travelers through the centuries. If you were out in the middle of the ocean in a ship and had no other way of telling where you were or what direction you were going, you could look up at night and figure out whether you were going north or south, simply by seeing the location of the North Star.

The North Star, the only star by which to determine latitude, helps navigators know more about how far they are from their destination. Look at the picture, which shows the Big Dipper moving around the North Star. No matter what position the Big Dipper is in, it still points to the North Star. This is a good thing to remember in case you are ever lost!

Fortunately for us, the North Star lines up quite nicely in the area of the North Pole. That gives us something beyond the Earth itself by which to measure our location. If you were to use the North Star as your fixed object and measure its altitude, you would be able to determine your latitude on the globe. This is precisely what the earliest explorers on the sea would do to find out how far north or south they were. You can imagine how disconcerting it must have been for those who first sailed so far south below the equator that they could no longer see the North Star!

Many years ago, navigators would stick their arms out straight and start counting fingers (fist over fist with the thumb tucked in) from the horizon to the sun or North Star to figure altitude and latitude. One finger is 4 degrees or 15 minutes, 4 fingers are 15 degrees or about an hour until sundown.

Using the above technique, go outside and measure the distance from the horizon to the sun. How long is it until sundown if each finger is worth 15 minutes? When the sun is down, go outside. Using your hands, measure from the horizon to the North Star. Remember, four fingers are 15 degrees. Tuck your thumb underneath when measuring. What is your latitude? Check your result with an atlas or a globe. How accurate were you? Perhaps you can now see why sailors were so happy to have more accurate methods of determining their location!

4. **You will need some tools to do the following measurement exercises. Get two rulers with good straight edges, and a protractor which has angles for a half-circle measured out in degrees.**

   a. **Go outside tonight and find the North Star. (Refer to a good astronomy book and a compass to help you, if necessary.) Then look for the horizon at its lowest point. Hold one ruler straight away from your face toward the horizon, sighting your eye along the length of the ruler to make sure you have it right. Use the other ruler to point straight at the North Star, having the two ends of the rulers closest to you meet. Then have someone hold the protractor with its straight edge along the straight edge of the ruler pointing at the horizon. Have that person look at the protractor and see which number of degree is at the bottom edge of the ruler pointing to the North Star. This number will show your latitude (assuming you are somewhere in the Northern Hemisphere). Check your finding with a globe or world atlas. How accurate were you? Write one paragraph describing your experience and findings. The previous experiment is the same as finding the altitude of the North Star. When you know the altitude of the North Star, you also know your latitude.**

   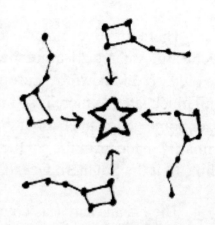

   b. **Using the method described above, find at least two other constellations or planets of interest to you and find their altitude. Remember that unlike the North Star, which stays at a fixed point in the sky, these other astral bodies will move with time as the night progresses. Wait an hour and then measure their altitudes again. How much have they risen or fallen during the past hour? Record your findings.**

Day 5

We will now look at the oceans of the world, because they were the most important waterways the early explorers took. Not only were new lands and new continents discovered by Europeans, but during the Renaissance the oceans offered a whole new area of discovery. What was once the fearsome "Ocean Sea" turned out to be one of the smaller of the oceans, the Atlantic, in comparison to the endless Pacific on the other side of the world. The Indian Ocean became a major trading route once Europeans ventured into it.

There are five major oceans to keep in mind: the Atlantic, Pacific, Indian, Arctic and Antarctic. Before the Renaissance and later explorations, the Atlantic was the only ocean known by Europeans. The Arctic and Antarctic were not mapped out until much later, as there is so much ice on them that they are hard to distinguish from land. Some geographers do not really think of the Antarctic as an ocean at all, as it is primarily made up of the southern tips of the other oceans. As a result, there are some who call it the Southern Ocean.

The oceans and seas cover about seven-tenths of the Earth's surface, with the Pacific covering about a third of the globe. Try to imagine what it must have been like for Magellan and his crew to cross the Pacific for the first time, not having any idea how big it was when they began. There must have been times when they felt they really were about to sail off the edge of the world!

When we talk about oceans and other waterways, there are a lot of names that can be confusing. What exactly is the difference between a channel and a strait, or a cove and an inlet? How about a sea and an ocean, for that matter?

In fact, there are no rules, although some geographers may argue this. Just as on land, similar forms can have different names. We might call a low part of land between a range of mountains a "pass" in one case and a "notch" in another. The only exception seems to be the five (or four, if you don't count the Antarctic) oceans, which generally seem to be agreed on as being oceans.

Although we cannot usually see it, the bottom of the ocean was of extreme importance to the early explorers. All ships and boats need a given amount of depth in order to sail safely. There are many hazards that prevent ships from simply sailing about anywhere there is water.

Just as we can look at a map of the land on Earth and see valleys and mountains, there are maps of the ocean floor that also show valleys and mountains. Interestingly enough, what we know to be land and islands are actually the peaks of the oceans' mountains, rising above the surface of the water. When you next take a bath, take a look at how your body fits in the water in the tub. Imagine that the bottom of the tub is the deepest part of the ocean, and that your body is the landforms rising from the bottom. Now look at the parts of your body that are rising above the surface of the water, such as your knees. They are just like islands.

We use the term *sea level* to describe the altitude of landforms such as mountains. Mount Everest, in the Himalayas, is the tallest mountain on land; we describe the altitude of its peak as being about 29,000 feet above sea level. The level of the oceans and sea generally stays the same throughout the whole globe (the exception being the tides), so it is a convenient way to measure the altitude of all landforms throughout the world. Mount Everest is not really the tallest mountain on earth. The tallest mountain is actually called Mauna Kea, and it is one of the Hawaiian Islands. Although it only rises about 13,800 feet above sea level, underneath it stretches down to the ocean floor far enough to give it a total height of about 30,000 feet.

Other important parts of the ocean floor are the *continental shelves* and *ocean basins.* If you are at the beach at low tide, you can often walk out quite far and the water only gradually gets deeper and deeper. You are on the continental shelf - a shallow part of the ocean that reaches out from the edge of the continents for miles before sloping suddenly down to the deep parts of the oceans, which are known as the basins. It is much as if you were in a swimming pool that has a shallow end and a deep end. If you start at the shallow end, you are on the shelf. At some point, the pool will start to dip down more quickly. This is like the continental slope. You then reach the deepest part of the pool, much like an ocean basin.

Continental shelves are vital parts of our ecosystem, as about 90% of the oceans' seafood comes from them. Their waters tend to be warmer and less turbulent than deeper ocean areas, sustaining many life forms.

No one knows for sure what the deepest part of the ocean is. The deepest ocean basins are about 20,000 feet deep. But in one basin there is a long hole called the Mariana Trench, and the bottom of it is 40,000 feet deep. This hole is more than seven miles deep, and could fit Mauna Kea and still have room to spare.

Two of the stickiest problems for sailors are coral reefs and sandbars. Some of these can be so large that they create a real barrier to passage, such as the Great Barrier Reef off the east coast of Australia. It is 1,250 miles long, and the early explorers to Australia, generally arriving from the east side, often got hung up trying to find a way through it. Coral reefs are formed from limestone built up over hundreds of thousands of years from the tiny skeletons of coral organisms. Although very beautiful, and an essential part of the oceans' ecosystem, they are often very sharp, usually causing extensive damage to a ship that runs into them.

Sandbars are places near coastlines where the ocean tides can cause a buildup of sand over time that will suddenly make the water shallower in a particular place. An early ship that landed on a sandbar often had to be given up for lost if the tides did not allow it to rise above the bar over time and sail off again. Many rusting hulks may still be seen close to shore as a result of boats having gotten stranded on a sandbar. Today we use tugboats and other such boats to try to pull a ship or boat off a sandbar.

Sounding is a method used to measure the depths of the ocean and other waterways. The earliest explorers would use a rope with a heavy object tied to the end (such as an anchor) and then tie knots or make some other kind of mark on the rope at equal intervals. They would drop the object overboard to see how much rope it took to get to the bottom. If as they sailed along, it seemed the ocean bottom was getting shallower and shallower, then there was a good chance that they were getting closer to land or to something dangerous, such as a sandbar or coral reef. If no land was in sight, the best course was to try to find deeper water again. You can imagine how this must have made for very slow going at times, as explorers tried to make their way through uncharted waters. Sounding is still used today, although we have more sophisticated techniques for measuring depth. It would be impractical to use a seven mile length of rope to measure the Mariana Trench! Instead we use devices lowered into the water which use *sonography*, or sound waves, to take pictures of the ocean floor. Sound waves are emitted, bounce off surfaces, and come back with information about how far away those surfaces are.

Just as we have maps to help find our way on land, navigators at sea use charts to find their way on the water. Charts are essential for ocean travel. It might not be to big a problem to run into a rock in a small pond if you are in a rowboat. But an oil tanker running into a rock or other obstacle in a far deeper part of water could cause extensive damage to ocean life and the nearby coastline. Even though the oil from an oil spill covers only the surface of the water, it blocks the sunlight which feeds the life below, making it difficult for whales and other sea life to come up to breathe, and seriously impacts birds.

If you look at a marine chart you will see that it is littered with little numbers, all over the water. These numbers show the depth of the water (measured in feet) at each particular location. Hazards are also charted, with symbols to show rocks and shipwrecks. Other helpful symbols are included, such as buoys and lighthouses, and where to find the location of radio signals that are emitted to help navigators. Sometimes an "S" is indicated to show where the bottom of the water is sandy. The contour of land is shown with a solid line, and large hazards such as reefs and sandbars are outlined with a dotted line. All charts have a *compass rose* on them; a circle showing where the cardinal directions north, south, east and west are, and an inner circle indicating magnetic north and the points of degree in between. Where magnetic north points on the compass rose will vary from chart to chart, depending upon the part of the ocean the chart is for.

The barest minimum of tools you would need to find your way around the ocean today is a compass and a marine chart for the area you are in. As long as you can determine where magnetic north is by using your compass, and match that direction up with the compass rose on the chart, you can have a good idea of which way you need to steer to get to where you need to go.

In general, we know that the equator is the warmest part of the world, and that as we move away from it towards the poles, temperatures get colder. There was an important discovery made by the early European explorers who first came to the West Indies. This was the Gulf Stream. All over the world, the oceans' waters are constantly moving in currents, much like the flow of a river. Warm water from the tropics is being pushed to colder climates, and then the colder water is brought back to the warmer areas. These currents flow in giant circles, taking up whole oceans. Ocean currents are essential for keeping the Earth's temperature in a relative balance so that life can be sustained throughout the world. If you were to look at a map of the Atlantic Ocean and the continents surrounded by it, you would see that the British Isles and the northern parts of eastern Canada are basically on the same latitude - the same distance - away from the equator. And yet the winters in northern Canada are far harsher then the winters in England. This is because the Gulf Stream, which starts with warm water from the Caribbean Sea, circles north and east away from North America, reaching Europe before the current then brings colder northern water back down again.

The Gulf Stream was very helpful to those returning from the New World. Even though the Gulf Stream does not go in a straight line from Florida to Spain, taking a more northerly roundabout way along the Gulf Stream saved time. Not only was the current in their favor, but the winds which helped cause this current would make the trip back relatively easy going. These winds were often referred to as the "Tradewinds." A hazard of the Gulf Stream however, is its habit of bringing hurricanes out from the Caribbean up the coast. Early explorers, treasure ships and traders would avoid sailing in late summer and fall, because this is the hurricane season.

The Gulf Stream made for an interesting sense of direction. For example, there are still people in New England who refer to Maine as "Down East," even though Maine is located to the north of them. This is because the Gulf Stream would make smooth sailing from Boston to Maine, being pushed downwind while sailing north!.

5. Choose one of the following projects:

a. **Explore sounding. Find a good-sized puddle after a heavy rainfall. If you are so equipped and inclined, you can also take a trip to a local lake or pond and go out in a boat. You may be able to do this exercise off of a long dock. At any rate, you need a relatively still body of water of some size. Bring a rope or strong cord with you, and tie to its end a rock or other object heavy enough to sink to the bottom, but light enough for you to pull out again. Tie small knots or brightly colored tape at three or six inch intervals, depending on how deep your body of water is. Put your knots closer together for shallower water. Now "sound" the puddle or pond by dropping the rock in, and noting how deep the water is there. How many knots are submerged in the deepest part of the water? How many inches is this? Sound different parts of the body of water, and make a chart showing your discoveries. If the lake or pond is too big, simply do a part of it, covering one area near the shore, for example. In any case, be sure to show the contours of the land where there is no water.**

b. **The next time you are taking a ride in the car, bring a compass with you that shows the cardinal directions. Before starting out, position the compass so the needle is pointing north. (This would be magnetic north.) As you ride, keep the compass in a fixed place. Watch the needle move as the car changes direction. Record your findings, describing your route and the direction, using approximate degrees, of each part of the trip.**

6. **Have your Home Teacher give you a spelling quiz. Review any words you miss.**

Extra Book Ideas:

See Lesson 34 for a list of books.

Extra Project Ideas:

- Make a pie chart showing the relative proportion of land to water on the globe.

- Find out more about modern maps, and their use of scale bars, locator grids and legends. Make maps of your room, neighborhood, or town.

- Find out more about any of these topics and write a report: the International Date Line and the time zones, coral reefs, the Tropic of Capricorn and the Tropic of Cancer, the world's ocean currents and their names, continental shelves, volcanoes and volcanic islands, tides and their relationship to the moon.

- Watch the video series about mapping by Patrick Stewart, called "The Shape of the World."

Social Studies/Art/ English~~~~~~~~Lesson 36

FINAL PROJECTS AND EXAM

Vocabulary Words

There are no vocabulary words for this lesson.

Spelling

Study all the words you have kept on your ongoing list this year. These are the words you missed in the previous quizzes. At the end of the week have your Home Teacher give you your final spelling quiz including all these words.

Grammar

Use complete sentences to answer all of your Social Studies questions.

Days 1 - 5

Read all of your assignments for the week ahead of time so you can plan your work.

1. **This week you will be completing a time line that shows an overview of all the civilizations and cultures you have studied this year. Use a piece of poster board that is large enough to fit all the information necessary. Begin with the Stone Age and go all the way through the Renaissance.**

   Before you begin, make an outline on a separate piece of paper so you can measure out your time line appropriately. On your final work, include illustrations for each civilization, and decorate the borders in the style of several of the cultures of your choice. Make this a real work of art.

2. Complete your world map. So far you have most of the continents in sections. Now add more sections to include the major oceans, seas, gulfs and bays. Add Australia, Antarctica and any other lands of interest to you. Add the time zones to your map. Take a photo of your map when it is completed, and send it to your teacher with the rest of your work.

3. You will need to refer to the world map that you have completed this year in order to answer these questions:

    a. Name the seven continents.

    b. On what continent did the Egyptians live?

    c. Where is the Indus River?

    d. Where is the Mediterranean Sea?

    e. On what continent is Persia?

    f. On what continent is the Yellow River?

    g. Where is the Nile River?

    h   On what continent are the Zimbabwe ruins?

    i. Describe where the island of Crete lies.

    j. On what continent and in what country is Athens?

    k. On what continent are the Alps that Hannibal crossed?

    l. What are the four major world religions, and in what countries and continents did they begin?

    m. On what continent was Pompeii?

    n. Where is Palestine?

    o. From what continent did William the Conqueror come?

p. On what continent did the Aztecs live?

q. What country was the focus of much of the Renaissance?

r. How many time zones do we have in the United States?

s. How many time zones are there in the world?

t. When traveling around the world, where is the point at which the date changes, and what is it called?

u. What are the major bodies of water in the world?

v. What groups of people have you studied from the continent of South America?

w. Where did the Reformation begin?

x. On what continent did Lief Ericsson land?

4. Choose one of the following projects:

a. At the end of the week, hold a Festival of World Cultures. You will need to do the following:

1) Prepare food from as many civilizations as you can. Your guests can enjoy sampling each of the foods.

2) Arrange an offering of games from ancient civilizations.

3) Display all of the craft projects you have done this year.

4) Design and make a costume that you would like to wear for this festival. Encourage others to wear costumes as well.

5) Make an invitation in the style of an ancient civilization that you have studied. Send a copy of your invitation to your teacher.

6) Invite family and friends to your festival. Perhaps some of your friends would like to help you prepare. Take lots of pictures and keep an accurate record of what you do at your festival. Write an essay in the first person, past tense in which you tell your teacher all of the details of your festival. Your teacher would love to see pictures.

The following suggestions may be helpful:

1) If you have this festival with a small group of friends and family, you may wish to serve the various foods as refreshments. However, if you plan to invite your whole neighborhood, you may wish to offer foods for sale.

2) If you have a small group, you will only be able to play one game at a time, explaining the game to your friends and telling them the country of its origin. If you invite the whole neighborhood, you can have various game booths. It would be fun (and helpful) to make signs telling about each of the games for the booths.

3) If you can get recordings of music from different countries, it would be nice to have the music playing in the background during the entire festival.

b. Write a three page essay in which you describe a civilization which is a composite of the many you have studied this year. Take what you think is the best from each of these civilizations and create a new one. Include the following information, along with several drawings:

1) The food they eat

2) The shelters they build

3) Special inventions they have made

4) Entertainment and games

5) **The clothes the people wear**

6) **Religious beliefs and ceremonies**

7) **The government**

8) **Customs and manners of the people**

9) **The status of men, women and children**

10) **The medical practices**

11) **Ways of making a living**

Present your ideas thoroughly and include details. This should be a civilization in which you would want to live! Make a beautiful cover page for your essay, and name the civilization you have created.

5. **Have your Home Teacher give you a final spelling quiz. Include all the words you have missed in your previous tests. Review any words you miss.**

CONGRATULATIONS !

**You have completed the
Ancient Civilizations/English Course.**

English Manual

Table of Contents

SENTENCE CONSTRUCTION

Every sentence must have a noun and a verb. A sentence should express at least one complete thought. It must begin with a capital letter and end with a punctuation mark.

1. The car went down the street.

    Car is a **noun**. *Went* is a **verb**. *The* begins with a **capital** letter. The sentence ends with a **period**.

2. The two main parts of a sentence are the **subject** and the **predicate**. The subject tells what the sentence is talking about and the predicate tells about the action of the subject. The subject contains a noun and the predicate contains a verb.

    Examples:
    Most dogs who run wild (subject) are vicious animals (predicate).
    The car (subject) went down the street (predicate).
    The brightly painted stretch limousine (subject) went racing around the corner at 80 miles an hour (predicate).

3. Sometimes the subject is not stated obviously, but is understood, such as in "Go away!" *You* is understood to be the subject.

SENTENCES

1. There are four kinds of sentences:

    a. A statement *tells* something and ends in a period. (**.**)

    b. A question *asks* something and ends with a question mark. (**?**)

    c. An exclamatory sentence *expresses* surprise, wonder or strong feeling and ends with an exclamation mark. (**!**)

    d. A command sentence gives *a command* or makes *a request* and ends in a period or an exclamation mark. (**.** or **!**)

2. An example of each kind of sentence:

    a. Today has been a beautiful day. (statement)

    b. Do you think tomorrow will be cold? (question)

    c. What a gorgeous day! (exclamation)

    d. Go clean the car! (command)

    e. Please leave at noon. (command)

3. Subjects and Predicates:

    a. The **subject** tells what the sentence is about. The subject includes a noun.

    Example:
      The big dog ran around the little room.
      The beautiful sun rose slowly over the high mountain.
      The gorgeous quilt was burgundy and mauve.

    b. The **predicate** tells something about the subject. It tells what the subject does, or did, is, or was. The predicate includes a verb.

    Example:
      The big dog *ran around the little room.*
      The beautiful sun *rose slowly over the high mountain.*
      The gorgeous quilt *was burgundy and mauve.*

NOUNS

A. A **noun** is the name of a person, place or thing.

   Examples: dog, park, piano, day, friend, bicycle.

B. There are five types of nouns:

   1. A **common noun** names a person, place or thing.

      Examples: hat, post office, car

   2. A **proper noun** names a particular person, place or thing.

      Examples: (Joan, Philadelphia, Mississippi River, New York City,
         Mojave Desert

   3. A **singular noun** names one person, place or thing.

      Examples: girl, cat

   4. A **plural noun** names more than one person, place or thing. (girls, cats,
      cities)

      a. To form the plural of nouns ending in *s, z, ch* or *sh,* add *es* to the singular.

         Examples: watch - watches, gas - gases, dish - dishes

      b. To form the plural of nouns ending in *x,* usually *es* can be added. Ox,
         oxen is an exception.

         Example: box - boxes

      c. To form the plural of most nouns that end in *f* or *fe* add *s* .

         Example: handkerchief - handkerchiefs

d. To form the plural of some nouns ending in *f* or *fe*, change the *f* or *fe* to *v* and add *es*.

Example: knife - knives

e. To form the plural of a noun ending in *y* after a vowel (*a,e,i,o,u*), add *s* to the singular.

Examples: boy - boys, bay - bays, ray - rays

f. To form the plural of a noun ending in *y* after a consonant, change the *y* to *i* and add *es*.

Examples: army - armies, navy - navies, daisy - daisies, fly - flies

5. A **possessive noun** shows ownership or possession.

a. Add an apostrophe and *s* to a singular noun.

Example: Bob - Bob's dog

b. To show possession in a plural noun that ends in *s*, add an apostrophe only.

Example: girls' dog

c. To show possession in a plural noun that does not end in *s*, add an apostrophe and *s*.

Example: men-men's

CAPITALIZATION

1. Always write the word *I* as a capital letter.

2. Capitalize words that refer to relatives when using them as a name or with a name.

   Examples:
   > Mary and Mother went to the store.
   > Joan and Uncle Peter will go later.

   a. Do not capitalize these words after possessive nouns or the words *my*, *our*, *his*, *her*, or *their*.

      Examples:
      > Mary took my mother and me to the store.
      > My aunt decided not to go with us.

   b. Use a capital letter to begin each word in the name of a person.

      Example: Mother's name is Leonora Wilhemina Collier.

   c. Use a capital letter to begin the name of a pet

      Example: I have a bird named Petey.

3. Capitalize a title such as Mr., Dr., General, or President.

   Examples: Mr. White, Dr. Jones, General Westmoreland, President Carter

4. Use a capital letter to begin each important word in the name of a place.

   Example: I am going to visit Washington's Crossing on the Delaware.

5. Use a capital letter to begin the name of a country, the name of a nationality, or a word made from the name of a country or a nationality.

   Examples: France, French, Europe, American, German, Germany, English, Indian

6. Capitalize days, months and holidays, but *not* seasons.

   Examples: Monday, Tuesday, January, February, Christmas, Easter, fall, winter

7. Capitalize the first word of a direct quotation.

   Example: Mother said, "When are you going to the store?"

8. Capitalize the first word and every important word in the title of a book, a story, a poem, or a song.

   Example: "Twinkle, Twinkle, Little Star"

VERBS

1. There are two kinds of **verbs**:

   a. One kind of verb shows action, and is called an **action word.**

      Examples: Run, walk, sit, stand, look, see

   b. The second kind of verb helps tell something about the subject and is called a **verb of being.**

      Examples: is, are, am, was, were, become, seem
      It *is* not too cold today.
      Yesterday *was* gorgeous.
      The roads *became* very slick in the rain.

2. Sometimes a verb is made up of more than one word. These additional words are helping words or auxiliary words.

   Examples: has, have, had, is, are, was, were
   The signal *was given* for the cars to proceed.
   She *is going* to the movies.
   The toys *are being* preserved.
   They *were going* to the bus.
   Nancy *was running* to see him.

3. Verbs have three common senses: **present**, **past**, and **past participle**. Tenses tell when the action takes place.

The principal tenses of some commonly used verbs:

Present	**Past**	**Past Participle**
do	did	done
see	saw	seen
give	gave	given
take	took	taken
go	went	gone
begin	began	begun
eat	ate	eaten
swim	swam	swum
throw	threw	thrown

The present and past tenses may be used without a helper. However, the past participle must have a helper.

Examples: has, have, had, is, am, are, was, or were
 I see the girl. (present)
 I saw the girl. (past)
 I have seen the girl. (past participle)
 I take off my hat in church. (present)
 I took off my hat in church. (past)
 I have taken off my hat in church. (past participle)
 She eats fruit every day. (present)
 She ate fruit every day. (past)
 She has eaten fruit every day. (past participle)
 They go to the park. (present)
 They went to the park. (past)
 They had gone to the park. (past participle)

PUNCTUATION

1. An abbreviation should always be followed by a period.

   Examples: Mr., Mrs., Dr.

2. Separate the day from the year by a comma when writing dates.

   Example: March 24, 1992

3. Use commas to separate the words or groups of words used in a series.

   Example: apples, pears, bananas, etc.

4. Separate the name of the person spoken to from the rest of the sentence by a comma or commas.

   Example: John, are you going to school today?

5. Separate *yes* or *no* with a comma when it is used as part of an answer.

   Example: No, I am not going to school today.

6. Use a comma after the greeting of a friendly letter.

   Example: Dear Geraldine,

7. Use a comma after the closing of a letter.

   Example: With warm regards,

8. Use a colon after the greeting of a business letter.

   Example: Dear Sir or Madam:

9. Underline the title of a book, magazine, or play when it is used in a sentence.

   Examples: The Once And Future King, Time, Macbeth

10. Use quotation marks to enclose the title of a song, a poem, a movie or a story if the title is used in a sentence.

Examples:
> "Listen to the Mockingbird" (song)
> "Fog" (poem)
> "Titanic" (movie)
> "How The Elephant Got His Trunk" (story)

Important Note: Titles of movies, plays, TV shows, operas or musicals are sometimes italicized, sometimes put in quotes, and sometimes underlined. See the section called "Titles" in this manual.

11. Use quotation marks around any part of the sentence that is a direct quote. (See the section called "Direct Quotations" in this manual for more information on quotes.)

Examples:
> Caitlin said, "I can't find my shoes."
> "Here they are," replied her mother.

CONTRACTIONS

A contraction is a shortened form of two words in which two words have been joined and one or more letters have been left out. An apostrophe is used to show where one or more letters have been omitted.

Examples:
> do not - don't
> would not - wouldn't
> should not - shouldn't
> cannot - can't
> you will - you'll
> I have - I've
> they would - they'd

CONJUNCTIONS

A word used to join two sentences together is called a connecting word or **conjunction**. *And, or, but, for, while, when, if, because,* and *after* are some of the conjunctions that can be used to join two sentences together. Often, a comma should be placed before a conjunction. When we join two sentences together, we call it a compound sentence.

Examples:
Henry walked to the store, *and* Mary rode her bike.
Henry walked to the store, *while* Mary rode her bike.
Henry walked to the store, *after* Mary rode her bike.
Mary rode her bike, *because* she did not want to walk to the store with Henry.

PRONOUNS

A **pronoun** is a word used in place of a noun. Some common pronouns are *I, my, mine, me, our, ours, we, us, you, your, yours, he, his, him, she, her, hers, it, its, they, their, theirs, them, themselves, herself, himself.*

ADJECTIVES

Adjectives describe nouns. They make sentences more interesting and provide important information. We can also think of them as picture words because they describe the appearance of people and things.

If you say, "The cat walked down the lane," it is not very interesting.

However, if you say, "The yellow cat walked down the winding, twisting lane," it becomes more interesting. *Yellow, winding, twisting* are called adjectives, and they describe the cat and the lane, which are the nouns.

Perhaps you are told, "You are supposed to meet a man at the station." This doesn't give much information. Adjectives can help. What if you were told this instead? "You are supposed to meet a huge old Frenchman at the new bus station." Now you have the information you need!

ADVERBS

Adverbs tell how, when, or where something is done. A sentence becomes much more interesting and informative when we use adverbs.

Example: The yellow cat walked slowly behind the bear down the winding, twisting lane.

Slowly and *behind* are adverbs, and tell about the verb, or HOW the cat walked.

Example: The huge old Frenchman lumbered noisily along beside me.

Noisily and *beside* are adverbs, and tell more about how the man moved.

Note: Some adverbs are also prepositions, when they describe a location.

Some common adverbs:

How	When	Where
quickly	late	near
slowly	early	far
softly	first	in
bravely	last	out
foolishly	later	behind
harshly	sometime(s)	here
silently	then	there

PREPOSITIONS

A **preposition** is a word that usually shows position or location.

Commonly used prepositions:

above	about	across	after
against	along	among	around
at	before	behind	beside
between	by	during	except
for	from	into	near
of	off	on	over
through	to	toward	upon
under	with		

A **prepositional phrase** is a group of two or more words that begins with a preposition and ends with a noun or pronoun.

Example: The clouds gathered in the sky before the storm.

In the sky and *before the storm* are prepositional phrases.

Note: Sometimes prepositions double as adverbs.

HOMOPHONES

Homophones are words that are pronounced alike but which are spelled differently and have different meanings.

Common homophones:

one - won	to- too - two	no - know
son - sun	by - buy - bye	rode - road
so - sew	in - inn	be - bee
its - it's	blue - blew	flour - flower
our - hour	ate - eight	there - their - they're
see - sea	here - hear	your - you're

SYNONYMS

Synonyms are words that are similar in meaning.

Common synonyms:

small - tiny	aid - help	worried - anxious
short - little	large - big	courteous - polite
grief - sorrow	happy - glad	close - near
close - shut	sick - ill	answer - reply
purchase - buy		

ANTONYMS

Antonyms are words that are opposite in meaning.

Common antonyms:

long - short	false - true	short - tall
many - few	difficult - easy	light - dark
loose - tight	cold - hot	small - big
cruel - kind	rough - smooth	early - late
slow - fast	young - old	wealthy - poor

DIRECT QUOTATIONS

The exact words said by someone are called a **direct quotation**. Always capitalize the first word of a direct quotation. Enclose the words of a direct quotation in quotation marks. The punctuation mark for the quote itself goes <u>inside</u> the quotation marks.

Examples:
"Go to the store," said Mother.
Kit replied, "I'll go now!"

In writing conversation, make a new paragraph each time there is a different speaker. A comma separates the non-quote part of the sentence from the actual quote.

TITLES

1. Enclose the title of a story, a poem, a song, or newspaper or magazine articles with quotation marks when used in a sentence.

2. Underline the title of a book, magazine, or newspaper when used in a sentence. Titles of movies, plays, musicals, operas, television shows are underlined or put in quotation marks when handwritten, or italicized when typed.

3. Begin the first word and every important word in the title of a book, a story, a poem, or a song with a capital letter.

DIRECT OBJECT

A **direct object** tells who or what received the action expressed by the verb.

Example: Chris kicked the ball.

Chris is the **subject**, *kicked* is the **verb** and if we ask the question, "kicked what?" we see that *ball* is the **direct object** because it received the action.

INDIRECT OBJECT

The **indirect object** tells to whom or for whom the action was done.

Example: Susie gave Tim the records.

Susie is the **subject**, *gave* is the **verb**, *records* is the **direct object**, and *Tim* is the **indirect object**. If we ask, "gave what?" we have *records* (direct object). If we ask, "to whom?" we have *Tim* (indirect object).

DICTIONARY

The words in a dictionary are listed in alphabetical order. When the first letter of two words is the same, we must look at the second letter to determine which word comes first in the dictionary. If the first and second letters are the same, we must look at the third letters, and so on.

The word at the left of the top of the dictionary page tells us the first word on that page. The word to the right of the top of the dictionary page tells us the last word on that page.

The words in a dictionary are divided into syllables with an accent mark to show which syllable should be accented.

A word may have more than one meaning. It is important to determine the correct meaning of a word from its use in the context of the sentence.

NEGATIVES

Words such as *no, never, not, no one, none, scarcely*, and *hardly* are called **negatives**.

1. Any word that ends in *n't* is also a negative, because *n't* is simply a contraction of *not*.

2. Only one negative should be used in expressing an idea.

    Examples:
    Kathy has no pen.
    Kathy hasn't a pen.
    Kathy does not have a pen.

3. It would be incorrect to say *Kathy hasn't no pen*. This would be a double negative, and makes a positive.

    Example: I wouldn't want no dogs for pets.

This contains a double negative, and actually means you wouldn't want to be without dogs for pets. You should use *any* instead of *no* because *wouldn't* is a negative, and you would not use *no* or there would be two negative words in the sentence.

Examples:
I wouldn't want any dogs for pets.
I do not want dogs for pet.

UNNECESSARY WORDS

1. Do not use a pronoun after a noun.

Example:
Kim she went to the zoo. (Incorrect)
Kim went to the zoo. (Correct)
She went to the zoo. (Correct)

This first sentence is incorrect because *Kim* and *she* are the same person. It is repetitious to say it this way.

2. The word *had* should never be used with *ought*.

Examples:
Sharla had ought better get a job. (Incorrect)
Sharla had ought to get a job. (Incorrect)
Sharla had better get a job. (Correct)
Sharla should get a job. (Correct)
Sharla ought to get a job. (Correct)

3. Never use *here* with *this* and *these* , or *there* with *that* and *those*.

Examples:
Jill is shoveling these here stones into the wheelbarrow. (Incorrect)
Jill is shoveling these stones into the wheelbarrow. (Correct)

The first sentence is incorrect because it is identifying the rocks twice. You would not say, "Pick up those there rocks." It should be, "Pick up those rocks."

WORD USAGE

Some words can be used alone, and some words need helpers, such as *is*, *are*, *was*, *were*, *has*, *have*, or *had*.

Words That Can Be Used Alone	Words That Need a Helper
came	come
gave	given
ate	eaten
did	done
went	gone
ran	run
saw	seen
drove	driven
wore	worn
tore	torn
broke	broken
spoke	spoken
chose	chosen
threw	thrown
knew	known
grew	grown
took	taken
sang	sung
rang	rung
brought	brought
	(never brang or brung)

1. Use *may* in asking or giving permission.

   Example: May we go to the park today?

2. Use *can* in expressing ability to do something.

   Example: She can do aerobics.

3. Use *let* to mean permit or allow.

    Example: I will let you go to the store.

4. Use *leave* to mean go away from.

    Example: We will leave the job soon.

5. Use *a* before a word beginning with a consonant sound.

    Example: A book is on the table.

6. Use *an* before a word beginning with a vowel sound.

    Example: An elephant is in the zoo.

PARAGRAPHS

Our purpose in learning to write paragraphs is two fold:

1. To help you organize and express your thoughts in a logical and planned way;

2. To help you create a concise piece of writing which will stand on its own as a complete entity. To accomplish these goals, three forms of paragraphs will be suggested. Much of the writing which you will be asked to do will concern itself with the basic questions:

> **Who?**
> **What?**
> **When?**
> **Where?**
> **Why?**
> **How?**

Always use these questions to guide your research so you have some basis for understanding the material read. Research is essentially the search for the answer to some questions; thus, these questions are good starting points.

PARAGRAPH FORMS

Writing, just as anything one builds, has a pattern. Good writing, like good music, is harmonious. Within a large written composition, the paragraph is a building block, the way a cell is a small part of a larger body.

1. Three-Sentence Paragraph:

    a. Topic sentence

    b. One major detail sentence

    c. Concluding sentence

    Example: Today was an exciting day. A Wells Fargo stagecoach arrived in our town. All the townspeople stopped what they were doing to go meet it.

2. Five-Sentence Paragraph:

    a. Topic sentence

    b. Three major detail sentences that support the topic sentence

    c. Concluding sentence

    Example: Today was an exciting day. A Wells Fargo stagecoach arrived in our town. It was the first scheduled overland contact with the East coast. On top was a large chest marked "U.S. Mail." All the townspeople stopped what they were doing to go meet it.

Compare this paragraph with the previous three-sentence one. See how much richer and exciting the event of the topic sentence becomes just by adding two more major details? Naturally, this communicates more.

3. Eight-Sentence Paragraph:

   a. Topic sentence

   b. Major detail sentence

   c. Minor detail sentence

   d. Major detail sentence

   e. Minor detail sentence

   f. Major detail sentence

   g. Minor detail sentence

   h. Concluding sentences

Example: Today was an exciting day. A Wells Fargo stagecoach arrived in our town. Six sweating horses and a triumphant driver brought it to a halt in the center of town. It was the first scheduled overland contact with the East coast. Usually our only contact comes by sea. On top of the stagecoach was a large chest marked "U.S. Mail." The last mail delivery was three months ago. All the townspeople stopped what they were doing to go meet it.

With this more detailed paragraph the reader senses the great importance of this event. More of the atmosphere, background, and anticipation are filled in. The minor details give depth and broaden the reader's perception and understanding of the topic sentence, "Today was an exciting day."

OUTLINING

Before beginning a report or essay, it's a good idea to make an outline. Brainstorm about your topic and jot down ideas to include in your report. The outline provides way to organize your ideas. It will save you a great deal of time when you write the report, as you will already know how to organize the information. You can change your outline if you find, once you're actually writing the report, that it doesn't meet your needs. Here is a sample outline:

I. The Main Idea

    A. Facts about the main idea.

        1. Supporting examples and details

    B. More facts

        1. Supporting examples and details

II. Second Main Idea

    A. Facts about the main idea.

        1. Supporting examples and details

    B. More facts

        1. Supporting examples and details

III. Third Main Idea

    A. Facts about the main idea.

        1. Supporting examples and details

IV. Conclusion

    A. Restatement and summary of main theme

A brief example of an outline might be:

I. Good nutrition is important for good health.

   A. Kinds of Food We Need

      1. Proteins: What, why, where, and how

      2. Fats: What, why, where, and how

      3. Carbohydrates: What, why, where, and how

   B. Vitamins

      1. What they are

      2. Why they are important

      3. Where they come from

      4. How they work in the body

   C. Minerals

      1. What they are

      2. Why they are important

      3. Where they come from

      4. How they work in the body

   D. Conclusion

Another approach to making an outline is to make a web. You can make a web with questions about your topic or with ideas and information you already have. Here is an example of a web outline:

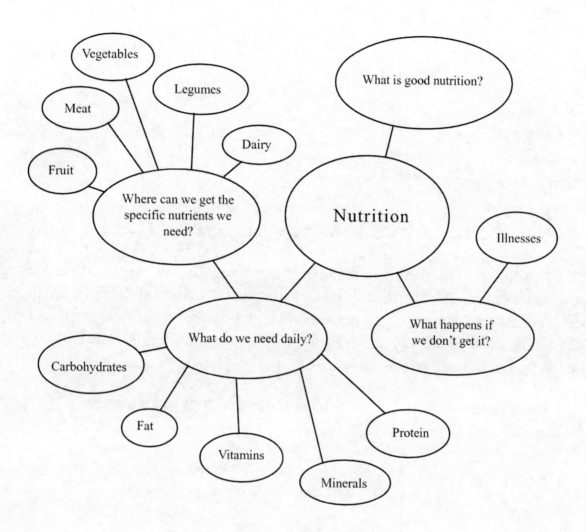

BUSINESS LETTER

Your Business
125 Main Street
Ojai, Ca 93023

April 29, 1999

Your Customer
Rosemary Lane
Hoboken, New Jersey 07890

Dear Students:

This letter is to inform you that a business letter has seven parts. Please notice that it has a return address (the address of the person writing the letter), a date, an inside address (the address of the person to whom you are writing), a greeting, body of the letter, closing, and signature. Please also notice the specific punctuation used for each part of the letter.

You should follow this format when writing a letter to a business.

Sincerely,

Owner

ADDRESSING AN ENVELOPE

Your Business
125 Main Street
Ojai, Ca 93023

> Your Customer
> Iris Lane
> Tulip, PA 19603

Please note that the return address goes in the upper left-hand corner of an envelope and the address of the person to whom you are sending the letter is in the center of the envelope.

WRITING A SHORT STORY

1. Make an outline of the following elements that go into every story. It's fine for you to change the order if it works better for you some other way. You may use either a traditional outline or a web outline. As you write the outline, you will need to consider how you plan to flesh out each of these areas in your story. Take notes on your ideas so you don't forget them.

    a. Plot - The series of events in the story.

    b. Characters and their personalities.

    c. The problems the characters have.

    d. Setting - Place and Time

    e. Climax - When the point of crisis of conflict is reached.

    f. Resolution - When things return to normal.

2. Keep a story in the same tense from beginning to end (present, past, or future).

Examples:

All the redbud trees are beautiful now in Virginia. Everywhere we look, we see purple. The woods are magnificent. (present)

The redbud trees were beautiful in Virginia during May. Everywhere we looked, we saw purple. The woods were magnificent. (past)

The redbud trees will be beautiful in Virginia during May. Everywhere we look, we will see purple. The woods will be magnificent. (future)

3. Tell a story from the first, second or third person point of view, but do not change in the middle of the story. Be consistent!

    a. First person: *I, we, my, mine, me, our, ours, us*

    b. Second person: *you, your, yours*

    c. Third person: *he, his, him, she, her, hers, it, its, they, their, theirs, them*

BIBLIOGRAPHIES

A bibliography is a listing of the books and other resources you used when researching information for a report or essay. A bibliography is put on a separate piece of paper at the end of the report. The list is ordered alphabetically with the author's last name first, starting at the left-hand side. It is followed by his or her first name, and then the title of the book. The title is underlined (if handwritten) or in italics (if typed). If there is a subtitle, it follows the title, separated by a colon. The name of the publisher is next, followed by the city where the book was published, and the year of publication. After the first line, all other lines of the listing are indented.

Example:

Carter, Dorothy Sharp. His Majesty, Queen Hatshepsut.
   Harper Collins Publishers. New York, 1987.
Macaulay, David. *Cathedral: The Story of Its Construction.* Houghton
   Mifflin. Boston, 1973.

If the book is part of a series of books by the same publisher, then the name of the series is given after the title.

Example:
> Biel, Timothy Levi. *The Crusades*. World History Series. Lucent Books. San Diego, 1995.

If there is more than one author, then the author whose name comes first in the alphabet is listed first, followed by the full name of the second author.

Example:
> West, Delno and Jean West. <u>Christopher Columbus: The Great Adventure and How We Know About It</u>. Atheneum Press. New York, 1991.

If you are using an article or an essay that is within a larger book or publication, such as the encyclopedia or a magazine article, then the author of the article is listed first, followed by the name of the article in quotations, and then the title of the larger publication, which is underlined (or italicized if typed). These are followed by the edition and volume number (if applicable), the year, and the page numbers where the article is found.

Example:
> Coates, John F. "The Trireme Sails Again." <u>Scientific American: The Origins of Technology</u>. (1997) pp. 56-63.

If the article in the magazine or encyclopedia does not give an author, then the title of the article is listed first in quotation marks, followed by the name of the larger publication, which is underlined, and the relevant page numbers.

Example:
> "Roman Catholic Church." <u>World Book Encyclopedia</u>. 14th ed., XIX, pp. 992-3.